PRINCETON SERIES ON THE MIDDLE EAST

Bernard Lewis and Heath W. Lowry, Editors

THE MIDDLE EAST ECONOMY:
DECLINE AND RECOVERY

*"Islam is the only world religion
founded by a successful businessman"*

Charles Issawi

The Middle East Economy: Decline and Recovery

Selected Essays by
CHARLES ISSAWI

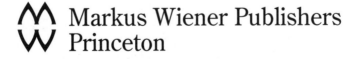 Markus Wiener Publishers
Princeton

FOR INFORMATION WRITE TO:
MARKUS WIENER PUBLISHERS
114 JEFFERSON ROAD, PRINCETON, NJ 08540

LIBRARY OF CONGRESS CATALOGING-IN-PUBLICATION DATA

ISSAWI, CHARLES PHILIP.
THE MIDDLE EAST ECONOMY: DECLINE AND RECOVERY:
SELECTED ESSAYS/BY CHARLES ISSAWI
PRINCETON SERIES ON THE MIDDLE EAST
SELECTED ARTICLES PREVIOUSLY PUBLISHED IN JOURNALS AND BOOKS
BETWEEN 1978/79 AND 1995.
INCLUDES BIBLIOGRAPHICAL REFERENCES.
ISBN 1-55876-102-0 (HC) ISBN 1-55876-103-9 (PB)
1. MIDDLE EAST—ECONOMIC CONDITIONS—1979.
2. MIDDLE EAST—ECONOMIC CONDITIONS—1945-1979.
I. TITLE. II. SERIES
HC415.15.I848   1995
330.956—DC20   95-16792   CIP

COVER DESIGN BY CHERYL MIRKIN
COPYEDITING BY SUSAN LORAND
THIS BOOK HAS BEEN COMPOSED IN CENTURY OLD STYLE BY CMF GRAPHIC DESIGN

MARKUS WIENER PUBLISHERS BOOKS ARE PRINTED ON ACID-FREE PAPER,
AND MEET THE GUIDELINES FOR PERMANENCE AND DURABILITY
OF THE COMMITTEE ON PRODUCTION GUIDELINES
FOR BOOK LONGEVITY OF THE COUNCIL ON LIBRARY RESOURCES

CONTENTS

ACKNOWLEDGMENTS

The contents of this volume have previously been published in various scholarly journals, conference proceedings, and books, and have been expanded and updated for this collection. The author gratefully acknowledges the following publishers:

Cambridge University Press for permission to reprint "The Modern Middle East in the World Context: a Historical View" from Georges Sabagh, ed., *The Modern Middle East in its World Context*, 1985; Center for Contemporary Arab Studies, Georgetown University, for permission to reprint "The Middle East in the World Economy: A Long Range Historical View," 1985; Cambridge University Press for permission to reprint "Technology, Energy and Civilization: Some Observations" from *International Journal of Middle East Studies* 23 (1991); ISIS Press for permission to reprint "The Ottoman-Habsburg Balance of Forces" from Halil Inalcik and Cemal Kafadar, eds., *Suleyman the Second and his Time*, 1991; St. Martin's Press for permission to reprint "Egypt, Iran and Turkey, 1800-1970" from Paul Bairoch and Maurice Levy-Leboyer, eds., *Disparities in Economic Development since the Industrial Revolution*, 1981; Center for Contemporary Arab Studies, Georgetown University, for permission to reprint "Egypt: Economic Evolution Since 1800" from Ibrahim Oweiss, ed., *The Political Economy of Contemporary Egypt*, 1990; Center for Lebanese Studies, Oxford, for permission to reprint "The Historical Background of Lebanese Emigration" from Albert Hourani and Nadim Shehadi, eds., *The Lebanese in the World*, 1992; Department of Near Eastern Studies, Princeton University, for permission to reprint "Iraq: A Study in Aborted Development" from *Princeton Papers in Near Eastern Studies*, Issue no. 1, 1992; Center for Contemporary Arab Studies, Georgetown University, and Croom Helm Publishers, for permission to reprint "The Japanese Model and the Middle East" from I. Ibrahim, ed., *Arab Resources: The Transformation of a Society*, 1983; Syracuse University Press for permission to reprint "The Adaptation of Islam to Contemporary Economic Realities" from Yvonne Yazbeck Haddad, Byron Haines and Elison Findly, eds., *The Islamic Impact* (Syracuse: Syracuse University Press,1984), pp. 27-45; M.E. Sharp, Publishers, for permission to reprint "The 1973 Oil Crisis and After" from the *Journal of Post-Keynesian Economics*, Winter 1978-79; Jean Batou

University, Geneva for "The Balkans and the Middle East," forthcoming in the Festschrift for Paul Bairoch.

The photographs in the text are reproduced courtesy of the following sources: ARAMCO World: 2, 30, 31, 35, 38-40; Arabic Republic of Egypt, Ministry of Culture: 7, 16, 20, 24, 25, 27, 28; German National Museum Nuremberg: 21, 22; Harvard University Art Museums: 17; Bernard Lewis: 23; Edition Neske private collection, Munich: 1, 4, 5, 8, 9-15, 17-19, 26, 29, 32-4, 37; Princeton University, Firestone Library: 3, 36; Turkish Historical Society: 6.

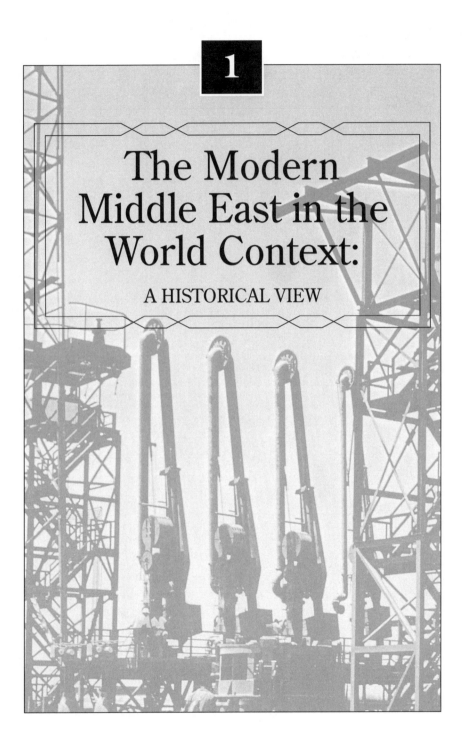

1

The Modern Middle East in the World Context:

A HISTORICAL VIEW

he world's earliest civilizations were born in the Middle East—in Iraq, Egypt, and Syria—which shows that, given the technology and social structure of antiquity, the region's climate and natural endowments must have been favorable. Indeed, even in the early Middle Ages the Middle East, Muslim and Byzantine, was still one of the two main centers of the world economy, the other being China under the T'ang and Sung dynasties. This is indicated by all the accepted criteria: urbanization, literacy, the production of books, the state of crafts, the level and crop mix of agriculture, and the monetization of the economy. In all these areas the Middle East stood far ahead of all other parts of the world, with the exception of China. We all know about this brilliant period, and I shall not elaborate the point any further.

But what is most advantageous at stages A and B may not be so at stage C, and with the development of technology, the growth of population, the discovery and exploitation of new lands and resources, and the emergence of bigger social units, the relative advantages of other regions began to loom larger.

Waterways and Water Power

A major advantage for countries we now call "developed" was the abundance of navigable waterways, in contrast to the Middle East, which has only the Nile and the much less serviceable Tigris and Euphrates. One can-

1 • Camel Caravan

not overestimate the part played by rivers, especially when supplemented by canals, in the development of China, India, Russia, Europe, and North and South America. It is true that extensive use of camel and mule caravans made possible a large flow of goods overland; thus on the Tabriz-Trabzon route, in the 1870s, pack animals carried some 25,000 tons of merchandise a year, the equivalent of seven or eight shiploads each way. But of course the volume of goods carried by caravans was much smaller and the costs much higher than by waterways.

A closely connected factor is the lack of waterpower in the region. The water mill seems to have been invented in the Mediterranean region[1] around the beginning of the Christian era, but for obvious reasons, it was used far less in the Middle East than in Europe. The role of the water mill in the economic development of Europe may be illustrated by three examples. First, "By 1086 William the Conqueror's Domesday Book records that the 3,000 settlements in England [whose total population was about

2 • Water wheel at Hama in Syria

1,100,000]—most of them very small—averaged nearly two mills apiece."[2] This means that not only was there a much greater concentration of power than could be provided by men or animals (2 to 5 hp compared to 0.1 hp for a man, 0.66 hp for an ox and 2 hp for a camel), but also that machinery was brought into every village and its workings demonstrated for the whole population. Second, in the course of the next three centuries water mills were put to an unprecedented variety of uses in the textile, metallurgical, lumber, and other industries, and stimulated numerous inventions or borrowings, such as the cam and the crank. Lastly, as late as 1860, water mills provided 60% of the total horsepower in French industry, and only slightly less in the United States; high rates also prevailed in Britain, Switzerland, and elsewhere. It may also be noted that windmills, which seem to have been invented in Iran in the sixth century, played a very minor role in the Middle East but an important one in Europe, where they were greatly improved and were transformed into the most powerful engines the world had yet seen, up to 8 hp.

Another weakness connected with the aridity of the Middle East is the paucity of forests, except in Turkey and northern Iran. This was a heavy handicap since, until well into the nineteenth century, wood was everywhere not only the most important source of energy but also the basic industrial material. Not only were houses, ships, and bridges built of wood, but also the machines used in manufacturing and mining. Indeed, in the United States streets were often paved with wood.

In addition, the Middle East is rather poorly endowed with minerals, except for oil, which assumed importance only in this century. Deposits of iron, copper, lead, gold, and silver are to be found in many countries, but they are almost always small. Coal is very scarce in the region, a fact whose importance may be gauged by considering that China has been burning coal since the fourth century and probably much earlier, and Western Europe since at least the thirteenth century.[3]

Last, and perhaps most important of all, is the fragility of the agricultural base in the Middle East. The larger part of the region has insufficient and very irregular rainfall, with violent annual fluctuations in production, the constant threat of droughts, and severe limits on expansion of cultivation; this applies to Iran, Iraq, Syria, and much of Anatolia. Irrigation provides a remedy, but its extent is strictly limited, and it usually requires elaborate and very vulnerable installations, such as the canals of Iraq and the qanats of Iran, which can be and often have been destroyed, with a consequent breakdown in the economy. The main exceptions in the Middle East are Egypt, with its splendidly regular and completely indestructible Nile, and the coastlands of Turkey.

The Role of Government

The social factors may be considered under three headings: the alien nature of government; the inhibiting role of government; and the social composition of government.

It is a commonplace that, for nearly a thousand years, the rulers of the Middle East have been of foreign, usually Turkic, stock. It may well be that those Turks gave the region better government than its own indigenous peoples had provided. And it is certainly true that this phenomenon is not peculiar to the Middle East—one can think of the Turks and Moghuls in India, the Manchus in China, the Spaniards in Latin America, and others. Even England had its French-speaking Normans and Plantagenets, and it comes as a shock to read of the great English king, Edward I, "that he understood, and occasionally spoke, English is almost certain"[4]—his mother tongue being French, of course. But while many foreign dynasties eventually took over the culture of their subjects, in the Middle East most did not last long enough to do so. This is connected with another factor ultimately derived from the aridity of the region, namely, the presence on its fringes of large groups of pastoralists whose cohesion and mobility have enabled them periodically to sweep over large territories. Little need be said on this subject, since it has been admirably described and analyzed by Ibn Khaldun.

> Bedouins are, of all peoples, the least fit for exercising political domination. This is because they are more nomadic than other peoples, moving more freely in the deserts and, because of their simple and rough ways, standing in less need of cereals and other agricultural products. This makes them less dependent on others and therefore less ready to submit to authority.
>
> In fact their chiefs are generally dependent on them, since it is their solidarity which defends [the community]. Hence these chiefs must humour them and avoid any form of coercion, for this might cause disunion and end in the destruction of the chief and of the whole community. In properly organized states, however, the rulers must be prepared and able to use force in order to check disobedience, else there will be confusion . . .
>
> They become fit for ruling only when religion has transformed their

character, driving out these [defects] and leading them to restrain themselves and to prevent other people from encroaching on each other's rights, as we said before.

An illustration of this is provided by the empire which the Bedouins founded on the basis of Islam. Religion provided for them a foundation for the state, in the form of a Canon Law whose prescriptions seek both the external and the internal welfare of the community. As the [early] Caliphs conformed their action to this law their power increased and their dominion spread. . . .

An Arab Philosophy of History: Selections from the Prologomena of Ibn Khaldun of Tunis, trans. by Charles Issawi (London, 1950), p. 59.

In many ways, the Arab bedouins may be included among the region's alien rulers. They too would eventually be civilized (or corrupted) by the bureaucracy and other institutions, but it usually took time and by then new nomads would come.

As regards the relation of government to society, a certain paradox may be observed. In late antiquity, while the Roman Empire broke down, the Byzantine and Sassanian empires survived, and their Arab conquerors soon succeeded in setting up a strong and fairly centralized government. And although the Arab empire soon broke up into many pieces the successor states remained quite strong. Hence, when in Western Europe the ground was cleared for the growth of numerous and vigorous independent centers of power and activity—Church, city states, feudal principalities, universities, guilds, and other associations—in the Middle East the continued power of the state discouraged such development. There were no independent city-states or universities; and guilds (whose existence before the Ottoman period has been questioned) were controlled by the government.

Middle Eastern governments refrained from interfering with many aspects of society, notably law, where Western governments, for instance, played the major role. But the inhibiting effect of the state in the spheres noted above deprived the region of those centers of independent activity which contributed significantly both to economic development and to the growth of political liberty in the West. Groups of producers—farmers, craftsmen, merchants, and others—did not have enough autonomy to establish associations and set up institutions that could further their interests and expand their economic base. And property was always insecure, as illustrated by the fact that so much trade and other economic activity

3 • Bay Mameluk

passed into the hands of foreigners or minority members, who enjoyed foreign protection and therefore were safeguarded against the arbitrariness of officials.[5]

Closely connected with this is the third factor, the social composition of government. At least since the fall of the Fatimid Empire, the state apparatus remained in the hands of soldiers and bureaucrats, with some assistance from the ulama. Their main concerns were fiscal and provisioning: to raise enough taxes to meet their salaries and other expenses, such as war, regardless of the effect on production; and to ensure that the cities were adequately provided with foodstuffs, again regardless of the broader economic consequences or of the effects on the farmers. With much more justice one can apply to the Middle East David MacPherson's indictment of Europe, written in 1805, that no judicious commercial regulations could be drawn up by ecclesiastical or military men (the only classes who possessed any authority or influence), who despised trade and consequently could know nothing of it.

The economic consequences were disastrous. The Middle East had no counterpart to the monasteries, which played such an important role in promoting European agriculture, and the Islamic land tenure system meant that after the early Middle Ages there were no progressive landlords and that peasants had little or no incentive to improve their agricultural methods.

The craftsmen were stuck in their old ways and the technical level of handicrafts may have actually declined; they certainly showed few signs of evolving into large manufactories, the way European ones did in the sixteenth and seventeenth centuries. Finally, there was competition from abroad. The lack of concern by governments in the Middle East led them to conclude with European countries treaties that allowed goods to enter freely upon payment of minimal duties, usually 3% to 5%. Some industries began to suffer from this competition as early as the fourteenth century.[6] Since most of these treaties, and the Capitulations,* were signed by the Mamluks and Ottomans at the height of their power, one must conclude either that those governments were uninterested in the economic consequences, or that they thought the damage done to the producers was a small price to pay for the benefits: larger imports of goods consumed by the ruling classes, or political objectives like alliances and support.

It is indeed striking to see how unconcerned Middle Eastern governments were with the broader objectives of commercial policy being pursued in Europe, like promoting exports to find markets for local products and to accumulate bullion, or restricting imports to protect local producers. No trace of mercantilism can be detected in Ottoman or Iranian policy until well on in the eighteenth century, when certain minor measures were taken by the sultan Selim III.

Partly because the ruling groups looked down on mercantile activities, leaving many of them to the Christian and Jewish minorities, and partly

---

*The Capitulations were treaties between the Middle Eastern and European states, granting the latter various extra-territorial and fiscal privileges.

because, in the eighteenth and nineteenth centuries, many members of these minorities managed to obtain foreign protection and to take advantage of the Capitulations, trade and shipping passed into their hands. This only increased the rulers' aversion to these and like occupations and made them further disinclined to give protection and encouragement to activities that could breed potentially hostile groups, as the Greeks had proved to be.

These governments did nothing to promote transport, except for the building of a few bridges and caravanserais in a few cities and along some main routes. No roads were paved, no canals were dug, and no ports improved.[7] In fact, many harbors deteriorated because of neglect, as, for example, in Alexandria; silting, as in Jaffa and Suwaydia; or even deliberate blocking, as in Sidon and Beirut in the seventeenth century. By 1800 the Middle East was economically far behind its main rival, Europe, and, as will be shown, behind several other regions as well.

Social conditions were equally bad. No improvement in education had taken place since the Middle Ages; indeed, at the highest level there had been a sharp deterioration, as may be seen by comparing the curriculum of Cairo's famous al-Azhar University in 1800 with the sciences studied in the eleventh century. The literacy rate in the Middle East must have been well below 5%. The first census figures we have for any country, namely Egypt in 1897, are 10.5% for men and 0.3% for women overall, that is, including children but also the much more highly educated foreigners and minorities. Hygienic conditions were as bad as anywhere in the world, and the region was periodically swept by devastating epidemics of cholera and the plague.[8]

Perhaps most serious of all was the complacency and arrogance of the ruling classes and of the religious establishment, which made them look with indifference, and even contempt, on the tremendous intellectual changes that had taken place in Europe. It was only when European soldiers had penetrated the Balkans and invaded Egypt that they began to take notice.[9] It is worth recalling that, in 1485, Bayazit II prohibited printing in Arabic and Turkish, although in Istanbul books were being produced in Hebrew, Greek, and various European languages. The first Turkish press was opened in 1729, closed in 1742, and reopened in 1784. In 1610 a press printing psalms in Syriac was set up in the Lebanese monastery of Qazhayya, and in 1702 an Arabic press was set up in Aleppo; but the beginning of Arabic printing may more properly be dated from 1822, in Muhammad Ali's Cairo.[11] Bonaparte had earlier brought an Arabic printing press to Egypt in 1798 and opened the Institut d'Egypte with a library.

Europe and the Middle East

To say that in the early modern period conditions in the Middle East were bad is not, however, very informative.

It is therefore necessary to compare the Middle East with other regions. One should start with Western Europe, since it was both the first region to modernize and the Middle East's closest rival. I shall be brief, since I have discussed this subject elsewhere.[11]

In explaining Western Europe's lead, E. L. Jones, in his excellent book, *The European Miracle*[12], stresses the following factors. First, the natural environment is favorable: Europe is less exposed to geographical disasters (e.g., earthquakes and volcanic eruptions), to climatic disasters (e.g., hurricanes, typhoons, droughts, etc.), to epidemics, locust invasions, and to human, crop, and animal diseases. Second, from a very early date, Europe had a pattern of dispersed settlement, nuclear families, and relatively late age at marriage; consequently less of its surplus was spent on the mere multiplication of life and more both on securing a relatively high level of living for its common people and on increasing its capital accumulation.

Three other sets of factors may be stressed: inventiveness; better economic practice and policy; and the great accretion of strength brought about by the discovery and colonization of the New World. Early medieval Europe far surpassed all other regions except China in its capacity to invent or borrow useful devices. Lynn White's superb study, mentioned earlier (cf. n.2 above), describes many such improvements. In agriculture there were the heavy wheeled ploughs, breast harnessing of horses, horseshoes, the common use of scythes, and the improvement of the harrow. The result was the development of the three-field system and the steady rise in grain yields, from levels far below those of the Middle East to far higher ones; at the same time Mediterranean Europe took over from the Middle East many tropical crops that had come there from Asia and Africa.[13] The use of water and windmills has already been mentioned. Shipbuilding improved steadily, and by the fifteenth century the Europeans were ready to launch their voyages of discovery. Armaments became more accurate and more deadly, giving Europe a decisive advantage in its encounters with other civilizations. Finally, starting with clocks and spectacles in the fourteenth century, Europe embarked on what may be called the high technology of the Middle Ages, and it has continued to lead the world until our times. In this context I should of course discuss the progress of European science, but this vast subject would take us too far afield. I should also mention the fact that by the late Middle Ages, western and southern Europe had a much higher rate

4 • Windmills and ships in the
German Hanse city of Rostock,
16th century using wind power and waterways.

of literacy than other parts of the world and that the lead widened steadily until the present century.[14]

As regards economics, Europe showed an early interest in numbers and the use of statistics. In the matter of economic practice we can point out such early developments as double-entry bookkeeping and insurance. We can also observe that European economic structures, like the political ones, were larger, more complex, and more durable than those of other cultures. Among many examples may be cited medieval guilds, banks, maritime convoys, and such institutions as the Hanseatic League, an alliance of German and northern European merchant city-states to protect and promote trade and commerce. Its Middle Eastern counterpart would be the Karimis, an organization of merchants dealing in spices and other goods, centered on the Indian Ocean but also active in the Mediterranean. The Karimis' volume of trade may have been even larger, but their overall position was weaker and they proved far more ephemeral.

Lastly, there is economic policy. Medieval European governments, like Middle Eastern ones until much later, were very much concerned with provisioning and the avoidance of famine. But in most city-states, to quote Cipolla, "There was a conscious effort to industrialize. At the beginning of the fourteenth century the conviction was widespread that industry spelled welfare. In a Tuscan

5 • *Fast sailing boat used by Southern European countries in the 15th and 16th centuries*

statute of 1336, statements may be read which might have been written by the most modern upholders of industrialization in the twentieth century."[15] Such national monarchies as England and France also took industrial and commercial needs into account, adopting appropriate measures to foster industries; they sought to increase exports with a large "value added" component and restrict imports of competitive goods, while encouraging imports that served as inputs into goods supplying important local needs or designed for export. Another manifestation of the same policy is the enactment of the Navigation Laws to stimulate local shipping; such laws were passed as early as the thirteenth century. The energetic measures taken to stabilize European currencies after the great inflation of the sixteenth century stand in striking contrast to the policy of the Ottomans and Safavids, and European taxes were somewhat more rational and less oppressive. Perhaps most important, property was far more secure in Europe than anywhere else in the world. The principal reason was probably the fact that producers—landlords, merchants, craftsmen, and industrialists—were more fully represented in government and had more influence on its policy than in other regions.

Japan and the Middle East

I shall also deal briefly with Japan, since I have discussed it too elsewhere at some length.[16] Perhaps the simplest way to point out the contrast between Japan and the Middle East is to say that early in the nineteenth century, well before it had been "opened up," Japan was a highly modernized country in every respect except technology. This may be studied under three headings: political, social, and economic.

Among the favorable political factors may be mentioned Japan's almost unparalleled ethnic, linguistic, and religious homogeneity, which has spared it many of the travails afflicting other societies. This homogeneity is reinforced by the extraordinary cohesion shown by the Japanese in both war and peace, and their readiness to subordinate their individual interests to those of a larger group, be they the state's or Toyota's. Japan achieved unity very early—by the seventh or eighth century—and by and large has succeeded in maintaining it. The central government exercised a fair measure of control over the land, enough to ensure peace and to carry out the few major public works that were deemed necessary. Village solidarity was also strong and much authority could be left to local bodies without endangering stability. After its unsuccessful invasion of Korea and its defeat by the Chinese at the Yalu river in 1593, Japan withdrew into itself and had three centuries of peace. Lastly, Japan produced a ruling class which eventually carried out what is perhaps the most spectacular modernization in history. Moreover, it was a ruling class that was willing to learn from others. In 1868, Prince Iwakura Tomomi led an amazing mission abroad. A large number of the most senior Japanese government leaders left their posts temporarily and visited the United States and Europe from 1871 to 1873 to learn about Western technology, government, business and society. They applied their newfound knowledge throughout the Japanese economy.[17]

The social record is even more impressive. For some 150 years Japan managed to keep its population constant at about 30 million, partly because of the usual Malthusian checks but also because of deliberate control by means of abortion and infanticide. Birth rates were distinctly below those of most other regions, including the Middle East, and so were death rates; more generally, health conditions seem to have been relatively good. Urbanization was extraordinarily high. By 1720, Tokyo had about one million inhabitants, matched only by London and Peking; Osaka and Kyoto had about 400,000 each; and some 12% of the total population lived in towns of 10,000 or more inhabitants, a figure higher than that for all but three or four European countries. Education was widespread, and by the 1850s "an estimated 40 per cent of the male population and 10 per cent of the female had achieved some degree of literacy." In the cities the figures were much higher, being put at 75% to 85% for males. One result was a very large publishing industry; in the 1780s some 3,000 titles were being published each year, editions of more than 10,000 were not uncommon, books were cheap, and both free and commercial lending libraries were active—conditions that compare favorably with the most advanced European countries.[18] Lastly, there was a keen intellectual curiosity and willingness to learn from other cultures, first China, then Europe. In the late seventeenth century some Japanese started learning Dutch, and in the eighteenth they began systematically to study Western technology, science, and painting; soon a small number of Japanese had become familiar with Newtonian physics and Western physiology.[19]

As regards the economy, perhaps the most striking aspect was the effort, sustained over several centuries, to raise agricultural output by using better methods, selecting seeds, experimenting with various types of organic fertilizers, introducing new cash crops, and so forth. An eighteenth-century book on agriculture had a first printing of 3,000 copies, and many books on agriculture went through several editions. As a result, Japanese yields were among the very highest in the world, and rose steadily.

Japanese handicrafts were at a very high level and were widespread in the villages as well as the cities. Because of Japan's isolation, these crafts were exposed to European competition far later than those of the Middle East, India, Latin America, or even China, and survived longer, to play an important part in the country's industrialization, particularly in the textile and ceramic industries but also in many other branches, through subcontracting. They also survived longer because of the peculiar pattern of Japanese development: the Japanese soon picked up European production methods but retained their traditional consumption patterns until very recently, whereas the people of the Middle East (and others) soon learned to consume *alla franga* but are only just beginning to adopt Western production methods. In the last few decades the pattern of consumption of the Japanese has changed, but their strong preference for homemade goods has persisted, to the chagrin of American and European exporters; in this area too the contrast with the Middle East is very marked.

Other economic matters that may be mentioned are the high degree of monetization and the well-developed credit institutions and instruments including paper money, checks, and even "future transactions in rice" in

Osaka in 1730. Double-entry bookkeeping, some of it on a very high level, was practiced, and what was possibly the world's first department store was established by the Mitsui family in Tokyo in 1683. Perhaps most striking is the prevailing work and profit ethic, attested in the large number of commercial, agricultural, and other books used in Japanese schools.[20] It should also be added that Japan had natural resources adequate for the preindustrial and early industrial period, including iron, copper, coal, wood, and water power, and that its navigable rivers and long coastlines greatly facilitated transport.

Russia and the Middle East

Comparison of the Russian and the Middle Eastern economies at the beginning of the nineteenth century would, at first sight, reveal little difference. Grain yields were somewhat lower in Russia,[21] the products of the handicrafts were inferior, urbanization was far lower, literacy little if at all higher, and transport costs distinctly higher. The main factors that had held up Russia's development for so long—isolation from Western Europe, the burden of an unhappy history, the huge distances and harsh climate which made it so difficult to exploit the country's vast riches, and the vicious institution of serfdom—still held the country in their grip. A closer look, however, reveals other factors at work which over the next hundred years were to produce a vast difference between the two regions.

First of all, Russia had, during most of its history, a strong government. The armies that had defeated the Swedish king, Charles XII, and raided the neighborhood of Stockholm, overpowered the Prussian king, Frederick II, occupied Berlin, and chased Napoleon all the way to Paris, and the navy that, sailing from the Baltic, had captured Beirut in 1772, presuppose an efficient bureaucracy, a good organization providing munitions and supplies, and a great capacity to raise taxes. During Peter the Great's reign tax collections increased fivefold, and they went on increasing under his successors. Moreover, the government was keenly aware of the need for economic and social development and had been taking many measures to bring this about. As early as 1569 some English industrialists were encouraged to build ironworks in Russia, and in the course of the next hundred years many enterprises in metallurgy, glass, sugar, and other branches were set up by foreigners, especially German craftsmen. In 1652 a special quarter, the sloboda, was established in Moscow for foreign craftsmen.[22] Peter made much greater use of the foreigners than his predecessors had, and he went further, implementing a mercantilist policy for developing the economy. Canals were dug, shipyards were built, and many industrial enterprises were undertaken. But, like his European contemporaries, Peter believed that the bulk of development would have to be carried out by private enterprise, and he set out to "manufacture the manufacturers," protecting them with high tariffs and other measures and encouraging them with loans and various privileges. In 1718 three colleges or boards (for business, manufactures, and mines) were created to oversee development and grant privileges to those qualified.[23]

Peter's successors continued to encourage industry and mining but gave private enterprise rather more scope.[24] As a result, the number of factories multiplied many times over and their average size increased. Russia's iron industry became, for some decades, the biggest in the world, and there was a large expansion in textiles, sugar, and some branches of the chemical industry.[25] A small number of entrepreneurs, mostly former merchants but some ex-serfs, also came to control large industrial enterprises in the Urals, Moscow, and elsewhere. This economic expansion was accompanied by a good deal of inventiveness. A list of Russian innovations in applied science and industry in the late eighteenth and early nineteenth centuries makes impressive reading, even after discounting for the Soviet tendency to claim Russian firsts in every field, from the invention of the wheel to the marvels of the twenty-first century.[26]

There was also much intellectual progress. The first printing press was established in 1553, although output remained small. Peter's approach to education was strictly practical: he opened engineering, naval, artillery, and mathematical schools, and founded a newspaper in 1703 called *News of Military and Other Affairs Worthy of Knowledge and Memory;* he founded the Academy of Sciences, opened just after his death in 1725. He forced the nobility to send their sons to government schools. Moscow University was founded in 1755 and was followed by four gymnasia. At the very beginning of the nineteenth century two more universities were established (at Kazan and St. Petersburg) and forty gymnasia.[27] Thus a base was laid for Russia's tremendous intellectual advance in the nineteenth century.

It is interesting to follow developments in the field of social thought. Even before Peter several economists had shown a good understanding of the situation in Russia, notably Ordin-Nashchokin (1605-80) and Pososhkov (1652-1726); in 1720, the latter wrote the important *Book on Poverty and Wealth.* In 1738 the first manual on agricultural economics was published.

The encyclopaedic mind of Lomonosov (1711-65) addressed historical and linguistic questions as well as those of natural science. In 1765 the Free Economic Society was established, and between 1787 and 1792 the *Commercial Dictionary,* the first economic encyclopaedia in Russia, was published.[28] It is worth noting that the Russian translation of Adam Smith's *Wealth of Nations* appeared in 1802-6, only twenty-six years after the English edition. Under Catherine, Nikolai Novikov (1744-1818) wrote some very incisive criticisms of Russian society, and his book enterprises published some 900 titles, while Alexander Radishchev (1749-1802) wrote his famous *Journey from St. Petersburg to Moscow.*[29] In 1820 the Imperial Library in St. Petersburg had 300,000 volumes, a figure exceeded only by the Royal Library in Paris, the Bodleian at Oxford, and the Archival Library in Munich.[30]

In other words, the heavy Russian dough was being leavened by both economic and intellectual progress. The results were soon to be visible, on the one hand, in Russia's cultural florescence, and on the other, in the industrial upsurge of the 1830s to 1850s.[31] The abolition of serfdom in 1861 made possible a swift capitalist development that registered the highest rate of industrial growth in the world, laid the world's second largest network of railways, began to improve land tenure and agricultural methods, spread education so that the literacy rate among recruits rose from 30% in 1888 to 68% in 1913,[32] and, but for the shattering effects of World War I, might well have carried Russia to some form of constitutional bourgeois government.

The Balkans

Today, by any economic or social criteria, this region is far ahead of the Middle East. Before World War I it was well ahead in the social field and in certain economic aspects, for example, industrialization and railway mileage, but not in others, such as per capita income or foreign trade. And yet around 1800 the Balkans were in most respects no better off than most of the Middle East. Grain yields may have been slightly higher.[33] Transport was probably no better: more carts were used and more rivers were navigable, but the terrain was muddier and rougher and camel transport was not available. In some areas, notably Bulgaria, handicrafts were more widespread, but the region lacked the high crafts of Istanbul, Cairo, Aleppo, and Isfahan.[34]

> If only absolute security for person and property could be obtained,
> I believe Bulgaria would be one of the most prosperous countries in
> Europe; and even as it is, I should be glad to think that the labouring
> poor of England and Ireland were as well off, well clothed and well
> housed, as the Bulgars.
>
> Henry C. Barkley, *Between the Danube and the Black Sea*
> (London, 1876), reproduced in D. Warriner, ed.,
> *Contrasts in Emerging Societies* (Bloomington, 1965), p. 222.

Literacy was probably slightly, though surely not much, higher, but urbanization was far lower.

The Balkans have one important natural advantage over the Middle East: higher and more regular rainfall, resulting in more forests, more water power, and more navigable rivers. But the secret of the area's better performance lies more in the political and social fields. First of all, the Balkans obtained independence from Turkey much earlier and, although Balkan governments were far from being models of stability or enlightenment, they were more responsive to their national needs. They helped the economy by giving protection, building infrastructure, and extending credit, and by bringing about some industrialization before World War I. Second, and more important, Balkan societies were far healthier than those of the Middle East. This may be observed in many aspects.

First and foremost, an enormous majority of peasants came to own their land, and since for a long time population density was light their plots were adequate. In Serbia, "old" Greece and Thessaly, and Bulgaria, land distribution came about with independence and the departure of the Turkish ruling class, and in Croatia with the Austrian reforms of 1848. Only Rumania had a large—and parasitic—landlord class and a very deprived peasantry, in spite of the agrarian reform law of 1864 and other measures taken by the Rumanian government.[35] As a result, many foreign travellers commented favorably on living standards and the prevalent social equality.[36] Another result of this equality, and of the development of cash crops for export to central and Western Europe,[37] was the growth of rural cooperatives, which both met some of the farmers' credit needs and helped them improve production.[38]

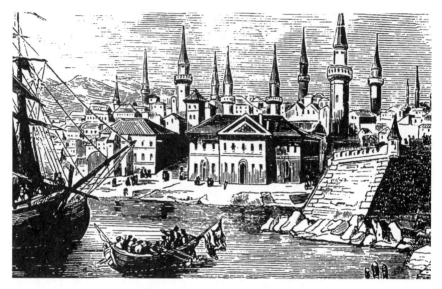

6 • Harbor in the Balkan town of Viddin

Second, the Balkan population was distinctly more educated than the Middle Eastern. Already in the seventeenth and eighteenth centuries students were sent to central and western Europe, books in the various vernaculars were printed in central and western Europe and sent to the Balkans, and many schools were established in Greece.[39] Trade with Austria and Italy also opened channels for new ideas, and Ragusa (now Dubrovnik) was a powerful center of the Enlightenment. After independence many schools were opened, general, monitorial and technical. By 1910, some 35% to 40% of children aged 5 to 14 were attending primary school, and secondary enrollments were also high; moreover, a large proportion of those in secondary and higher education were engaged in technical training.[40] By 1907 Greece had achieved a literacy rate of 39% and Bulgaria of 34%, compared to Egypt's 7%, and even lower figures for the rest of the Middle East; by 1927 the figures were 60% for Bulgaria and Greece compared to 15% for Egypt and 8% for Turkey.[41] Third, birthrates began to decline shortly before World War I, and by the 1920s and 30s had fallen to low levels.[42]

Greece was the most disadvantaged country in terms of resources, and its inhabitants have therefore always engaged in trade and shipping. Already by the eighteenth century Greeks accounted for a very large proportion of Ottoman trade and shipping as well as of southern Russian. Greeks were also extensively employed in the Ottoman bureaucracy. A Greek bourgeoisie came into being early and played an important role in the political, cultural, and economic development of both Greece and its neighbors.

Lastly, the Balkan countries profited from the emigration of hundreds of thousands of their citizens to the New World, Russia, Egypt, and elsewhere. Money was remitted, skills were acquired, and new ideas were brought back. Of all the Middle Eastern countries only Lebanon enjoyed this stimulus, though mention may be made of the Iranians in the Caucasus.

Latin America

Latin America is too complex an area to discuss here, and therefore only two countries will be considered, Argentina and Mexico, which may be taken to represent, respectively, the empty, temperate, and fertile southern region, and the densely settled area of ancient civilizations in the north.

In the eighteenth century, Buenos Aires grew into a town of more than 50,000 as a port of entry for the great silver-mining center of Potosi, in present-day Bolivia. After independence Buenos Aires developed into an export center for hides, wool, and other animal products, and after 1860 began to attract large amounts of capital and immigrants, enabling Argentina to lay down 35,000 kilometers of railways by 1914 and to become a major exporter of wheat and meat. By 1914 Buenos Aires had 1.5 million inhabitants and real wages there were higher than in Paris. Large-scale industrialization began in the 1880s and continued at a rapid rate until the end of World War II. The growth of GNP was such that Argentina compared favorably with Australia and Canada, and its culture was almost on a European level. All this, *dependencia* theory notwithstanding, presents no problem for the old-fashioned economic historian who believes in development based on the export of a staple product.[43] The real mystery is why Argentina has performed so poorly since the last war, and one theory is that politics in general, and Juan Peron in particular, have much to answer for; however, the effect of falling export prices should not be underestimated.

Mexico did not have Argentina's assets—immensely fertile land, abundant and regular rainfall, and navigable rivers—and its history has been much more checkered, starting with the shrinkage of the Indian population from perhaps 20 million in 1500 to 1 million in 1600.[44] But what should be stressed is that around 1800, Mexico was richer and much better educated than the Middle East.

As regards wealth, in the eighteenth century Mexico experienced a great upsurge in both population and production, including mining, agriculture, and handicraft industry.[45] Available figures suggest that per capita GDP in Mexico was from a third to a half that in the United States—and it may be noted that Mexico accounted for about one-half of the total population and product of Spanish America.[46] Mining technology was quite advanced and improved steadily, the handicrafts were active, the big estates received much capital investment, and trade, both legal and contraband, was very large; there were many substantial merchants (some with a capital approaching $500,000) who gave and took extensive credit.[47]

All this does not of course mean that the level of living of the masses was high. First, there was the enormous unrequited drain of silver to Spain: for 1785 the total for the colonies has been put at $30 million, compared to $6.5 million for India in the same year.[48] Second, there was the vast inequality due to ethnic composition and social stratification. At the end of the eighteenth century one-fifth of Mexico's population was Spanish and another fifth of mixed race; three-fifths were Indian, a figure comparable to that for a few parts of Spanish America, but much higher than for others[49]. At the top of the social pyramid were some estates worth $2 to $3 million.[50]

This wealth made it possible to support an impressive educational establishment. Printing presses were set up at the Conquest, as early as the 1550s universities were opened in Lima and Mexico City and by the end of the colonial period there were more than twenty institutions of higher learning, including a College of Mines opened in Mexico in 1792; among them they had conferred 150,000 degrees.[51] They were modeled on Salamanca, then one of the largest (7,000 students) and most active universities in Europe.[52] In addition many students went abroad, not only to Spain but to France, Italy, and England.[53] And of course Spain was always part of the European cultural stream, even if it was somewhat of a backwater. As a result, Latin Americans participated very fully in the Enlightenment—in philosophy, physics, mathematics, and biology—and were familiar with (and often critical of) the works of Descartes, Newton, Locke, Leibnitz, Adam Smith, Buffon, Franklin, and others. This is brought out very clearly by a study based on the theses written by students at the rather small University of San Carlos in Guatemala.[54] In addition, intellectuals applied themselves to local problems, ranging from botany and medicine to economics.[55]

Clearly, Latin America was well ahead of the Middle East in 1800. The great destruction and anarchy following independence, with local wars and foreign intervention, however, set the region back. To take two examples, it was only around 1880 that the 1810 level of silver output was regained; and the University of Mexico was closed repeatedly between 1833 and 1865, and finally shut down in the latter year. The region had to start its upward climb painfully again in the last decades of the nineteenth century.

China and the Middle East

Until the eighteenth century, China was always at the forefront of economic, technological, and even scientific progress. It had also produced a highly educated society. Printing had been practiced on a large scale since the seventh century, and in the eighteenth and nineteenth centuries "perhaps 30 to 45 percent of the males and only 2 to 10 percent of the females (possessed] some ability to read and write."[56] Following a series of shattering internal and external shocks in the first half of the nineteenth century, the society broke down and China experienced nearly a century and a half of intense disruption. It is now set to become once again one of the most dynamic societies in the world.

By now it seems clear that the Middle East entered the nineteenth century at a disadvantage, economically and socially, compared to the other regions surveyed. We still need to ask, however, why the Middle East did not catch up in the next two centuries. The reasons are to be sought in both external and internal factors.

Impact of Europe

As regards the external, the Middle East was subjected to a very powerful European impact in the political, economic, and social spheres.[57] This had many beneficial results. Foreign trade multiplied many times over, agricultural output expanded greatly, new crops were introduced, railways and ports were built, hygiene improved noticeably, and the foundations of modern education were laid down. The region began to modernize at an accelerating pace. But in addition to the usual painful disruptions accompanying any change, there were several adverse developments—though nothing, I should hasten to add, comparable to the earlier drain of bullion from Latin America and India, the export of slaves from Africa, and the Opium War and its aftermath in China.

First of all, as in all parts of the world, improved hygiene and mechanical transport, which reduced famines, led to population growth, through a drop in the death rate; in the Middle East, however, the birth rate started declining much later than elsewhere, and in fact in many countries it still shows no signs of decrease. The result has been an explosive population growth that has put great strain on resources. Second, again as in all parts of the world, the handicrafts suffered from the competition of machine-made goods, and many were ruined; however, reindustrialization—the setting up of modern factories—started later in the Middle East, and was much slower there than in Russia, the Balkans, Latin America, Japan, India, and, in some respects, China. This was partly due to the smallness of internal markets and the paucity of natural resources, infrastructure, capital, and skills; partly to the baleful effects of the Commercial Treaties, which prevented tariff protection; and partly to the lack of interest of governments, whether national (with the conspicuous exception of Muhammad Ali) or foreign. It was only in the 1930s and more particularly after the World War II that the region began to industrialize.

Third, there was the huge volume of public debt, most of which was squandered. Again, the Middle East is not unique in this respect, the record of the Balkans and Latin America being equally poor (but not that of Russia, India, and Japan). Whether the Middle East was treated more harshly than other regions in its terms of debt settlement is moot: Egypt probably was, but Turkey was not. The large amount of private capital that flowed in was, on the whole, used productively.

Fourth, to a particularly high degree, economic development in the Middle East was implanted by foreigners and remained confined to an enclave. The region not only took capital and technology from abroad; it imported a bourgeoisie and a skilled working class as well. Except for members of the religious minorities, few Middle Easterners participated in the expanding modern sectors of the economy—foreign trade, finance, mechanical transport, mining, and later industry—which were financed and run by Europeans. As a result, the natural resources of the Middle East were developed, but not the human resources. Moreover, in contrast to Russia, the Balkans, and Latin America, foreigners did not eventually blend with the population through intermarriage and permanent residence. And it was only in the 1930s and 1940s that a national Muslim bourgeoisie emerged.

One more point should perhaps be added. Because of its political situation, the Middle East in some ways had the worst of both worlds. Unlike Japan, Russia, the Balkans, and Latin America, the countries of the Middle

East did not enjoy independence, with the chance to make and also to learn from mistakes. Nor were they subjected to the kind of control that led to much development by the British in India, the Russians in Azerbaijan, the Japanese in Taiwan, or the Americans in the Philippines. Instead, most often, there was the influence of rival powers jealously watching and checking each other, preventing railway building in the Ottoman Empire and Iran and thwarting other schemes. Of course, the experience of North Africa shows that direct foreign control, too, can lead to much development of resources with very little benefit to the indigenous population.

To these external factors must be added an internal one, which is best described as a lack of sustained interest in economic development. It is true that the governments were greatly handicapped by the Capitulations, Commercial Conventions, foreign pressures, and lack of funds; but it cannot be seriously argued that they could not have done more to promote the economy and especially education. Even more striking is the indifference of the people themselves. After all, it does not take much money to teach children—or adults—how to read and write, but it does take work. One should note that in Western Europe, Japan, and elsewhere the raising of literacy rates to the first crucial 40% or 50% was achieved not by the state but by churches and other social agencies. Here one can contrast the very limited efforts made by the ethnic Turks, Arabs, and Iranians not only with those of their Balkan neighbors and others but also with those of their minorities—Greeks, Armenians, Jews, and Christian Arabs. The minorities were economically much more successful, a fact partly due to foreign help and protection but also to the numerous schools they set up and their pursuit of technical and professional education.[58] One more point may be briefly made. The vast majority of Middle Easterners who went to study abroad did not go in for science, economics or, except for a small number of engineers, technology. Most of them studied law, and a few studied medicine and letters. This too must have had an adverse effect on economic development.

In the last fifty years or so this dismal picture has changed markedly. Industrialization has spread rapidly and has been greatly strengthened by the development of oil, which has generated vast income and skills and provided raw materials and fuels. The infrastructure has been vastly expanded and is now approaching adequacy. Land reforms have transformed the ancient, vicious agrarian structure. The economy has been wrested from foreign hands and is now run by nationals.

Hygiene has considerably improved and life expectancy has doubled to

7 • Street scene in Heliopolis, Egypt in the 1950s

sixty years. The region is beginning to draw on the enormous resources, hitherto almost unused, of half its population as women participate much more actively in economic and social activity. Perhaps most encouraging of all is the progress in education, best indicated by the fact that adult literacy, which just after World War II averaged about 20%, has risen to 50% or more. At the higher level, the region now has tens of thousands of men and women trained in science, technology, economics, and statistics, some of whom are doing excellent work. The progress in education can be traced, chronologically and comparatively, in the illuminating tables compiled by Richard Easterlin, showing school enrolment rates per 10,000 inhabitants.[59] If we take a figure of 1,000 as indicating the level of primary education that allows a country to absorb technology and therefore embark on rapid economic development, we can see that the three major Middle Eastern countries—Egypt, Iran, and Turkey—reached that level by 1960; as late as 1930 the figure was only 300 for Turkey, less for Egypt, and far less for Iran. By contrast, Western Europe had reached it by the first half of the nineteenth century, the United States still earlier, Japan and Russia at the turn of the century, and the larger Latin American countries in the 1920s or 30s.

Of course the Middle East is still beset by tremendous problems: explosive population growth, urban hypertrophy, lagging agricultural production, the stifling grip of the government over the economy. And it is truly sad to see the waste of resources on unending wars and ever-accumulating armaments. But it is not excessively optimistic to state that the foundations of economic and social development have at last been laid.

I should like to conclude with one more observation. Hitherto, my analysis of the region's economic and social performance has been confined to physical and social factors. I should like to make a brief excursion into the treacherous realm of mentality. Oversimplifying and generalizing wildly, one can say that whereas the Greeks were interested in ideas, the Romans in organization, the Chinese and Japanese in things and organization, and the Europeans in ideas and things, the Middle Easterners have been interested in words, but also in God; and, as a Middle Easterner reminded us, "The Word was God." The latter interests do not tend to promote economic and social development. But consider what they have enabled the region to achieve: the Sumerians and Egyptians started the whole process of civilization; the Phoenicians invented the alphabet and initiated the mercantile city-state economy which, as Hicks points out, was the most important economic development since the establishment of agriculture.[60] The Jews, Persians, and Arabs between them gave most of the world's great religions. Add to this some of the finest art and literature. These contributions surely outweigh a certain deficiency in the technological, economic, and social fields, especially since there is nothing that decrees that the region will not do better in those fields in the future than it has in the past. Furthermore, we do live in a time when many have come to realize that economic growth and technological development are not the most important things in the world.

NOTES

1. Lynn White, *Medieval Technology and Social Change* (Oxford: Clarendon Press, 1962), p. 155.

2. E. Reischauer and J. Fairbank, *East Asia, The Great Tradition* (Boston, 1960), p. 178; *The Cambridge Economic History of Europe,* Vol. II (Cambridge, 1952), pp. 125, 160, and 434.

3. L. Salzman, *Edward I* (London: Constable, 1968), p. 190.

4. See Charles Issawi, "The Transformation of the Economic Position of the *Millets* in the Nineteenth Century," in Benjamin Braude and Bernard Lewis, eds., *Christians and Jews in the Ottoman Empire* (2 vols.; New York, 1982).

5. E. Ashtor, "L'Apogée du commerce vénitien," in Hans-Georg Beck, Manoussos Manoussacas, and Agostino Pertusi, eds., *Venezia, Centro di Mediazone tra oriente e Occidente, Secoli XV-XVI* (Florence, 1977).

6. Somewhat more seems to have been done by the Ottomans in the Balkans than in the Middle East; see Halil Inalcik, *The Ottoman Empire: The Classical Age, 1300-1460* (New York, 1973), pp.146-50.

7. For a partial list of plagues see Charles Issawi, *An Economic History of the Middle East and North Africa* (New York, 1982), pp. 97-9.

8. For examples of lack of interest see Charles Issawi, "Europe, the Middle East and the Shift in Power," reprinted in idem, *The Arab World's Legacy* (Princeton, 1981), pp. 118-19; for an excellent general discussion, see Bernard Lewis, *The Muslim Discovery of Europe* (New York, 1982).

9. Bernard Lewis, *op. cit.,* pp. 50 and 306; Philip Hitti, *History of Syria, Including Lebanon and Palestine* (New York & London, 1951), pp. 676-7; Johannes Pedersen, *The Arabic Book* (Princeton, 1984), pp. 131-41.

10. Issawi, "Europe."

11. E. L. Jones, *The European Miracle* (Cambridge, 1981).

12. On this see Andrew Watson, *Agricultural Innovation in the Early Islamic World* (Cambridge and New York, 1983). It may be noted that in England as early as the thirteenth century scientific treatises on agriculture and estate management began to be circulated; see George Trevelyan, *History of England* (London & New York, 1947), p. 153.

13. Carlo Cipolla, *Literacy and Development in the West* (Harmondsworth, 1969), passim.

14. Carlo Cipolla, "The Italian and Iberian Peninsulas," *Cambridge Economic History of Europe,* Vol. III (1941), p. 413, and more generally pp. 408-19; see also Vol. IV (1967), chap. 8, and Vol. V (1977), chaps. 7 and 8.

15. Charles Issawi, "Why Japan?" in Ibrahim Ibrahim, ed., *Arab Resources* (Washington, D.C., 1983), pp. 283-300.

16. Edwin L. Harper, "Do We Need an Industrial Policy?" in Michael Wachter and Susan Wachter, eds., *Removing Obstacles to Economic Growth* (Philadelphia, 1984), p. 460.

17. C. E. Black et al., *The Modernization of Japan and Russia* (New York, 1975), pp. 82-5, 106-9; Herbert Passin, Society and Education in Japan (New York,

Columbia University, 1965), pp. 11-61; Nan [Ivan] Morris, *The Life of an Amorous Woman* (London, 1964), pp. 26-7.

18. Donald Keene, *The Japanese Discovery of Europe* (Stanford, 1969), passim.

19. For details see Issawi, "Why Japan," pp. 294-5.

20. See Jerome Blum, *The End of the Old Order in Europe* (Princeton, 1978), pp. 144-5; Issawi, *An Economic History*, p. 119.

21. Peter Lyashchenko, *History of the National Economy of Russia* (New York, 1949), pp. 269 and 833-55; Hermann Kellenbenz, "The Organization of Industrial Production," *Cambridge Economic History of Europe*, V. 529.

22. See Simone Blanc, "The Economic Policy of Peter the Great," in William Blackwell, ed., *Russian Economic Development from Peter the Great to Stalin* (New York, 1974), pp. 23-49.

23. See Arcadius Kahan, "Continuity in Economic Activity and Policy During the Post-Petrine Period," in Blackwell, *Russian Economic Development*, pp. 51-70.

24. For figures and details see Lyashchenko, pp. 292-304 and 329-39 Kahan, pp. 61-3.

25. See Lyashchenko, pp. 328-9 and 425-6; Roger Portal, "The Industrialization of Russia," *Cambridge Economic History of Europe*, Vol. VI (1965), pp. 801-63.

26. Joseph Roucek, ed., *Slavonic Encyclopaedia* (New York, 1949), p. 267; Richard Pipes, *Russia under the Old Regime* (New York, 1974), p. 123.

27. Lyashchenko, pp. 837-41; see also *Bol'shaia Sovetskaia Entsiklopedia* (2nd ed.; Moscow, 1949-57), s.v. "Lomonosov," "Ordin-Nashchokin," and "Pososhkov."

28. Joseph Schumpeter, *History of Economic Analysis* (New York, 1954), p. 193; Pipes, pp. 256-8.

29. Cipolla, *Literacy and Development*, p. 109.

30. V. K. Yatsumsky, "The Industrial Revolution in Russia," in Blackwell, *Russian Economic Development*, pp. 109-36; Lyashchenko, pp. 327-39.

31. Cipolla, *Literacy and Development*, p. 118.

32. See figures for 1862-1912 in John Lampe and Marvin Jackson, *Balkan Economic History, 1550-1950* (Bloomington, 1982), p. 188.

33. See Doreen Warriner, ed. *Contrasts in Emerging Societies* (Bloomington, 1965), p. 3 and *passim;* see also *La Révolution industrielle dans le Sud-Est européen* (Sofia, 1976), pp. 146-50 and *passim.*

34. Warriner, pp. 3-16 and *passim;* L. S. Stavrianos, *The Balkans since 1453* (New York, 1958), pp. 296-7, 478-9; Lampe and Jackson, pp. 184-9.

35. For Serbia, see Warriner, pp. 302-8; for Bulgaria, ibid, pp. 255-6 and 273-5.

36. Bruce McGowan, *Economic Life in Ottoman Europe* (Cambridge and New York, 1981); Lampe and Jackson, pp. 159-201.

37. Ibid., pp. 198-200, 305-6, and 369-75; and pp. 264-7 and 363.

38. Stavrianos, pp. 146-8.

39. See tables in Lampe and Jackson, pp. 502-4.

40. UNESCO, *Progress of Literacy in Various Countries* (Paris: UNESCO, 1953).

41. Marvin Jackson, "Comparing the Balkan Demographic Experience, 1860 to 1970," *Journal of European Economic History,* 14 (Fall 1985), 223-72.

42. See Jonathan Brown, *A Socioeconomic History of Argentina, 1776-1860* (Cambridge and New York, 1979), pp. 225-34 and *passim;* also Laura Randall, *An Economic History of Argentina in the Twentieth Century* (New York, 1978).

43. D. A. Brading, *Miners and Merchants in Bourbon Mexico, 1763-1810* (Cambridge, 1971), pp. 1-3; James Lockhart and Stuart Schwartz, *Early Latin America* (Cambridge and New York, 1983), p. 36.

44. Brading, pp. 14-18; Lockhart and Schwartz, pp. 306-8.

45. Brading, pp. 18-19; Fernand Braudel, *The Perspective of the World* (New York, 1984), p. 421.

46. Brading, pp. 94-100, 120-5, 131-9, 216; Lockhart and Schwartz, pp. 142-8.

47. Braudel, p. 421.

48. Lockhart and Schwartz, p. 342; John Chance, *Race and Class in Colonial Oaxaca* (Stanford, 1978), passim.

49. Brading, pp. 294-8.

50. John Lanning, *The University in the Kingdom of Guatemala* (Ithaca, N.Y., 1955), p. 3; *Enciclopedia Universal Illustrada* (Barcelona & Madrid), s.v. "Mejico," "Peru."

51. John Elliott, *Imperial Spain,* 1469-1716 (London, 1963), p. 118.

52. Lockhart and Schwartz, p. 411.

53. John Lanning, *The Eighteenth Century Enlightenment in the University Of San Carlos de Guatemala* (Ithaca, N.Y., 1956).

54. Lockhart and Schwartz, pp. 344-6.

55. Evelyn Sakakida Rawski, *Education and Popular Literacy in Ching China* (Ann Arbor, 1979), p. 23.

56. Issawi, *An Economic History,* passim.

57. On this subject, see Issawi, "Transformation of the Economic Position."

58. Richard Easterlin, "Why Isn't the Whole World Developed?" *Journal of Economic History,* 41 (March 1981), 1-17.

59. J. R. Hicks, *A Theory of Economic History* (Oxford, 1969), p. 39.

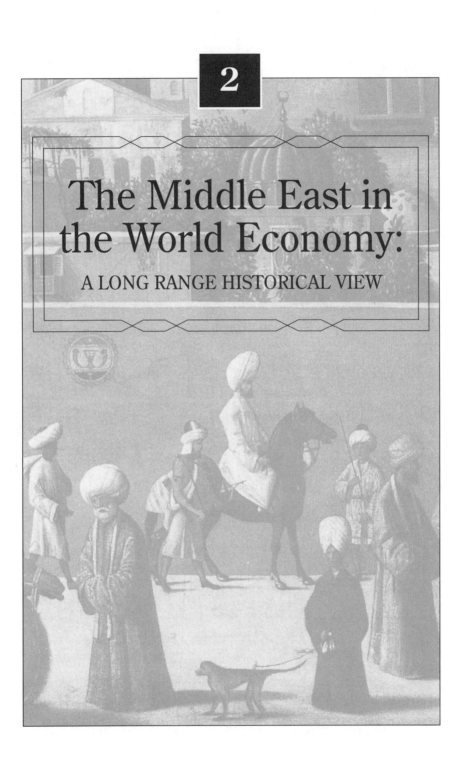

2

The Middle East in the World Economy:

A LONG RANGE HISTORICAL VIEW

ive distinct centers of civilization developed in the 3,000 or 4,000 years before the Christian era, each with its own peculiar economic structure and policy: Mesopotamia, Egypt, Syria, Iran, and Anatolia. Egypt and Mesopotamia had one fundamental economic feature in common: both depended on an irrigated agriculture. This meant that continuous, concerted, and disciplined efforts had to be sustained to preserve the irrigation canals, dams, and drains, and it is no coincidence that we see in the Tigris-Euphrates and Nile valleys the first cities, the first states, the first bureaucracies, the first systems of writing, the first calendars, and the first systematic measurements and calculations in human history. Irrigated agriculture produced the surplus that was required to support cities, bureaucrats, soldiers, priests, scholars, poets, artists, and all the paraphernalia of civilization. It also supported a large body of craftsmen, and the museums show that a high level was reached in textiles, pottery, glassware, metalwork, carpentry, and numerous other crafts.

Egypt and Mesopotamia

There were and are certain differences between Egypt and Mesopotamia; some persisted for millennia and others may still be discerned. First, Egypt is splendidly defended by wide and barren deserts, and has therefore enjoyed much longer periods of immunity from foreign invasion. Second, to quote Sir William Willcocks, an eminent engineer who worked in Egypt and Iraq as well as India, "Of all great rivers, the Nile is the most gentlemanly." Its annual rise and fall are regular and predictable, in sharp contrast to the thoroughly villainous Tigris and Euphrates which, since Noah's time, have caused untold devastation; moreover, the Nile flood occurs at a time much more favorable for agriculture. The Nile is far less salty than the Tigris and Euphrates, and therefore causes much less salination of the soil. The annual Nile flood drains itself, whereas the slope of the Mesopotamian plain is such that elaborate drainage canals have to be built and constantly cleared; when, as so often happened, this was neglected owing to a breakdown in government, tribal incursions, or other causes, much land went out of use.

8 • The Nile

Finally, the prevailing winds along the Nile blow from the north, which means that one can sail upstream and float downstream. This has given Egypt what all other parts of the Middle East lack-an inland waterway comparable to those of Europe, America, Russia, India, and China—and has immensely promoted both its political unity and economic activity.

One other difference is worth noting. From very early times, Mesopotamia, in contrast to Egypt, had private ownership of land. Moreover, a small group of private traders and bankers came into being, again in contrast to Egypt, and it was they who developed the great caravan trade that was eventually to link Syria, Arabia, the Black Sea region, Iran, India, and China; for, unlike Egypt, Mesopotamia lacked many essential raw materials, such as stone and metals, and had to acquire them by trade. Perhaps it is not a coincidence that it was in Mesopotamia that the concept of law evolved, and that such codes as that of Hammurabi were elaborated, a fact of immense significance for the future development of mankind; after all, a very large part of these codes deals with economic transactions and economic justice.[1]

Anatolia, Syria, and Iran

The other three centers—Anatolia, Syria, and Iran—may be discussed more briefly. In all three, agriculture was rainfed, which implies a smaller surplus and much greater fluctuations in crops, but also a smaller chance of total breakdown. At least as early as the third millennium B.C., Anatolia was exporting metals—copper, silver, and later, iron—to Mesopotamia and

Syria in exchange for textiles and other manufactures.[2] Syria also supported a citied economy in the fourth millennium B.C., an economy about
which we are just beginning to learn thanks to the discovery of the volumi-
nous archives of Ebla, a town near Aleppo.[3] Much more distinctive, however,
were the coastal Syrians, the Phoenicians, who were the first great traders
of antiquity. From an early date, Syrians and Phoenicians traded actively
with Mesopotamia and Egypt, exporting wood, textiles, glass, and other
manufactures, and secured the privilege of occupying special quarters in
certain cities in Egypt. Later, they vastly extended their activity, founding
colonies in North Africa and Spain and sailing as far as Britain and West
Africa.[4] Indeed, the account given by Herodotus—who was highly skeptical
on the subject—makes it almost certain that the Phoenicians circumnavi-
gated Africa at the request of the Egyptian Pharaoh, Necho, around 600 B.C.

As for Libya [Africa], we know that it is washed on all sides by the
sea except where it joins Asia, as was first demonstrated, so far as our
knowledge goes, by the Egyptian king Neco, who, after calling off the
construction of the canal between the Nile and the Arabian gulf, sent
out a fleet manned by a Phoenician crew with orders to sail round and
return to Egypt and the Mediterranean by way of the Pillars of Heracles.
The Phoenicians sailed from the Red Sea into the southern ocean, and
every autumn put in where they were on the Libyan coast, sowed a
patch of ground, and waited for next year's harvest. Then, having got in
their grain, they put to sea again, and after two full years rounded the
Pillars of Heracles in the course of the third, and returned to Egypt.
These men made a statement which I do not myself believe, though
others may, to the effect that they sailed on a westerly course round the
southern end of Libya, they had the sun on their right-to northward of
them. This is how Libya was first discovered to be surrounded by sea,
and the next people to make a similar report were the Carthaginians.

Herodotus, *The Histories, Book Four: Circumnavigation of Africa,*
trans. Aubry de Selincourt (Harmondsworth, 1954), pp. 283-4.

This concentration on trade and manufacture was unique in antiquity;
in Gordon Childe's words, "A much larger proportion of the Phoenician
population must have been engaged in industry and commerce than in the
predominantly agricultural states of Egypt, Babylonia, Assyria and Hatti.[6]
This social structure was reflected in Phoenician political institutions.

It is probably no coincidence that the alphabet was invented and spread by these merchants. I have my own theory on the subject. We know that in Ugarit, the home of the oldest known alphabet, five different scripts, including cuneiform and hieroglyphics, were in use. One day a Lebanese businessman, appalled by the cost of keeping five clerks, said, "There must be a better way of doing business. Think!"-and invented the alphabet.

Iran's numerous contributions to the economic development of the Middle East include the building of dams and subterranean canals (*qanat*), and the introduction of many plants from India. But perhaps more important was the expansion of the market. The Persian Empire was by far the largest the world had yet seen; it included the whole of the Middle East and extended to India and Central Asia.

Royal roads and posts linked the various provinces to the capital, weights and measures were standardized, uniform gold and silver coins were minted, and a canal linking the Nile to the Red Sea was completed. As a result, trade expanded greatly. In the words of Ghirshman, "The volume of trade in the sixth and fifth centuries B.C. surpassed anything previously known in the ancient East, but its main feature was that, instead of the luxury goods of earlier periods, trade was concerned above all with ordinary, everyday products, household articles and cheap clothing. Thus the development of industry was increasingly directed to the services of all classes of society in the Empire."[7] Moreover, commerce with other regions seems to have been on a larger scale than before—in particular with India, South Arabia, and Greece.[8]

The Hellenistic World

Alexander's conquests brought Greece, with its incomparable art, thought, and technology, into the heart of the Middle East. Hundreds of Greek cities were founded by him or his successors—from Alexandria of Egypt to Alexandria Areion (that is, Herat) in Afghanistan, and from Antioch in Syria to Antioch-in-Persis on the Gulf-and the number of Greek and Macedonian settlers must have run into the hundreds of thousands. However, the inflow of Greeks soon fell off sharply and many of the more remote cities declined. In the economic field, the Hellenistic period saw two important developments. First, the resources of the Middle East seem to have been more rationally and intensively developed than ever before. Second, the scope and range of trade among the different parts of the Middle East and with other regions was greatly expanded.[9]

The first process can be observed most clearly in Egypt, on which material is far more abundant than on the other countries. With the help of an efficient bureaucracy, the Ptolemies planned and managed the economy so as both to maximize its output and develop its productive potential. Irrigation was expanded by the introduction of the waterwheel (*saqiya*), Archimedean screw (*tanbur*), and other devices; the cultivated area was extended; and new plants were introduced, including vines, olives, various fruits, and improved varieties of wheat. Mines were more intensively exploited. The quality of the handicrafts, notably pottery, textiles, and metalwork, was improved. The productive power and output of the country were augmented considerably, though it may be added that the bulk of the increase was absorbed by the Greek ruling class and that the level of the mass of the Egyptian population probably showed little, if any, improvement. The same process seems to have occurred, to a lesser extent, in the other Hellenistic regions—Syria, Mesopotamia, and Anatolia—but at least in Syria, Hellenization struck deeper roots and may have brought greater material benefits as well.

Trade was facilitated by the excellent harbors, of which the one at Alexandria, with its famous lighthouse, was the most important.[10] Land routes were patrolled and traffic flowed on them more freely. Coinage was everywhere of the highest quality, making exchanges easier; in addition, Egypt had a network of royal banks and the other regions were served by city, temple, or private banks. Another favorable factor was the widespread use of two international languages: Aramaic in the Fertile Crescent, and the Greek Koine in the whole Hellenistic world.

International trade expanded in all directions: first, in the Mediterranean, primarily with Greece, but soon also, on a rising scale, with Carthage, Sicily, and Italy; second, with India, Arabia, and East Africa, by a combination of sea and caravan routes; and third, with Central Asia, connecting with the silk caravans to China. The Middle East imported spices, silk, slaves, and other goods for which it seems to have paid mainly by exports of manufactures. Two main routes were in use: the Red Sea route, through South Arabia and from there to the southern Syrian ports or to Egypt; and the Gulf route, terminating in the northern Syrian ports. Rivalry between the Ptolemies and Seleucids for control of these routes was intense, and it continued to be an important factor in the politics of the region until early modern times.

The Roman Period

Under the Romans, law and order were enforced severely, but effectively. Magnificent roads were laid and it is no coincidence that the Arabs in the east, like the Germans in the north, took the word *strata* into their languages as *sirat* and *strasse,* or *street,* respectively. The cisterns built by the Romans still serve villages and towns in Syria and Transjordan. The frontier of cultivation was pushed far into the steppe. And one could continue in this vein.

In this period, the Middle East played a leading part in the economy of the Empire, and also in the world economy. The population of Egypt, Syria, and Asia Minor was probably well over 20 million, or about one-third of that of the Empire.[11] If we add a purely conjectural—but probably rather conservative—figure of 10 million for Iraq, Iran, and Arabia, the Middle Eastern population of over 30 million would represent a seventh or an eighth of the estimated world population,[12] a ratio that has not been attained since that time. In agriculture, Egypt exported to Rome 140,000 tons of wheat each year, and Tunisia twice as much; Syria and Mesopotamia usually more than met their needs for grain; and olive oil was exported from Tunisia and Anatolia.[13] In handicrafts, Egypt was a large exporter, to both East and West, of papyrus, linen, and glassware, and it processed and re-exported Oriental spices to the Mediterranean lands. Syria was equally active in linen and woolens and its glass manufacturers went further, exporting know-how and founding branches in various European provinces. Anatolia, principally Pergamum, was the source of parchment and was also famous for its woolens.[14] Trade with India and the Far East became much more active after the Greeks had become familiar with the pattern of the monsoon winds in the first century B.C., and, according to Strabo, 120 ships participated in the trade. The Roman Empire imported spices, incense, silk, Persian carpets, and other products, mainly through the Red Sea route via Egypt or southern Syria, but also partly over the land route from Central Asia through Iran. Its exports—linens, metals and metalware, and glassware—did not quite cover its imports, and a drain of bullion to the East, estimated by Pliny at 100 million sesterces (about 5 million 1938 dollars), ensued. Needless to say, the Indian trade enriched many communities in the Middle East, including Muza in Yemen, Alexandria in Egypt, Petra and Palmyra in Syria, and, most important for the future, Mecca, the merchant republic where the Prophet Muhammad was born in 571 A.D.[15]

The Arab Conquest

The Arab conquest led to a drastic re-orientation of Middle Eastern trade. The Mediterranean, which had been the main link binding the Roman Empire, was split into two antagonistic, and usually warring, halves, the Christian and the Muslim.[16] Together with the depopulation and impoverishment of Europe, this split greatly diminished economic exchanges between the two regions. But the Middle East was more than compensated by the establishment of the Arab Empire, which stretched from the Pyrenees to Central Asia and India and had an area of nine to ten million square kilometers, or about two and a half times that of the Roman Empire; however, a much larger proportion consisted of deserts, and the inhabited area may have been around two million square kilometers, compared to, say, three million for the Roman Empire. At the peak of the Arab Empire, around the tenth century A.D., its population may have been about 35 to 40 million, or rather less than two-thirds of the Roman.[17] By then the Arab Empire had broken down into a multiplicity of states, but its religious and cultural unity remained: it had a common set of laws based on the *shari'a,* and a *lingua franca,* Arabic. Men and goods continued to move very freely

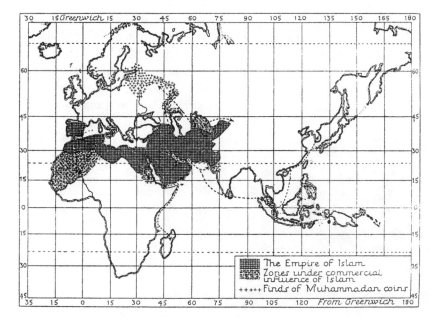

9 • *The world of Islam*

across the political borders.

The establishment of the Arab Empire also promoted trade in another way. By their eastern conquests the Arabs abolished two borders: between Iran and northern India, and between the Iranian and Roman Empires. The latter had constituted a serious obstacle to trade because the Romans levied heavy duties, reaching 25 percent at certain times, on imports from Iran, and one may presume that the Parthians and Sassanians also had their customs taxes. Still more important, relations between the two empires were usually hostile, and the Romans and Byzantines strongly resented their dependence on Iran for goods (coming overland or through the Gulf) from India, Central Asia, and China. They made great efforts to divert as much traffic as possible to the Red Sea route, which they or friendly states such as Ethiopia controlled. Under Islam, all these obstacles were removed-though the rivalry between the Red Sea and Gulf routes persisted-and trade with the East flourished as never before.

In addition, thanks to the founding of the Arab Empire, the geographical position of the Middle East in the world shifted, if a solecism may be allowed. The Islamic realm lay in the center of the Eastern Hemisphere, adjacent to all the major civilizations of the time (Western Europe, Byzantium, India, and China) as well as to the hinterlands of Eastern Europe and Africa, and trade and other contacts with all these regions were active.

The goods traded with the East (India, Indonesia, and China) showed little change. Spices continued to be imported, probably in much larger quantities, both for the Middle East's own consumption and for re-export to Europe. Teak and other kinds of wood were imported from India, and porcelain and silk fabrics from China. Silkworms had been smuggled out of China in the sixth century and silk was soon being produced in Anatolia, Syria, and especially the Caspian provinces of Iran.[18] In return, the Middle East exported to India and the Far East "costly fabrics of linen, cotton or wool, including rugs; metal work and iron ore,"[19] as well as pearls, incense, ivory, and, since its exports did not cover its imports, bullion.

10 • Arab ship bound for India

Most of this trade was carried in Arab and Persian ships. These ships are mentioned in Chinese sources at least as early as the seventh century A.D., and in the eighth and ninth centuries their number seems to have been very large. A sizable Muslim trading colony developed in Canton that actually captured and sacked the city in 758 A.D. With few exceptions, notably the expeditions that reached as far as East Africa at the beginning of the fifteenth century, the Chinese did not sail further west than the Straits of Malacca, and most of the shipping of the Indian Ocean was conducted by Arabs and Persians.[20]

The Middle East also carried out an active overland trade, up the Volga and other Russian rivers, with the Baltic, importing furs, wax, and slaves, and exporting manufactured goods. Hoards of early Islamic coins have been found in the Baltic area; in charity to the Vikings, one may presume that these were partly acquired by trade rather than pillage![21]

I saw with my own eyes how the Rus had arrived with their wares, and pitched their camp along the Volga. Never did I see a people so gigantic: they are tall as palm trees, and florid and ruddy in complexion. . . . [They] wear a garment of rough cloth, which is thrown over one side, so that one hand remains free.

Every Rus carries an axe, a dagger, and a sword, and without these weapons they are never seen. Their swords are broad, with wavy lines, and of Frankish make. From the tip of the fingernails to the neck, each man of them is tattooed with pictures of trees, living beings, and other things.

The women carry, fastened to their breast, a little case of iron, copper, silver, or gold, according to the wealth and resources of their husbands. Fastened to the case they wear a ring, and upon that a dagger, all attached to their breast. About their necks they wear gold and silver chains.

They come from their own country, anchor their ships in the Volga, which is a great river, and build large wooden houses on its banks. In every such house there live ten or twenty, more or fewer. Each man has a couch, where he sits with the beautiful girls he has for sale. He is as likely as not to enjoy one of them while a friend looks on.

Michael Crichton, *Eaters of the Dead:*
The Manuscript of Ibn Fadlan, Relating His Experience with the
Northmen in A.D. 922 (New York, 1976), pp. 32-33.

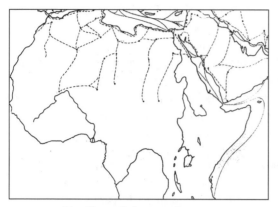

11 • Trans Sahara trade routes

With East Africa, the existing trade was greatly developed by the spread of Islam and the emigration of Arabs and Persians who settled along the coast and controlled the main towns, down to the limit of the monsoon, in Madagascar and Mozambique. The Middle East exported cloth, weapons, glass, and trinkets, and imported wood, ivory, palm oil, and gold. It also imported slaves in substantial numbers; most of these remained in the countries bordering the Red Sea and Gulf, but some went on to India and even China.[22]

The trans-Saharan trade, with the Sudan and Central and West Africa, also expanded. Great caravan routes crossed the whole of Africa north of the Tropical forests: from Sennar and Darfur to Egypt;[23] from Bornu to Tripoli; from Kano to Tunis; from Timbuktu to Tunis, Sijilmasa, and Fez; and from Ghana to Fez and Mogador (al-Sawira). The main imports of North Africa from sub-Saharan Africa were gold, ivory, pepper, and again in large numbers, slaves. Exports consisted of salt, weapons, copper, textiles, glassware, and trinkets.[24]

A very important landmark in the economic history of the Middle East was the introduction, in the pre-Islamic or early Islamic period, of a set of valuable crops from India, the Far East, and Africa. These included rice, sorghum, cotton, sugar cane, and numerous fruits and vegetables such as oranges, lemons, artichokes, spinach, eggplants, and many others. Most of these crops required systematic irrigation and other adaptations, as well as substantial investment and labor input, if they were to survive in the colder, drier Mediterranean, and their diffusion across North Africa to Europe was quite slow.[25] They brought with them their Persian-Arabic names, as did damson from Damascus, and apricot and shallot from Ascalon. Another Middle Eastern contribution was coffee, which seems to have been introduced into Yemen from Ethiopia during the Islamic period and spread throughout the Middle East in the fifteenth century, and then to Europe.[26]

I have often wondered who were the greater benefactors of mankind, the Arabs who gave it coffee or the Chinese who gave it tea, and decided in favor of the Chinese. For coffee is good when one is well, but tea is good in sickness and in health.

Still more important were exports of manufactured goods. Islamic society was highly urbanized, with a rich upper and merchant class and numerous courts that patronized the handicrafts and provided a market for their wares. Moreover, the population seems to have grown appreciably in the eighth to tenth centuries, expanding both the market and the labor force-a phenomenon that was both cause and effect of the Agricultural Revolution of that period. In addition, technological progress was achieved in several fields, notably textiles.[27] There were large exports of silk, linen, cotton, and woolen goods to Europe, as is attested by both the records and such words as damask (from Damascus), gauze (from Gaza), muslin (from Mosul), tabby (from the Attabi quarter of Baghdad), baldachin (also from Baghdad), fustian (from Fustat, a suburb of Cairo), taffeta, atlas, and oth-

12 • Linen mill in the Islamic period

ers; words for many colors and dyes, such as lilac, crimson, scarlet, and aniline, are also Middle Eastern. Other handicrafts also gave loan words to Europe, and examples include damascene in metalwork; morocco and cordovan in leather; balsam, benzoin, and julep in drugs; alcohol, arsenic, alkali, and alembic in chemistry; and admiral and arsenal in navigation. Middle Eastern ceramics and glassware were highly prized in Europe, as were papyrus and then paper. Papermaking was introduced into the Middle East by Chinese prisoners captured in 751 A.D.; it spread slowly across North Africa and Europe, reaching England probably in the fifteenth century.[28] The word ream is derived from Arabic, as are several terms used in trade and finance, such as magazine, tariff, douane, and probably cheque.

Middle Eastern exports brought in a large amount of specie, notably gold from West Africa and silver from Europe and Central Asia. This helped to improve the currency and monetize the economy, and may also have stimulated production.[29] One can, however, surmise that a substantial proportion of this inflow was re-exported to India and the Far East.

The Rise of Europe

From a very early date, Middle Eastern trade with Europe was carried almost solely by European traders in European ships. Even the Jewish traders seldom went beyond Sicily and Spain, and tended to have dealings with Christian merchants, not with their European co-religionists.[30] By 1050 A.D., the Europeans had established their supremacy in the Mediterranean and, to all intents and purposes, kept it thereafter. By the eighteenth century, even the coastal trade of the Middle East and North Africa was largely in European hands.[31] From the seventeenth century on, Greek merchants went to Venice, where they settled in the Fondaco dei Grechi. Other Greeks and Serbs, as well as a few Turks, traded across the land borders with Austria.[32] In the early nineteenth century, Greek, Armenian, and Jewish merchants from the Middle East opened trading houses in Marseilles, Manchester, London, and elsewhere.[33] The Eastern trade (that is, within the Middle East and overland to India), however, remained in Muslim hands until well into the nineteenth century.

Shipping was only the first of the many fields in which technical superiority and economic supremacy passed from the Middle East to Europe. From the twelfth century, Europe began to improve its agriculture; to show much more inventiveness than the Middle East; to apply mechanical power on a much larger scale, including breast harnessing, watermills, and windmills (the latter having been invented in Iran probably in the seventh century); and to pursue much more effective economic policies.[34] The result was a startling reversal of roles: Europe began first to produce and then to export to the Middle East the articles it had previously imported from that region, and Middle Eastern exports to Europe came increasingly to consist of raw materials or semi-finished goods. One can say that the Middle East was drawn as a peripheral unit into the emerging world economy, of which Western Europe was the center.[35]

A few examples of the reversal are illustrative.[36] First, as regards manufactured goods, by the fourteenth or fifteenth century the Middle East started importing paper from Europe, mainly Italy, and has continued to do so. A little later the same process took place with regard to high quality glass. Sugar, formerly a Middle Eastern monopoly, was grown successively in Sicily, Spain, and Portugal, then in the virgin lands of Madeira, the Azores, and Cape Verde, and later in the New World, and the Middle East began importing the cheaper refined sugar of France and other countries. The same happened with coffee, a Middle

13 • Spray of the coffee plant

Eastern monopoly that was broken by the Dutch, who transplanted shoots to the East Indies; by the eighteenth century the Middle East was almost certainly importing more coffee than it exported.

In addition, Europe began supplying the Middle East with high-technology goods, notably clocks and spectacles. Carlo Cipolla is correct in pointing to the shipment of a clock in 1338 as the first example of the export of European machinery.[37]

The same reversal took place in textiles. By the fourteenth century, "most Near Eastern industries were no longer able to compete with Western manufactured goods, imported by Italian and other merchants."[38] Export of linen from Egypt to Europe seems to have stopped in the seventeenth century, owing to European competition. Silk fabrics, which the Middle East had exported to Europe on a large scale, faced European competition in the thirteenth century, and by the fifteenth century, the Middle

East imported silk. Cotton cloth and yarn held up better, but in the second half of the eighteenth century the industry was hit by heavy duties on imports to France and by Indian competition. Early in the nineteenth century, machine-made cotton, woolen, and silk fabrics poured in, devastating the Middle Eastern handicrafts. In the meantime, the Middle East had become an important supplier of raw cotton, silk, and, to a smaller extent, wool to Europe.

New Trade Routes and Disasters

Europe struck two further blows at the sources of the Middle East's wealth. By sailing to West Africa, the Portuguese diverted much trade, in both goods and slaves, away from the Saharan routes; one should not, however, exaggerate the decline of the latter until the nineteenth century.[39] More important was the Portuguese circumnavigation of Africa and ascendancy in the Indian Ocean, which eliminated much Arab and Persian ship-

14 • Arrival of the Venetian ambassador. in Cairo

ping and, for a couple of centuries, destroyed Muslim domination of the East African coast. By the seventeenth century, the Dutch had firm control over the sources of East Indian spices, and they diverted round the Cape the trade from which the Middle East had made such large profits for some two thousand years.

It is important to note that the decline of the Middle East was caused not only by the rise of European economic power—there was no question of the superiority of European political or military power until the eighteenth century—but also by its own shortcomings. Like Europe, the Middle East and North Africa were devastated, in the fourteenth century, by the Black Death; but, for reasons that are not clear, their population, unlike that of Europe, does not seem to have bounced back. Weakening government control and prolonged wars, including the Crusades, the Mongol and Tatar invasions, and the Turco-Persian conflicts, caused much damage to the productive powers of the region, notably Iraq's irrigation works, which did not recover until the present century. The cultivated area shrank and the quality and quantity of handicraft wares fell off. These processes were accelerated by the extortionist and short-sighted policy pursued by most Middle Eastern governments, control over which had passed, around the twelfth century, from civilians to soldiers. As a result, the Muslim bourgeoisie, which had been both rich and enterprising, was reduced to impotence.[40]

But although the Middle East was relegated to the periphery of the world economy, until the eighteenth century it continued to be an important component of the system. It remained as the main supplier of cotton to Europe until the development of American production in the nineteenth century, and it was a very important source of silk even after the growth of the India and China trade. Other articles that were exported were wool, hides, coffee, and, when crops were good, cereals. Owing to the very low import duties levied by the Ottoman government, the Middle East was also a large market for European goods. It is estimated that at the beginning of the seventeenth century the Levant trade accounted for half of France's total foreign trade,[41] and the "Levant trade was regarded as of such special value that the [French] Ambassador to the Porte was often appointed not by the Foreign Secretary but by the Minister of Finance and Trade."[42] However, the expansion of European trade in the seventeenth and eighteenth centuries greatly reduced the share of the Middle East; for France, it had fallen to about six percent of the total by 1789, and for Britain the figure was much lower. It is worth noting that, as in the past, Europe's imports from the Middle East exceeded its exports to the region, and the balance continued to be covered by a flow of bullion, much of which eventually made its way to India, a country with which the Middle East seems to have had a negative balance of trade.

The 19th-century Recovery

The nineteenth century saw an economic upsurge in the Middle East, an expansion in its agricultural production, and a sharp rise in its foreign trade. Between about 1800 and 1913, Turkey's exports and imports rose seven-fold (in current prices), Iran's eight-fold, and Egypt's forty-fold; for Syria, the corresponding figure was about twenty-fold, and for Iraq, from the 1860s to 1913, sixteen-fold. But these figures refer to sea trade only. Since their land trade was probably stagnant, or may even have declined, the total increase for Iraq and Syria must have been much smaller. The total for the countries listed may have been about £10 million around 1800 and £120 million in 1913, a twelve-fold increase. Total world trade is estimated to have risen from £340 million in 1820 to £8,360 million in 1913, or about 25 times; the Middle East's share, therefore, fell from about 3 percent to under 1.5 percent-surely a lower figure than at any time in its long history. It may be added that, for both the Middle East and the world, the real increase was greater than that in current prices, since price levels fell over the period.[43]

The composition of Middle Eastern trade showed some change. Exports of manufactured goods almost disappeared and each country gradually concentrated on a few, or even one, raw material: cotton in Egypt; tobacco, dried fruits, and cotton in Turkey; silk and opium in Iran; wheat and barley in Syria and Iraq; silk in Lebanon; oranges in Palestine; and coffee in Yemen. There was a large increase in the import of textiles and other manufactured consumer goods, which devastated the old handicrafts of the region. In general, the region's exports lagged behind its imports and it had to export large quantities of bullion accumulated in previous generations.

The Middle East also attracted a relatively large amount of capital investment. On the eve of World War 1, the total public and private debt of the Ottoman Empire was about £T182 million, of Egypt over £E200 million, and of Iran about £30 million, or a little over $2,000 million in all.[44] At that time total long-term foreign investment in the world was about $44,000 million.[45] In other words, the Middle Eastern share was about 5 percent of the whole, a large figure compared to the region's share of world population (45 million out of 1,900 million, or about 2.5 percent), or of agricultural and industrial production. But it should be noted that over half the capital inflow was in the form of public debt and that by far the greater part of this was wasted, which means that the region was saddled with a heavy burden in return for benefits that were disproportionately small.

It may be added that the Middle East attracted very little migration, except for a small inflow into Egypt. This forms a sharp contrast with neighboring North Africa, where hundreds of thousands of Frenchmen, Italians, and Spaniards settled.

Transport and Location

But there was one field in which the importance of the Middle East increased: international transport. By the late 1820s, European steamships had reached the Middle East through the Mediterranean, and in the early 1830s, Russian and Austrian steamers called at Istanbul and British India steamers at Suez. These lines were connected by the overland route through Egypt, which finally won over the rival one through Syria and Iraq.[46] As a result, Egypt got its first railway in 1851, before Sweden. Even

15 • The opening of the Suez Canal with Empress Eugénie of France, wife of Napoleon III.

more important was the Suez Canal, which opened in 1869. This not only cut the distance from London to Bombay by half and to China by a quarter but, by enabling ships to sail narrower and much more traveled seas than those on the journey round the Cape, gave a great stimulus to steam navigation.[47] By the 1880s, the Canal was handling nearly two-thirds of Britain's trade east of Suez, and half of India's total trade.[48] And when the bulk trade between Europe and Asia, for which the Canal had been primarily designed, began to flag in the 1930s, a new and far more valuable freight was found in the form of oil from the Gulf to Europe. Just before its nationalization in 1956, the Canal was carrying 13 percent of world shipping and 20 percent of tankers.

The Middle East also played an important part in the development of air transport, particularly from the 1930s to the 1960s. An airline map of the world shows a funneling through the region of an enormous amount of traffic between North Africa and Europe, on the one hand, and the Indian Ocean area, with prolongations to the Far East and Australasia, on the other.

Oil and Money

At present, the Middle East has become synonymous with oil and, very recently, money. The extraction of oil in the Middle East-in Egypt and Iran-began just before World War I, but at the outbreak of World War II the region's annual output was only 120 million barrels, or 6 percent of world production. Iran accounted for the bulk of output, followed by Iraq, Bahrain, and Egypt. However, by then large deposits had been discovered in Arabia, and by 1960, the Middle East's proven published reserves of oil, 163 billion barrels, amounted to 61 percent of total world reserves, and Middle Eastern output to 2 billion barrels, or 26 percent of world output. By 1980, Middle Eastern reserves had climbed to 386 billion but, owing to the more rapid discovery of reserves in other parts of the world, its share of the world total had fallen to 60 percent. Middle Eastern output in 1979 amounted to 8.6 billion barrels, or 37 percent of world production. At present, the Middle East accounts for half the world's oil exports.[49]

This huge increase in oil production, and in the revenues accruing from oil, naturally resulted in a large expansion in the region's foreign trade. In 1948, the Middle East's imports amounted to $2.2 billion, or 3.5 percent of the world total, and its exports to $2 billion, or also 3.5 percent; Egypt accounted for one-third of the region's trade. In the following 25 years, the growth of Middle Eastern trade kept pace with that of world trade, and its percentage share showed very little change. The sharp rise in oil prices in the 1970s, however, led to a rapid increase in both the absolute and relative value. By 1975, Middle Eastern exports stood at $82 billion and imports at $72 billion. In 1977, exports amounted to $109 billion, or 10 percent of world trade. This compares with its population share of just under 4 percent-160 million out of a world total of 4,200 million. By then, the largest trading nations were the major oil producers: Saudi Arabia, Iran, Iraq, and Kuwait.[50] It should be added that, apart from oil, long-staple cotton and citrus fruits are the only items in which the Middle East's share of world trade is at all significant.

As mentioned earlier, starting in the nineteenth century the Middle East had a persistent deficit in its balance of trade. This was partly covered by services, such as tourism, pilgrimage, and transit trade, partly by remittances from abroad, but mostly by capital inflow. Allied Army expenditures in the two world wars enabled several countries, notably Egypt, to accumulate large balances of foreign exchange and thus reduce their indebtedness, but by and large the region was a substantial capital absorber. This situation persisted until very recently. As late as the early 1970s, only a few small countries with a large oil production, notably Kuwait and Saudi Arabia, had a surplus in their current account and accumulated funds abroad. In 1973 and after, there was an explosion in oil prices and revenues; in 1978 revenues were nearly $100 billion, in 1980 they were $200 billion, and, even after the recent decline in output and prices, they are still well over $100 billion. This converted the major producers into large capital exporters. In 1982, the official net foreign assets of the major Arab oil-producing countries (including Algeria and Libya) stood at $184 billion.[51]

It is outside the scope of this study to discuss the enormous impact of the oil price revolution on the Middle Eastern societies. On the one hand, there has been a sharp acceleration in economic growth, a huge increase in investment—much of it mismanaged—and a great expansion in education, health, and other social services. But on the other hand, this unprecedented and unparalleled accrual of wealth has, in many countries, strained the social fabric beyond endurance. The revolution in Iran, in my opinion caused mainly by this factor, may be only the harbinger of several others.[52]

This very quick trip through history shows that, for several millennia, the Middle East was at the very center of the world stage. In the few hundred years between the sixteenth and twentieth centuries, it drifted to the wings. Now, it has once again been recalled, by a mysterious providence, to the center. How long it will keep that position is not for me to say.

NOTES

1. H. W. F. Saggs, *The Greatness that was Babylon* (New York, 1962), pp. 196-232, 269-98; A. Leo Oppenheim, *Ancient Mesopotamia* (Chicago, IL, 1964), pp. 83-95; Joan Oates, *Babylon* (London, 1979), pp. 11-15; see also Karl Polanyi et al., *Trade and Market in the Early Empires* (Chicago, IL, 1957).

2. O. R. Gurney, *The Hittites* (London, 1954), pp. 80-88.

3. Chaim Bermant and M. Weitzman, *Ebla* (New York, 1978).

4. Sabatino Moscati, *The World of the Phoenicians* (New York, 1968); see also Ezekiel, Ch. 27: vs. 3-25.

5. Herodotus, *The Persian Wars,* IV-42 (New York, 1947), p. 306.

6. Gordon Childe, *What Happened in History* (London, 1943), p. 146.

7. R. Ghirshman, *Iran* (London, 1954), p. 186, see also pp. 181-88; A. T. Olmstead, *History of the Persian Empire* (Chicago, IL, 1948), pp. 83-85, 299-301; Hans Wulff, *The Traditional Crafts of Persia* (Cambridge, MA, 1966), pp. 246-50.

8. M. Rostovtzeff, *The Social and Economic History of the Hellenistic World* (Oxford, 1941), 1:83-90.

9. *Ibid., passim,* and especially 1:351-602 and 2:1026-1312.

10. See the description in E. M. Forster, *Alexandria* (New York, 1961), pp. 141-53.

11. These figures are derived from Julius Beloch, *Die Bevölkerung der Griechisch-Römischen Welt* (Leipzig, 1886), amended by the estimates in Tenney Frank, ed., *An Economic Survey of Ancient Rome* (Baltimore, MD, 1938), Vols. II and IV, and M. I. Finley, *Aspects of Antiquity* (New York, 1968), pp. 155 and 199; for a discussion of Roman population statistics, see A. H. M. Jones, *Ancient Economic History: An Inaugural Lecture* (London, 1948), and Peter Brunt, *Italian Manpower:225 B.C.-A.D. 14* (London, 1971).

12. United Nations, *The Determinants and Consequences of Population Trends* (New York, 1953), p. 81.

13. Frank, *An Economic Survey of Ancient Rome,* 2:480-85; 4:42-50, 127-29, 611.

14. *Ibid.,* 2:328-46, 4:189-92, 817-25.

15. *Ibid.,* 2:344-45, 4:200-202; A. H. M. Jones, "Asian Trade in Antiquity," in D. S. Richards, ed., *Islam and the Trade of Asia* (Oxford, 1970), pp. 1-10; Irfan Shahid, "Pre-Islamic Arabia," in P. H. Holt et al., eds., *The Cambridge History of Islam* (Cambridge, UK, 1970), 1:9-11.

16. Charles Issawi, "The Christian-Muslim Frontier in the Mediterranean," *Political Science Quarterly* (December 1961), reprinted in Issawi, *The Arab Legacy* (Princeton, NJ, 1981).

17. Issawi, "The Area and Population of the Arab Empire: An Essay in Speculation," in A. L. Udovitch, ed., *The Islamic Middle East, 700-1900* (Princeton, NJ, 1980), reprinted in *The Arab Legacy.*

18. *Encyclopaedia of Islam* (new edition) sv. "Harir."

19. Hourani, *Arab Seafaring in the Indian Ocean* (Princeton, NJ, 1951), p. 70.

20. Hadi Hasan, *A History of Persian Navigation* (London, 1928), p. 99; Geoffrey Hudson, "Medieval Trade of China," in D. S. Richards, ed., *Islam and the Trade of Asia,* pp. 159-67; E. Ashtor, *A Social and Economic History of the Near East in the Middle Ages* (Berkeley, CA, 1976), pp. 106-9, 147-48, 275-76.

21. Sture Bolin, "Mohammed, Charlemagne and Ruric," *Scandinavian Economic History Review,* 1 (1953); see also the map in Sir Thomas Arnold and Alfred Guillaume, *The Legacy of Islam* (London, 1931), p. 78.

22. Reginald Coupland, *East Africa and its Invaders* (Oxford, 1938), p. 35; see also Charles Issawi, *The Economic History of Iran* (Chicago, IL, 1971), pp. 124-28.

23. Charles Issawi, *The Economic History of the Middle East* (Chicago, IL, 1966), pp. 465, 473-76.

24. See the excellent account and map in A. G. Hopkins, *An Economic History of West Africa* (New York, 1973), pp. 78-87.

25. Andrew Watson, *Agricultural Innovation in the Early Islamic World* (Cambridge, UK, 1983).

26. *Encyclopaedia of Islam* (new edition) sv. "Kahwa."

27. Ashtor, *A Social and Economic History of the Near East in the Middle Ages,* pp. 86-100.

28. Thomas Carter and L. Carrington Goodrich, *The Invention of Printing in China* (New York, 1955), pp. 137, 247-50.

29. Ashtor, *A Social and Economic History of the Near East in the Middle Ages,* pp. 80-86.

30. S. D. Goitein, *A Mediterranean Society, Vol. 1, Economic Foundations* (Berkeley and Los Angeles, CA, 1967). 1:209-17.

31. Robert Lopez, *The Birth of Europe* (London, 1967), pp. 284-91; Hélène Ahrweiler, *Byzance et la Mer* (Paris, 1966); Ekkehard Eickhoff, *Seekrieg und Seepolitik Zwischen Islam und Abendland* (Berlin, 1966); Issawi, *The Economic History of the Middle East,* p. 37; Issawi, *The Economic History of Turkey* (Chicago, IL, 1980), p. 152.

32. Charles Issawi, *The Economic History of Turkey,* pp. 57, 270-72; and Bruce McGowan, *Economic Life in Ottoman Europe* (Cambridge, UK, 1981), chapter 1.

33. Charles Issawi, "The Transformation of the Economic Position of the Millets in the Nineteenth Century," in Benjamin Braude and Bernard Lewis, eds., *Christians and Jews in the Ottoman Empire,* 2 vols. (New York, 1982), 1:270-72.

34. For a fuller discussion, see Issawi, "Europe, the Middle East and the Shift in Power," *Comparative Studies in Society and History* (October 1980), reprinted in *The Arab Legacy.*

35. For a powerful statement of this view, see Immanuel Wallerstein, *The Modern World System* (New York, 1974).

36. Charles Issawi, "The Decline of Middle Eastern Trade," in D. S. Richards, ed., *Islam and the Trade of Asia,* pp. 245-66, which has full references, reprinted in *The Arab Legacy.*

37. Carlo Cipolia, *Clocks and Culture* (London, 1967), preface.

38. E. Ashtor, "L'apogée du commerce vénitien," *Venezia Centro di Mediazione* (Florence, 1977), 1:318-21.

39. Hopkins, *An Economic History of West Africa,* pp. 82-83.

40. Charles Issawi, "The Decline of Middle Eastern Trade"; Goitein, *A Mediterranean Society,* pp. 266-72; Ashtor, *A Social and Economic History of the Near East in the Middle Ages,* pp. 169-331.

41. For a full account, see Paul Masson, *Histoire du commerce français dans le Levant au XVIIe siècle* (Paris, 1896), and Masson, *Histoire du commerce français dans le Levant au XVIIIe siècle* (Paris, 1911).

42. Harold Nicolson, *The Evolution of Diplomacy* (New York, 1962), p. 82.

43. Albert A. Imlah, *Economic Elements in the Pax Britannica* (Cambridge, MA, 1958), pp. 94-98 and 189; Charles Issawi, *The Economic History of the Middle East and North Africa,* pp. 24-25.

44. Vedat Eldem, *Osmanli Imparatorlugunun iktisadi sartlari bir tetkik* (Istanbul, 1970), pp. 190-91; A. E. Crouchley, *The Investment of Foreign Capital in Egyptian Companies and Public Debt* (Cairo, 1936), passim; L.A. Fridman, *Kapitalistichiskoye razvitiye Yegipta* (Moscow, 1963), p. 13; Charles Issawi, *The Economic History of Iran* (Chicago, IL, 1971), pp. 356-61, 370-72.

45. United Nations. *Capital Movements During the Interwar Period* (New York, 1950).

46. Halford Hopkins, *British Routes to India* (New York, 1928).

47. Max Fletcher, "The Suez Canal and World Shipping," *Journal Of Economic History* (December 1958).

48. D. A. Farnie, *East and West of Suez* (Oxford, 1969), pp. 171, 306, 354-56.

49. For details, see Charles Issawi and Mohammed Yeganeh, *The Economics of Middle Eastern Oil* (1962) and *British Petroleum, BP Statistical Review of the World Oil Industry* (annual).

50. United Nations, *Statistical Yearbook;* United Nations, *The Direction of Trade.*

51. International Monetary Fund, *International Financial Statistics;* see also a special issue of *Arab Studies Quarterly,* "The Impact of Money" (Winter/Spring, 1984).

52. For a fuller discussion, see Charles Issawi, "Economic Trends in the Middle East and Future Prospects," in United States 96th Congress, 2nd Session, Joint Economic Committee, *The Political Economy of the Middle East* (Washington, D.C., April 21, 1980), and other papers in the same volume.

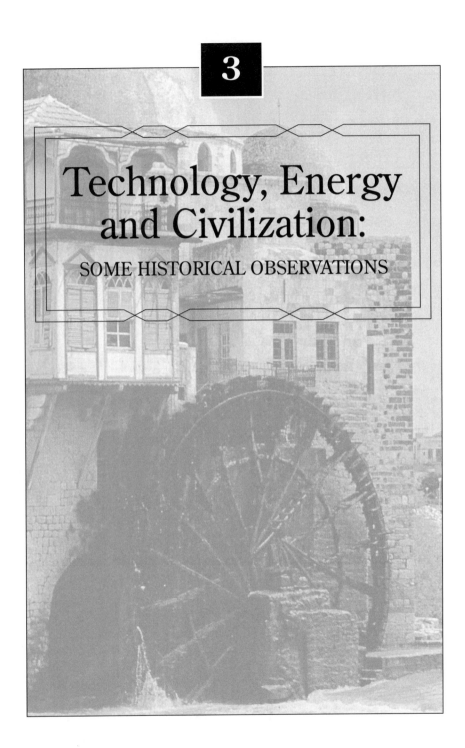

3

Technology, Energy and Civilization:

SOME HISTORICAL OBSERVATIONS

he degree of development (or, if you prefer, material civilization) of any society is set by the size of its surplus (the total amount it produces minus the amount needed for the bare subsistence of the population) and the uses to which the surplus is put. In Emerson's words, "The question of history is what each generation has done with its surplus produce. One bought crusades, one churches, one villas, one horses and one railroads." The size of the surplus is, in turn, determined by four factors: the amount of energy available to the society, the society's technology, the mix of its economy, and the size of its population. Until comparatively recently, energy was, with the important exception of sailing ships, provided exclusively by human or animal power.[1] Two important steps forward were the invention of the watermill and that of the windmill; their development will be discussed later. Nevertheless, it has been estimated that until the Industrial Revolution, some 80-85 percent of total energy was provided by plants, animals, and people.[2] This means that the basic factors determining the amount of energy available to a society were the amount of land (arable, pasture, and woodland) it had at its disposal and the land's productivity. Land "was not simply the principal source of food for the population [the other being the seas and rivers] but also virtually the sole source of the raw materials used in industrial production"—fibers, hides, hair, wood, and so forth; almost all industrial workers were engaged in processing agricultural materials. Wood was, moreover, not only the prime source of heat but the main construction material—along with bricks and stone—and was also used to make ships, bridges and industrial tools and machines. In other words, land met all four of humanity's basic needs: food, shelter, clothing, and heat.[3]

Until at least the end of the first millennium A.D., there is every reason to believe that the productivity of Middle Eastern (the term is used here to cover Egypt, Iraq, geographical Syria, and Turkey) agriculture was at least as great as that of Europe, and that the amount of energy available to it was at least as large. For one thing, the warmth of the climate both reduced the amount of food, clothing, and heat necessary for survival and stimulated plant growth. For another, the development of agriculture in the Middle

East between, say, 700 and 1100 had been remarkable: new crops such as silk, cotton, sugarcane, rice, sorghum, and numerous fruits and vegetables were introduced from India, the Far East, and Africa; irrigation was greatly extended, partly offsetting the region's greatest handicap, aridity; and large investments were made in agriculture.[4] Figures on total production or on yields per acre are, of course, very tentative. However, Ashtor puts the yield-to-seed ratio for grain in Egypt at 10 to 1, and contrasts it with 2-2.5 to 1 in Western Europe in Carolingian times. Bolshakov accepts these figures and believes that Syria's yields were 1.5 times those of Europe. It is also worth noting that the yield-to-seed ratio of 5-6 to 1 typical of Turkey and Syria in the mid-19th century compares favorably with yields for 16th-century European countries other than the Netherlands, Northern Italy, and England—and there is no reason to believe that Middle Eastern yields had risen appreciably between the 16th and 19th centuries. For Egypt, yields were far higher—14-15 in 1800, according to the calculations of Napoleon's experts.[5]

In Upper Egypt, the proportion of the total cultivated area planted to fodder crops may be put at one-sixth, in the Delta at one-third. It is the latter province which supplied the ox and buffalo hides sent to France and Italy. The only lands in Egypt which are allowed to rest are those that do not recieve natural flooding or artificial irrigation.

As for fertility, each hectare receives 155 liters of wheat seed and yields, in an ordinary year, 2,325. In our most fertile departments in France, 2 hectoliters of seed are used per hectare and the yield is 20 hectoliters. In other words, land in Egypt yields 14 or 15 for every 1 sown whereas our best provinces yield only 10 and our worst 3. Thus, estimating the fertility of land by the ratio of crops to seeds per given area, the fertility of Egypt may be put at 15 and the average for France at 6.5; in addition it should be noted that our lands need artificial fertilization whereas the countryside along the Nile needs only natural flooding.

The average price per hectoliter of wheat in Egypt is about 4 francs 30 centimes; in France it is today 14 francs 59 centimes. The average ratio of prices is therefore 10 to 33.

P.S. Girard, "Mémoire sur l'agriculture, l'industrie, et le commerce de l'Egypte" (Paris, 1809-22), quoted in Issawi, *The Economic History of the Middle East 1800-1914* (Chicago and London, 1966), p. 377.

Another indication of the high productivity of agriculture in the Middle East is the very large size of its cities. Baghdad, Cairo, Constantinople, Damascus, and Aleppo far outclassed European cities until at least the 17th century, and the Middle Eastern urbanization rate was probably higher than in European states until the 18th or 19th century, with a few exceptions such as the Netherlands and Britain.[6] This indicates that Middle Eastern agriculture was more productive, since it could sustain a larger non-agricultural population-unless of course it shows greater exploitation of peasants, which may well have been the case at certain times and places; O. G. Bolshakov argues convincingly that this was very high.

The size of the surplus available to the Middle East is indicated by its monuments, both pre-Islamic (such as the Pyramids, Karnak, Persepolis, Ba'albak, the Sasanian palace at Ctesiphon, Aya Sophia, and the walls of Constantinople) and Islamic (the mosques and citadels of Cairo, Damascus, and Aleppo). It is also indicated by the amount that must have been dissipated in wars and luxury consumption.

After about A.D. 1200 the paths of Europe and the Middle East began to diverge sharply: Europe continued to advance at an unprecedentedly rapid rate, while the Middle East stagnated and, in some respects, deteriorated. I am aware that the latter terms are, nowadays, frowned upon, but they seem to me accurately to describe the situation in economics, technology, and intellectual activity. To what extent this stagnation was the result of external shocks, such as a series of invasions leading to the breakdown of order (e.g., the Crusades and the Mongol invasions), the Black Death, and the diversion of the trade routes, and to what extent they were the result of such factors as the replacement of civilian government by the military and increasing social and intellectual rigidity, cannot be discussed here.

Two observations may, however, be made. First, as was seen so clearly by the British classical economists (Adam Smith, Ricardo, Malthus, and J. S. Mill), the operation of the Law of Diminishing Returns threatens every agrarian society with stagnation (or, as they put it, with the Stationary State). This can be staved off only by bringing increasing amounts of new land under cultivation or by constant technological progress. One implication of this has recently been cogently stated by E. A. Wrigley:[7] in an Organic Society, namely, one that derives its energy primarily from the produce of land, the amount of energy available per capita will, eventually, decrease. Second, the agricultural base of the Middle East is particularly precarious. Rainfall is scarce and irregular, and irrigation works are fragile and easily destroyed, and are also subject to deterioration by salination. Hence, with weakening government, invasions, and the infiltration of the ever-present nomads, agricultural production must have been greatly reduced. The main exceptions are Egypt, with its reliable and indestructible Nile, and the rainy coastlands of Turkey, and it is no coincidence that these two areas formed the basis for the two major states of the late medieval and early modern period, the Mamluks and Ottomans.

In Europe, by contrast, the picture was one of steady technical progress resulting in increasing amounts of available energy. The most important innovations were in agriculture, starting in the very early Middle Ages: use of the heavy wheeled plow, breast harnessing of horses, horseshoes, the replacement of the sickle by the scythe, the improvement of the harrow and, consequently, the development of the three-field system.[8] All this enabled Europe to put to use its rich but heavier soil which, together with its steadier and more abundant rain, raised its agricultural productivity well above that of the Middle East. The trend is brought out by the rise in the yield-to-seed ratio of the four main grain crops in England: from 3.7 in 1200-1249 to 7 by the 16th century, a figure surely higher than that of any Middle Eastern country, except Egypt, until this century.[9] At the same time, Mediterranean Europe enriched its agricultural production by introducing the crops that had previously been brought into the Middle East. Later Europe was to profit from the energy-rich crops of the New World, notably potatoes and maize.[10] Some of these crops, in turn, made their way to the Middle East between the 17th and 19th centuries.

Europe also supplemented its energy resources with two powerful instruments, the watermill and windmill. The working rate of an overshot water wheel was 2-5 horsepower, and of a post windmill 2-8.[11] Watermills seem to have been invented in the Mediterranean just before the Christian era.[12] For obvious reasons, their use in the Middle East remained restricted. Moreover, the Muslims continued to use the primitive "Greek" or "Norse" (vertical axis) watermill, as distinct from the superior—Vitruvian" (horizontal axis) type used in Europe from late Roman times onward. In the words of a leading authority: "Apart from its use in irrigation, the water wheel never became a principal prime-mover in the Muslim world." A few examples may, however, be noted: near Baghdad, in the 10th century, there was a floating mill for paper making, and in Basra there were some tide mills; the water wheels of Hama are well known, and there were also some at Antioch.[13]

For the Ottoman period a vast amount of information on water mills is

16 • A waterwheel at Hamah, Syria

available in the *defters* (government registers), since they were taxed; unfortunately, no systematic study has yet been made of the records. Data published by Huri Islamoglu-Inan are, however, indicative.[14] For a group of villages in the Tokat region, she lists 269 water millstones in the 1520s and 354 in 1574. The number of taxpayers was 11,319 and 26,353, respectively; multiplying by 5, to take into account women, children, the military, government officials, and slaves, all of whom were tax-exempt, this represents a total population of, say, 57,000 and 132,000, respectively. In other words, there was one water millstone per 212 inhabitants in the 1520s and one per 373 inhabitants in 1574. These figures are distinctly higher than that of 195 per mill (not millstone) for England in 1086; presumably in England, as in Turkey, many mills had more than one stone.

Moreover, those figures are probably well above the average for the Asian part of the Ottoman Empire, since the Tokat area receives a high amount of rain and is full of streams and rivers. In Palestine, in 1596-97, for instance: it is interesting to note that mills—and this means water mills, because hand mills were not taxed—are to be found frequently in the *liwa'* Safad and *qada'* Hawran; some occur also in *liwa's* Lajjun and Ajlun, a certain number in *liwa'* Nablus (where there is a marked concentration of mills in the wadi Faria and its tributary valleys), but there are no taxed mills in the *liwa's* of Quds and Ghazza. Although places which are suitable for the construction of water mills in these two southern *liwa's* are less frequent than in the north, they should at least occur in certain places. There must be another, still unknown reason for the fact that no mention is made of any mills in these two *liwa's*.[15]

In order to quantify this statement, the breakdown by villages of the *liwa'* Safad—the most populous and best watered of the *liwa's*—was studied. Total receipts from the tax on mills (*tahun*) were 2,616 *akçes*; the tax rate was 60 *akçes* per millstone per year or 30 per half year (i.e., in the rainy season only);[16] assuming an average of 45 *akçes*, this gives a total of 58 millstones. The population of the *liwa'* of Safad was put at 82,570,[17] which means 1 millstone for every 1,424 inhabitants. This figure may, however, understate the number of mills, since in the 1553-57 regional *defters*, in addition to the mills listed in the village entries, groups of mills are shown.[18] However, it does suggest that watermills were infrequent in Palestine Another check is provided by the relatively dry province of Malatya, for which a 1560 *tahrir defteri* is available. The total number of taxpayers was 31,148;[19] of these, the vast majority were households, so an estimate of about 150,000 for total population seems reasonable. The total number of

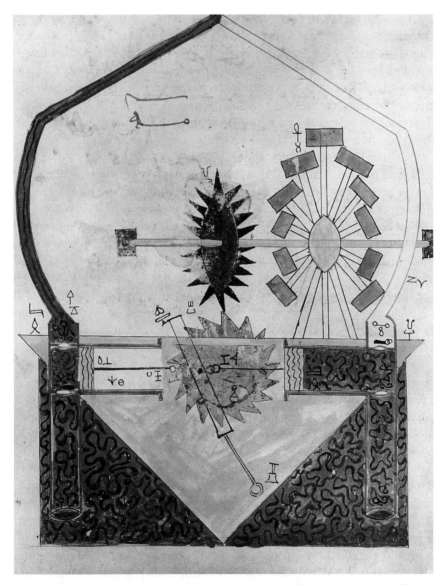

17 • Illustration of a reciprocating pump with two cylinders copied repeatedly in the Muslim world during the Middle Ages

millstones (*asyab*) was 326, including an estimate for a few where the tax yield was given but not the number. In other words, there was 1 millstone per 460 inhabitants.

One can therefore conclude that, in the 16th century, at the height of Ottoman prosperity, the Middle East had distinctly fewer mills per capita than 11th-century England. Moreover, a large number of the mills listed operated for only half the year, owing presumably to a shortage of water, which means that their contribution to energy was much lower. This conclusion is reinforced by the fact that, owing to their flat terrain, neither Egypt nor lower Iraq can have had any significant number of mills, and that the desert and semi-desert regions were similarly devoid of them.

Even in the 19th century almost no use was made of water power for industrial purposes. In the course of my research on the various countries, I came across only two references. In 1870, a cotton mill was established at Antioch using the power of the Orontes, but it soon closed down; and in 1879, a French consul reported from Izmir: "In this same spot, where water is abundant and can provide motive power, several attempts have been made to establish first a paper mill, then a glass factory, a spinning mill and a tannery. But all these attempts remained fruitless." It is not clear whether the factories in question were designed for water power or steam.[20]

In Europe, by contrast, watermills were widespread. In 1086, according to the Domesday Book, the 3,000 settlements in England—most of them very small—contained 5,624 mills, some of which were used for other purposes than grinding corn.[21] Assuming an average horsepower of 3, this represents an aggregate horsepower of about 17,000, or the equivalent of 170,000 "slaves," to use Levasseur's expressive term.[22] Since England's population was about 1,100,000, and its labor force, in male equivalents, was probably below 500,000, this represents an addition of about 0.015 horsepower per capita, or one-third, to the labor force. Moreover, those "slaves" did not require feeding and could work much longer hours. Their contribution to the surplus was therefore far greater. One should add that, thanks to those mills, machinery was brought into almost every village, giving the whole population a demonstration of its workings and uses. In the next three centuries, everywhere in Europe watermills were put to a variety of uses, in the textile, metallurgical, wood, and other industries, and they stimulated a number of inventions or borrowings, such as the cam and the crank. It may be pointed out that as late as 1860, 60 percent of total horsepower in French industry and only slightly less in the United States was provided by watermills; high rates also prevailed in Britain (in spite of the spread of steam), Switzerland, and elsewhere.

The fate of the windmill was similar. It was probably invented in Central Asia in the 5th century and is mentioned in the celebrated conversation between 'Umar and Abu Lu'lu'a in 644.[23] These windmills, however, had a vertical axis and low efficiency. They were used in various parts of the Middle East and are occasionally mentioned by geographers and historians, but seem to have gone out of use in the Middle Ages.[24] At the end of

18 • *Windmill in Arabia*

the 18th century, Napoleon's experts noted that some seven or eight windmills had been set up in Alexandria by Europeans, and al-Jabarti mentions the ones put up by the French in Cairo as an unfamiliar phenomenon. Writing in 1907, the British consul in Aleppo stated, "The windmill has often been tried, but has always failed in consequence of the continual shifting of the wind, which rushes down the gullies of the neighboring hills." A few mills were built in Palestine in the 18th and early 19th centuries, and more were built by Jewish and German immigrants.[25]

Until the last years of the 19th century only animal or manpower was used for drawing water from wells in Palestine. For drinking water a rope and a bucket would be used, and for irrigation as well as drinking there was the water hoist (Ar. *Shaduf* or *shalaf*) or the waterwheel. For drawing reasonable amounts of water, even just for drinking purposes, these devices were effective only in shallow wells. The water hoist (pumping wheel), operated by animal power, would raise a series of clay jugs, and later wooden boxes cast in a framework of iron bars. When full of water, a 1-meter-long row of such jugs or boxes would weigh up to 70 kilograms. This limited the capability of the animal (usually a mule), so that water could not be drawn from more than 10, or at most 12, meters deep.

In Petah Tikva in 1900, there were 28 wells. Two were used exclusively for drinking water—one equipped with a pump operated by hand and the other (the wind pump in Yehud) inoperative by then. Of the other 26 wells, 23 irrigated orchards of a total area of 923 *dunams.* The

Rothschild orchards amounted to 348 *dunams,* with another 70 *dunams* being then prepared for planting. They were irrigated by one waterwheel, one locomobile, and three internal combustion engines. Another 18 orchards with a total area of 575 *dunams* were irrigated by 20 wells equipped with 17 waterwheels, one hand pump, and two engines. . . .

The technical difficulties involved in pumping water for irrigation were now taken up by Leon Stein, an engineer by profession and the owner of the first modern mechanical workshop in Jaffa. Apparently in 1904 he developed a filter that prevented the infiltration of sand into the pipe of the pump. It was a fine, dense copper net that was installed on the pipe and allowed the passage of water but not sand. This simple device facilitated the use of mechanical pumps instead of the water-pumping wheels. As a result, an intensive planting activity was launched in the orange plantations in general, but most of all in Petah Tikva.

The filter was distributed all over the country only after it had been tried successfully in one of the orchards of Petah Tikva. But it proved to be a mixed blessing. The fast and intensive pumping quickly exhausted the wells, so that they would take many hours to refill. To overcome this problem the wells had to be dug even deeper so that more abundant groundwater could be reached. This led to the introduction of another innovation. Instead of digging deep in the water-carrying level, the well would be dug up to the top of the water-carrying level and from there drilling would start into the groundwater.

A new type of well thus developed: deeper, more abundant in water and dug only in its upper part. It was designated a "Jewish" or "dry" well, as opposed to the "Arab" or "wet" well, with water visible on its bottom.

Shmuel Avitsur, "The Contribution of Early Petah Tikvah
to the Agricultural and Industrial Development of Eretz Yisrael,
1878-1917", *Cathedra* 10, January 1970.

In Europe, however, the windmill—first referred to in the 12th century and probably introduced from the Middle East—was developed almost beyond recognition, and was widely diffused.[26] In flat areas lacking water power, batteries of windmills supplied huge amounts of concentrated energy, and in the Netherlands in particular they played a vital part in drainage and industry.

Wood, water, and wind provided the motive force for what the late Lewis Mumford,[27] following Patrick Geddes, called the Eotechnic economy and E. A. Wrigley termed the Advanced Organic Economy. The achievements of this economy, especially in the Netherlands and England, were spectacular. As Wrigley pointed out, in England between 1600 and 1800, population more than doubled and agricultural output per head rose, but the labor force in agriculture stayed more or less constant, implying a large increase in productivity. This meant that the proportion of the working force in agriculture fell to about 40 percent, releasing huge numbers for employment in industry, shipping, trade, and other services, and swelling the urban population to an unprecedented size.[28]

A hardly less important factor was the difference in the demographic pattern between the Middle East and Europe; this question will be discussed only briefly since it has received extensive coverage elsewhere. In the Middle East, as in most parts of the preindustrial world, early marriage was the rule, and both birth rates and death rates were very high. This combination is wasteful since a substantial investment is made in children (in the form of food, clothing, shelter, care, etc.) who do not live long enough to enter the labor force and start repaying society. This pattern still prevails, with one important difference. Most women marry before the age of 20,[29] and birth rates are very high, about 45-50 per thousand; however, thanks to improved hygiene, more abundant food, better transport, and greater security, death rates have fallen sharply, to about 10-15 per thousand. The result has been very rapid population growth, exceeding 30 per thousand in some countries.

In Europe, on the other hand, where nuclear (rather than extended) families seem to have prevailed from Neolithic times, marriage took place at a later age. Thus, in England in 1637-80, the median marriage age for yeomen was 27-28 and for their wives 24-25—and many remained single; in 17th-century France the marriage age in rural areas, for both men and women, was in the late 20s—and there were very few illegitimate births![30] As E. L. Jones put it, "Our concern is to account for Europeans persistently holding population growth a little below its maximum and keeping land back for livestock husbandry and woodland uses, thereby holding their consumption levels a little above those of Asia."[31] Needless to add, the greater emphasis on woodlands and livestock meant that much greater amounts of energy were available, in the form of wood and draft animals, than in, say, the rice fields of India or China or the wheat and barley lands of Egypt and Iraq. Moreover, of course, anything that holds population back increases, correspondingly, the amount of energy available per capita and the size of the surplus.

The preceding analysis suggests a further observation: the economic surge of Europe, compared to other parts of the world, is best accounted for by internal factors. Trade made large profits, the loot of empire was substantial, and the colonization of the Americas brought in huge accretions of resources. However, the main explanation is to be sought elsewhere. Europe enjoyed incomparable natural advantages, such as lower exposure to earthquakes and other disasters, equable climate, and adequate rainfall. Its supply of both woods and arable land was abundant. Its steady and accelerating technological progress enabled it to produce ever increasing amounts of energy. Its population pattern was such that a greater amount of the surplus it produced was converted into both human and physical capital—which in turn raised output—rather than into what Latin American economists have called "vegetative growth." Here, as E. L. Jones has cogently argued, lies the explanation of the "European Miracle." In Ragnar Nurkse's words, "Capital is made at home."

The combination of more favorable natural resources and greater amounts of physical and human capital meant that European productivity (first in agriculture and then in industry) was higher than that of what are now known as the less developed countries (LDCs). As pointed out by W. Arthur Lewis, here lies the origin of what has been denounced as the "unequal exchange" between Europe and the LDCs, namely, that the product of an hour of European labor exchanges for the product of more than one hour of LDC labor.

However, one further obstacle remained. Wrigley has persuasively maintained that even the Advanced Organic Economy was subject to the Law of Diminishing Returns and, with population growth, therefore faced the prospect of stagnation. The Stationary State that the British classical economists so feared was not just a nightmare. Indeed, Wrigley maintains that the Netherlands experienced such stagnation in the 18th century, and that Britain might have done so a little later.[32] However, the latter nation was saved by a transition to a Mineral Based Energy Economy, thanks to the use of coal which provided practically unlimited amounts of energy. The result may be illustrated by a few figures. In 1800, the aggregate power of steam engines in Britain may have been 10,000 horsepower—a far smaller figure than for waterpower; by 1850, however, there was about 500,000 horsepower of stationary engines and 790,000 horsepower of mobile engines, mostly in the form of railway locomotives.[33] In other words, every member of the labor force (of, say, 9,000,000) had 1.4 "steam slaves" at his disposal, not to mention the "water slaves." By 1900, the figure for Britain was about 14,000,000 horsepower, or about 9 "slaves" per worker. By contrast, except for railways, which started in the 1850s, and tugboats, the Middle East hardly participated in the steam revolution until very recently. One example is illustrative: in Egypt in 1941 the capacity of all the machinery in the country was about 1,900,000 horsepower, or about 0.1 horsepower per capita and an estimated 2.5 "mechanical slaves" per head of working population. Moreover, it should be remembered that, at least until the 1930s, Egypt was the most mechanized and industrialized country in the Middle East.[34]

Of course things have now changed dramatically. The Middle East (in the broader sense) contains over half the world's most important source of energy, oil. In addition, oil, and its associated product, gas, provide the raw material for the increasingly important petrochemical industry—not to mention huge amounts of foreign exchange. The energy constraint has been suddenly lifted. Simultaneously, however, we have discovered that, because of the nature of contemporary technology, the main constraint nowadays is no longer energy or other physical resources but the degree of development of human resources; this is convincingly shown by the examples of Japan, Switzerland, South Korea, and many other countries. Fortunately, much of the advanced technology (e.g., in bioengineering) can be transferred without too much difficulty to the LDCs. In this respect the Middle East is lagging badly, and it is toward the building of its human capital through education, health, and the emancipation of women that its efforts must now be directed.

NOTES

1. In Europe the working rates were: a man, 0.1 horsepower; a donkey, 0.25; a mule, 0.5; and an ox, 0.66; for a camel the figure is 2. See A. R. Ubbelohde, *Man and Energy* (London, 1963), pp. 50-52.

2. Carlo Cipolla, *The Economic History of World Population* (London, 1964), p. 46.

3. See E. A. Wrigley, *Continuity, Chance and Change: The Character of the Industrial Revolution in England* (Cambridge, 1988), p. 18 and passim.

4. For an extensive discussion, see Andrew M. Watson, *Agricultural Innovations in the Early Islamic World* (Cambridge, 1983), passim.

5. E. Ashtor, *A Social and Economic History of the Near East in the Middle Ages* (Berkeley and Los Angeles, 1976), p. 50; O. G. Bolshakov, *Srednevekovyi gorod Blizhnego Vostoka* (Moscow, 1984), pp. 234-35, 265. For European yields, see B. H. Slicher van Bath, *Yield Ratios, 810-1820* (Wageningen, 1963), passim. For Middle East ratios, see Charles Issawi, Economic History of Turkey (Chicago, 1980), pp. 214-15; Charles Issawi, *The Fertile Crescent* (New York, 1988), p. 273; and Charles Issawi, *The Economic History of the Middle East* (Chicago, 1966), p. 377.

6. See figures in Charles Issawi, "Economic Change and Urbanization in the Middle East," in Ira Lapidus, ed., *Middle Eastern Cities* (Berkeley and Los Angeles, 1969), reproduced in Charles Issawi, *The Arab Legacy* (Princeton, N.J., 1981), pp. 289-307.

7. Op cit.

8. Lynn White, *Medieval Technology and Social Change* (Oxford, 1965); "The Expansion of Technology," in Carlo Cipolla, ed., *The Fontana Economic History of Europe* (London, 1972), vol. I, p. 144; Lefebvre des Noëttes, *La force motrice animale à travers les ages* (Paris, 1924).

9. Van Bath, *Yield Ratios,* pp. 16ff.

10. Alfred W. Crosby, Jr., *The Columbian Exchange* (Westport, Conn., 1972).

11. Ubbelobde, *Man and Energy,* pp. 50-52.

12. K. D. White, *Greek and Roman Technology* (Ithaca, N.Y., 1984), pp. 55-56; see also R. J. Forbes, "Power," in Charles Singer, ed., *A History of Technology,* vol. II (Oxford, 1957).

13. Forbes, "Power," pp. 608-14. For a more detailed account of watermills in medieval Syria, see Muhsin D. Yusuf, *Economic Survey of Syria during the Tenth and Eleventh Centuries* (Berlin, 1985), pp. 74-77. Yusuf found no evidence of windmills.

14. Huri Islamoglu-Inan, "State and Peasants in the Ottoman Empire," in Huri Islamoglu-Inan, ed., *The Ottoman Empire and the World Economy* (Cambridge, 1987), pp. 151-52.

15. Wolf-Dieter Hütteroth and Kamal Abdulfattah, *Historical Geography of Palestine, Transjordan and Southern Syria in the Late 16th Century* (Erlangen, 1977), pp. 32-33.

16. Ibid., p. 72; in 1571, the rates in the vilayet of Tripoli were the same; see Robert

Mantran and Jean Sauvaget, *Règlements fiscaux Ottomans* (Paris, 1951), p. 76; identical rates prevailed in Malatya in 1560.

17. Hütteroth and Abdulfattah, *Historical Geography,* p. 43.

18. I owe this information to Bernard Lewis, who kindly went with me through a defter covering the nahiyes of Jira, Tibnin, Shaqif, and Akka; we counted 78 mills, many with two or four stones.

19. Refet Yinanç and Mesut Elibüyük, *Kanuni Devri Malatya Tahrir Defteri,* 1560 (Ankara, 1983), p. xiii.

20. Issawi, *The Fertile Crescent,* p. 379; Issawi, Economic History of Turkey, p. 276.

21. Forbes, "Power," p. 610.

22. E. Levasseur, *La population française* (Paris, 1889-92), vol. III, p. 74, cited in Wrigley, *Continuity, Chance and Change,* p. 76.

23. Al-Tabari, *Tarikh,* ed. M. J. de Goeje et al. (Leiden, 1879-1901), vol. 1, p. 2722.

24. Forbes, "Power," pp. 615-17. There is, however, a reference to a tax on windmills in an Ottoman qanunname in the collection edited by O. L. Barkan.

25. Issawi, *Economic History of the Middle East,* p. 377; 'Abd al-Rahman al-Jabarti, *Aja'ib al-Athar fi-al-Tarajim wa-al-Akhbar* (Beirut, 1978), vol. II, p. 231; Issawi, *Fertile Crescent,* pp. 272, 340; S. Avitsur, "Wind Power in the Technological Development of Palestine," in David Kushner, ed., *Palestine in the Late Ottoman Period* (Jerusalem-Leiden, 1986), pp. 231-44.

26. Forbes, "Power"; and Rex Wailes, "A Note on Windmills," in Singer, *History of Technology,* vol. II, pp. 623-28. For one example among many, see the efforts made by Venice to introduce and develop windmills in the 13th and 14th centuries (E. Ashtor, "The Factors of Technological and Industrial Progress in the later Middle Ages," *Journal of European Economic History,* 18, 1, pp. 27-29).

27. Lewis Mumford, *Technics and Civilization* (London, 1934).

28. Wrigley, *Continuity, Chance and Change,* pp. 12-17.

29. In Egypt in 1947, less than 1 percent of women in the age group 45-49 had never been married and only 20 percent in the age group 20-24 (see United Arab Republic National Planning Committee, Memorandum 448, cited in Charles Issawi, *Egypt in Revolution* [London, 1963], p. 78).

30. H. J. Habakkuk. "The Economic History of Modern Britain," *Journal of Economic History* (December, 1958); Robert Forster, "Achievements of the Annales School," *Journal of Economic History* (March, 1978).

31. E. L. Jones, *The European Miracle* (Cambridge, 1981), p. 14; see also Peter Laslett, "Characteristics of the Western Family Considered Over Time," *Journal of Family History* (1977).

32. Wrigley, *Continuity, Chance and Change,* pp. 34-67.

33. David Landes, "Technological Change and Development in Western Europe, 1750-1914," in H. J. Habakkuk and M. Postan, eds., *Cambridge Economic History of Europe* (Cambridge, 1965), vol. VI, pt. 1, p. 334.

34. The aggregate horsepower of all licensed machines was 1,038,000; of these, 336,000 were in irrigation and drainage. This figure does not seem to include

railways. There were 655 locomotives in the state railways which, assuming an average of 1,000 horsepower, represents 655,000 horsepower; and 184 locomotives in the light railways which, assuming an average of 500 horsepower, represents 92,000 horsepower. Allowing another 200,000 horsepower for street cars, motor vehicles (which may not be included in the total), and other machinery gives a total of about 1,900,000 horsepower. Egypt's population was about 17,000,000, and its labor force, in male equivalents, may be put at about 7,700,000. This means that every worker had 0.25 horsepower at his disposal, or 2.5 "mechanical slaves" (see Egypt, Ministry of Finance, *al-Ihsa al-Sanawi*, 1941/42, pp. 304-9, 716). Calculations for 1930 show almost identical results, and for 1920, when the aggregate power of licensed machines was 614,000, the results are much lower; see ibid., 1921/22, 1929/30.

4

The Ottoman-Habsburg Balance of Forces

n the 16th century two great empires dominated the Western world: the Ottomans and the Habsburgs, with their Austrian and Spanish branches. They fought for mastery of the Mediterranean and made deep incursions into each other's territory: in North Africa, Hungary and elsewhere. The century ended in what was essentially a stalemate.

The purpose of this chapter is to analyze the material, human and technical resources available to either side around 1550.

A comparison of the main indicators of power shows that, at the time of Süleymân, the Ottoman and the combined Habsburg empires were quite evenly matched. We may consider Area, Population, Agriculture, Minerals, Manufacturing, Transport and Economic Organization.

I. Area

The area of the Ottoman Empire was distinctly larger than that of the Habsburgs.

However, the addition of the enormous territories in the Americas that were under effective Spanish control by the 1550s, and which were of the order of 5,000,000 square kilometers, more than made up the difference.[1]

Ottoman Empire[2]

Europe	about	1,000,000	square kilometers
Anatolia	about	750,000	square kilometers
Arab provinces (inhabited areas only)			
	about	750,000	square kilometers
		2,500,000	

Spanish Habsburg

Spain	about	500,000	square kilometers
One half of Italy	about	150,000	square kilometers
Netherlands etc.	about	50,000	square kilometers
		700,000	

Austrian Habsburg[3]	about	250,000	square kilometers

19 • The Habsburg Empire under Charles V, mid-sixteenth century, without the American territories.

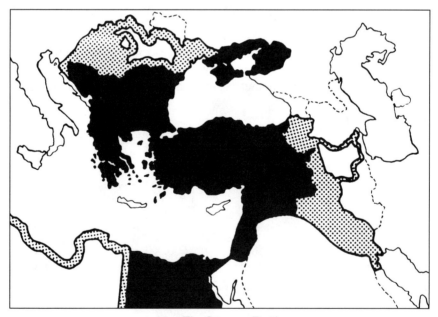

20 • The Ottoman Empire

II. Population

For the Ottoman Empire, quite reliable figures have been provided by Ö. L. Barkan and M. A. Cook.[4]

For Spain and its European possessions, too, reliable figures are available.[5] But for the Austrian Habsburg Empire there is a dearth of information in the sources just enumerated and in such standard works as that by Tremel. Mols puts the population of the "Danubian Countries" at 5,500,000 in about 1500 and 7,000,000 in about 1600, or say, an average of 6,250,000 for around 1550.[6] From this a deduction of some 1,250,000 may be made for that part of Hungary occupied by the Ottomans, leaving about 5,000,000. The Atlas of World Population puts the population of the Habsburg Empire at 7,000,000 in 1550 and 8,000,000 in 1600.[7]

As regards the Americas, estimates of the pre-Columbian population differ hugely, from some 13,000,000 to over 100,000,000, but all agree that there was a catastrophic decline following the Spanish conquest and estimates for around 1550 put the combined total for Mexico and Peru at around 4,000,000.[8]

Ottoman Empire

Europe	about	8,000,000
Anatolia	about	6,000,000
Arab provinces	about	6-7,000,000
	about	20-21,000,000

Spanish Habsburg Empire

Spain	about	9,000,000
One-third of Italy	about	4,000,000
Netherlands etc.	about	2,000,000
	about	15,000,000

Americas	about	4-5,000,000
Austrian Habsburg Empire	about	5-6,000,000

It will thus be seen that, leaving aside the Americas, the combined Habsburgs had a population almost exactly equal to that of the Ottomans.

Two more points may be made. First, in all three empires population was growing, at not too dissimilar rates. Barkan puts the population of the Ottoman Empire around 1600 at 30 million. Mols shows a Spanish and

21 • Vienna during the Turkish Siege of 1529

Portuguese growth from 9,300,000 in 1500 to 11,300,000 in 1600 and a "Danubian" growth from 5,500,000 to 7,000,000. This means that the age structures were probably similar and that the proportion of men of working and fighting age must have been about the same. Secondly, the Ottoman Empire was much more urbanized than the Habsburg ones. No European city had a population approaching that of Istanbul (about 400,000) or Cairo (200,000-300,000) or even Aleppo (probably over 100,000); of all the Habsburg cities only Naples approached the 100,000 mark; Seville, Cordoba, Granada, Barcelona, Antwerp, Brussels, Ghent, Palermo, and Messina had around 50,000 inhabitants and Vienna and Prague probably less.[9]

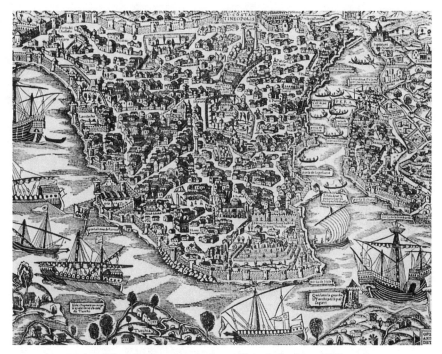

22 • G. Vavassore's plan of Istanbul, circa 1520

III. Agriculture

Since in all the areas surveyed the bulk of the land was devoted to grain and since the New World crops (particularly maize and potatoes) had not yet established themselves, the most meaningful index for comparison is the yield-to-seed ratio for wheat, which was by far the most widespread crop. However, it should be noted that this ratio does not necessarily reflect yields per acre, since sowing practices differed in various localities.

The only Ottoman figures I have so far found relate to the mid-nineteenth century, and average 5 or 6 to 1 in both Anatolia and Rumelia.[10] There is no reason to believe that sixteenth century yields were appreciably lower, since no significant improvements had been introduced in the intervening period. In the Arab provinces the yield was probably lower, except in the fertile, irrigated Nile valley where it was much higher.

For Spain, the earliest figure, 3-4 to 1, refers to Catalonia in 1533-1548; by 1780 it had risen to 5.[11] There is no reason to believe that the national average for Spain was higher than the figure for Catalonia. In Italy, however, yields were distinctly higher-5-6 or over-and in Belgium higher still, averaging 10.9 in 1586-1602.[12] For Austria in the eighteenth century a 3-5 yield prevailed.[13] As for earlier figures, in the mid-sixteenth century yields of 2 or less were recorded in various parts of Hungary, rising to 3.5 in the seventeenth century, and in 1651-1700 to 3-4 in parts of Czechoslovakia.[14]

There is therefore every reason to believe that Ottoman yields were as high as, or higher than, those in the Habsburg lands. Given its wide range of climates and terrain (from the Balkans to the Nile valley), the Ottoman Empire may also have had a greater variety of crops. It was generally a net exporter of wheat (from Egypt, Rumelia, and Rumania), livestock (North Africa), cotton (from Cyprus, Syria and Greece) and silk (mainly re-exports from Iran).[15]

IV. Minerals

All three empires were well-endowed with minerals. The Ottomans drew ample supplies of iron, copper, lead, mercury, and silver from both the Balkans and Anatolia.[16] The main deficiency was tin, which was imported from Britain and elsewhere. Spain was very rich in minerals: iron in the Basque provinces, lead, silver, copper in Huelva, mercury in Almaden and other lesser minerals. Belgium and Italy were also well-endowed with minerals. And, of course, there was the huge influx of gold and silver from America.

The Austrian Habsburgs were even more fortunate. Their mountainous lands contained an ideal combination of minerals, untouched by Roman exploitation, thick forests providing building timber, charcoal and pitprops, and water power to drive the increasingly complex machinery that was installed in the Middle Ages and early modern times. Bohemia, Silesia and Hungary supplied gold, silver and copper, and Styria, Carinthia, Tyrol and Bohemia had large iron mines.[17]

It should be noted that mining technology in Europe was more advanced and innovative than in the Ottoman Empire. The amalgamation process for separating silver from its ore was introduced in Spain and its colonies early in the sixteenth century. For iron smelting, the use of blast furnaces also spread from the Netherlands to Galicia, Styria and other parts of Europe at the same time and water driven machinery was increasingly used to crush ores and drain mines.[18] The Ottomans tried to keep up with such developments, but tended to lag behind.

V. Manufacturing

On both sides textiles were the leading industry. The Ottomans had such great centers as Istanbul, Bursa, Cairo, Aleppo, Damascus and Salonica. The Spanish Habsburgs also had large centers in Castille, Andalusia and Catalonia, and more important ones in Belgium, North Italy and Naples. The main Austrian centers were Bohemia and Silesia.

In this field too the technological superiority of Europe was already apparent. In textiles the Ottomans tended to import the more valuable woolens and silks and to export cheaper cottons, or textile fibers. Other goods, such as glassware and paper, that had formerly been exported from the Middle East were now imported. In the use of water, and especially wind power, Europe was far more advanced than the Middle East and coal was beginning to be used, for instance in Belgium.[19] In metallurgy and armaments, the Ottomans tried hard to keep up with Europe by using the services of converts to Islam; we do not hear of a reverse flow of men or techniques. And, of course, European industry, mining, commerce, finance, and even agriculture were beginning to profit from the diffusion of printing which, in the Ottoman Empire, was restricted to non-Arabic scripts.

VI. Transport

Little need be said on this subject. Both sides suffered from a lack of navigable rivers, the Nile and Danube being the main exceptions, but both the Ottomans and the Spanish Habsburgs used coastal navigation very extensively - the Austrian Habsburg Empire was, of course, landlocked. On land, the Ottomans had the advantage of using the camel, whose load was twice that of the horse or mule;[20] on the other hand, Europeans made much more use of carts and carriages. And on the seas there seems little doubt that European ships, including Spanish, which had to sail Atlantic waters, were definitely superior to the Mediterranean galleys and other vessels which constituted the Ottoman navy and mercantile marine. For the same reasons, the art of navigation was more advanced in Europe.

VII. Economic Organization

Only two brief observations will be made under this heading. On the one hand one has the impression—fortified by what Andrew Hess has said —that the Ottoman monarchs had a much tighter control of their economy than did the Austrian, or even the Spanish, Habsburgs and that they could mobilize a larger proportion of total resources. One also has the impression that the deficits in the Ottoman state budgets were much smaller than those in Spain. There does not seem to be anything comparable to Philip II's huge loans or to his spectacular bankruptcy of 1575. It is true that the Ottoman akçe was steadily debased but the loss in its value between 1500 and 1700 does not seem to have been greater than that of the Spanish maravedi; however, it was much greater than the decline in the Austrian pfund-pfennig.[21] But, as against that, economic institutions and methods in the private sector—including banks, companies, insurance and accountancy—were distinctly more developed in the Habsburg empires than in the Ottoman.

VIII. Concluding Remarks

The preceding analysis suggests that, in the great conflict pitting the Ottomans against the combined Habsburgs, the protagonists were evenly matched. The population, resources and—to a lesser extent—technologies on either side were roughly equal. The additional handicap imposed on Turkey by wars with Iran was offset by that imposed on Spain by the wars with France.

After about 1580, however, Spain tacitly withdrew from the fight against the Ottomans, leaving Austria to bear the brunt of the battle, along with such allies as it could muster. And here the discrepancy was very great—a 10 to 1 advantage in area and 3 or 4 to 1 in population in favor of the Ottomans. No wonder that Austria remained on the defensive until the end of the seventeenth century, particularly after it threw its armies into the Thirty Years War.

There was much resemblance between the Austro-Hungarian and the Ottoman empires. Both were multi-ethnic, polyglot states, harboring many sects and held together by common loyalty to a sovereign and an overwhelmingly predominant religion (Islam, Catholicism). But in addition there was a symbiotic relation between them. The Austrian Habsburg Empire arose as a response to the Ottoman invasion. After the collapse of Hungary at Mohács, it became the main defense of Europe. With the decline of the Ottomans, it expanded in the Balkans—and also in Poland. But by then it was no longer fulfilling an essential function, and the center of the action had shifted to Western Europe—to the Netherlands, France and Great Britain. Eventually, both the Habsburg and the Ottoman empires succumbed to the same enemy: Nationalism, born of the French Revolution, Romanticism and the economic and social changes that were taking place in Europe. The first to respond were the Balkans—the Greeks, Serbs, Rumanians and others. Then came the turn of the Central Europeans—the Czechs, Hungarians and Croats. These movements exacerbated the nationalism of the dominant groups, the Turks and the Germans, and the result was intense struggle in both empires. Both were shattered by the First World War and their dynasties were swept away almost simultaneously.[22]

23 • Der Türkische Kaiser (The Turkish Emperor)

Notes

1. Present day Mexico, Peru and Chile total some 4,000,000 square kilometers. Central America and the larger islands of the Caribbean total over 500,000 and to this should be added large portions of Venezuela, Colombia and Argentina.

2. For assumptions and sources see Charles Issawi, "The Area and Population of the Arab Empire," in *idem, The Arab Legacy* (Princeton, 1981), pp. 37-38.

3. Present day Austria (83,000) and Czechoslovakia (127,000) plus Silesia and a small portion of Hungary.

4. Ömar Lütfi Barkan, "Essai sur les données statistiques des registres," JESHO 1 (1957), pp. 9-36; M. A. Cook, *Population Pressure in Rural Anatolia* (London, 1972).

5. J. Nadal, *Historia de la Poblacion espanola* (Barcelona, 1966); Roger Mols, "Population in Europe 1500-1700," in Carlo Cipolla (ed.), *The Fontana Economic History of Europe,* Vol II, 1974, pp. 15-82; Karl Helleiner, "The Population of Europe," in E. E. Rich and C. H. Wilson (eds.), *The Cambridge Economic History of Europe,* Vol. IV, pp. 1-95.

6. *Op. cit.,* p. 38.

7. Colin McEvedy and Richard Jones, *Atlas of World Population* (Harmondsworth, 1978), p. 91.

8. N. Sanchez-Albornoz, *La Poblacion en America Latina* (Madrid, 1973), pp.54-66.

9. See H. Inalcik, EI2 s.v. "Istanbul"; Janet Abu Lughod, *Cairo* (Princeton, 1971) p. 131; André Raymond, *Grandes villes arabes à l'époque ottomane* (Paris, 1985); for the European figures see Helleiner, *op. cit.,* p. 81.

10. Charles Issawi, *The Economic History of Turkey* (Chicago, 1980), pp. 214-215.

11. B. H. Slicher Van Bath, *Yield Ratios* 1310-1820 (Wageningen, 1963), pp. 42, 60.

12. *Ibid,* p. 42; *Fontana History, op. cit.,* p. 616.

13. Ernst Wangermann, *The Austrian Achievement, 1700-1800* (London, 1973), p. 24.

14. Van Bath, *op. cit.,* p. 61; *Fontana History, op. cit.,* pp. 602-604.

15. Fernand Braudel, *The Mediterranean* (2 vols., New York, 1972), pp. 593, 585, 84, 117, 156, 209, 559, and 362-565.

16. Robert Anhegger, *Beiträge zur Geschichte des Bergbaus im osmanischen Reich,* 2 Vols. (Istanbul, 1943-1945); Ahmet Refik, *Osmanli Devrinde Türkiye Madenleri* (Istanbul, 1931); see also Charles Issawi, *The Economic History of Turkey, op. cit.,* pp. 273-298.

17. John U. Nef, "Mining and Metallurgy in Medieval Civilization," *Cambridge Economic History of Europe,* vol. II (Cambridge, 1952), pp. 433-441 and 469-473; see also Ferdinand Tremel, *Wirtschafts und Sozial Geschichte Österreichs* (Vienna, 1969).

18. Domenico Sella, "European Industries," in *Fontana Economic History, op. cit.,* p. 395; Nef, op. cit., pp. 458-469.

19. A. Rupert Hall, "Scientific Method and Progress of Techniques," in *Cambridge*

Economic History, vol. IV, *op. cit.,* pp. 103; Charles Issawi, "Technology, Energy and Civilization," (chapter III, above).

20. Charles Issawi, *The Economic History of Turkey, op. cit.,* p. 177.

21. See the graphs drawn by Frank Spooner in *Cambridge Economic History of Europe, op. cit.,* Vol. IV, p. 458; for the Castilian budget in 1574 see Geoffrey Parker, *Spain and the Netherlands* (London, 1979), p. 32; for the Ottoman budgets of 1564-65, 1591-92, 1597-98, 1648 and 1650 see Bernard Lewis, *Islam in History* (London, 1973), p. 210.

22. H. A. L. Fisher, *A History of Europe* (London, 1936), pp. 729-735.

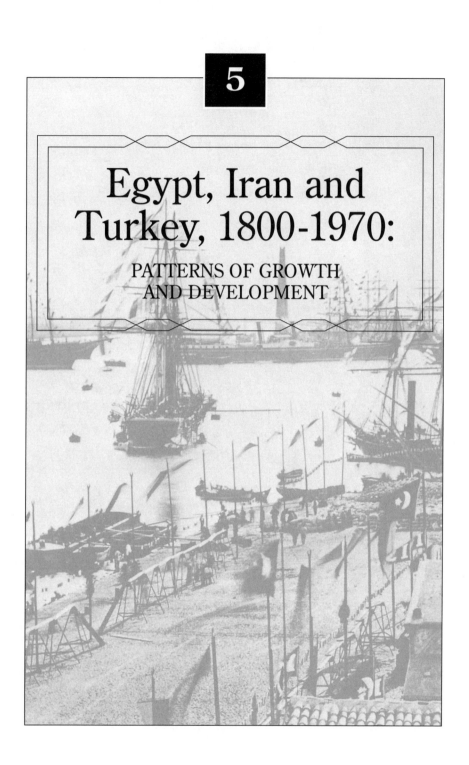

5

Egypt, Iran and Turkey, 1800-1970:

PATTERNS OF GROWTH AND DEVELOPMENT

n assessment of the relative economic performance of Egypt, Iran and Turkey[1] from 1800 to 1970 is more meaningful than most such comparisons. Throughout the period, the three countries have had populations of much the same size and degree of development, and around 1800 their per capita incomes must have been roughly equal and their economic structures basically similar. Until the Oil Revolution of 1970-73, which drastically changed their relative positions, there was no significant difference in their resource endowments. All three share a common historical and cultural legacy: each had originated one of the major ancient civilizations, each had greatly contributed to the formation of Islamic society and culture, and all three had experienced the stagnation and decline that characterized the Middle East in the modern period. Lastly, all three were integrated in the world economy at much the same time and subjected to the same major forces: the thrust of European imperialism, the expansion of world trade, the spread of mechanical transport and electric communications, the flow of vast amounts of foreign capital, the unsettling Western ideas of nationalism, secularism and political liberty, and the influx of hundreds and thousands of Europeans with the technical, business or administrative skills required for the modernization of society which the Middle Eastern governments were, with various degrees of commitment and success, attempting to carry out.

This chapter falls into two parts. In the first, an appraisal is made of the economic development of the three countries at certain significant dates: 1800, 1860, 1913, 1950 and 1972. The second consists of an analysis in terms of some factors that may account for the differences observed.

1800

The end of the eighteenth century marks a low point in the economic history of the Middle East. Population had declined from its late medieval and early modern levels, standing at some 3.5 million in Egypt, 6 million in Turkey (1831) and perhaps 5 million in Iran. The cultivated area had shrunk, and many villages and their surrounding fields had been abandoned. The crafts were still active, but their technology had stagnated and

24 • The court of Al-Azbar Mosque. Gatherings of scholars can be seen inside.

in many quality had fallen off; moreover some branches were already suffering from the competition of cheaper or better European goods. As for trade with Europe—which is the only one about which we have any information at present—it was definitely diminishing in Egypt, where both British and French merchants were leaving the country, and in Iran, where the East India Company's business had declined so much that it was planning to close down its establishments in the Gulf. The Ottoman Empire's trade with Europe grew appreciably between 1715 and 1790, but this was largely attributable to the development of the Balkan provinces; the trade of Izmir showed a comparable increase, due partly to the diversion of the Persian silk trade from Aleppo, but otherwise no trend can be discerned in the trade of Istanbul or Anatolia. At the outbreak of the French Revolution Egypt's trade (exports plus imports) with Europe may have totalled £0.6 million and Turkey's £1.5 million, while Iran's total trade in 1800 was put at £2.5 million. The Revolutionary and Napoleonic Wars greatly reduced the trade of Egypt and Turkey and the War of Greek Independence led to further diminution in Turkey's trade. This economic decline was accompanied by reduced intellectual activity. One has only to compare the curriculum of the leading Muslim university, Al Azhar in Cairo, with the sciences taught in the heyday of Islam, or to recall the fact that when Muhammad Ali started his reforms he could not find a single native Egyptian who knew any European language, to realize how low Egypt had fallen. Iran was no better off but in Turkey there had been some hopeful developments in the eighteenth century, including the introduction of a Turkish printing press, some translations from European works and the opening of Western-type military academies.

Many causes led to this decline, of which only one will be mentioned here: the breakdown of government. In Iran this occurred early in the eighteenth century, with the collapse of the Safavi dynasty and the Afghan and other invasions. In Egypt anarchy grew steadily throughout the same century. And in the Ottoman Empire the central government gradually lost its control until, by the beginning of the nineteenth century, it was confined to a small area in Europe and Asia Minor centered on Istanbul.

1860

On the eve of the American Civil War, which by creating a shortage of cotton was to stimulate Egyptian growth so greatly, the Middle East presented a very different picture. Steam navigation had linked Egypt, Turkey and the Levant with Europe for nearly three decades, though Iran was still unprovided for. Steamers were also sailing on the Nile and Tigris-Euphrates, as well as the Aegean and Black Sea waters. Telegraphs had been laid down in Egypt and Turkey and would soon be in Iran. Some 500 kilometers of railway had been built in Egypt and work was under way on the Izmir-Aydin Line. The Ottoman Empire had been opened up by the Anglo-Turkish Commercial Convention of 1838 (applied to Egypt in 1841) and Iran by the Russo-Persian Treaties of 1813 and 1828 and the Anglo-Persian Treaty of 1841; these replaced the former monopolistic, prohibitive and arbitrary practices with non-discriminatory, permissive provisions and very low import duties. European merchants increasingly supplied the expertise, market connections and short-term finance required by the import-export trade. At the same time various reformers—Muhammad Ali in Egypt, Mahmud II and the "Men of the Tanzimat" in Turkey and Amir-i-Kabir in Iran—were attempting to modernize their countries.

All these developments began to integrate the various parts of the Middle East, in different degrees, in the international trade network. Foreign trade expanded, in Egypt from about £2 million in 1823 to over £5

25 • The Port of Alexandria in the 19th century

million in 1860, in Iran from about £2.5 million in 1800 to some £5 million and in Turkey from £5 million in the 1840s to £25 million in the 1870s. On the export side, the growth was due to greater output and sales of cash crops like cotton in Egypt and silk and opium in Iran and Turkey. By far the greatest increase in imports was that of cotton and other textiles, which drove many handicraftsmen out of business. There was also a rise in imports of colonial goods such as sugar, coffee and tea. Except under Muhammad Ali in Egypt, almost no capital goods were imported.

The years 1861 to 1866 mark an important turning point in the history of Egyptian cotton production. When the period began some half a million cantars were being grown on perhaps 250,000 feddans; five years later the harvest had increased four times in size, the area by five, and from then on cotton became once and for all the crop which absorbed the major portion of Egyptian energies and the overwhelming share of its export earnings. The cause of this sudden metamorphosis was the American Civil War which, by depriving the European textile industry of the greater part of its supplies of American cotton on which it was largely dependent, drove up the price of cotton to enormous heights and conferred great prosperity on those countries which, like

Egypt, were able to take advantage of the favourable situation . . . The period of cotton boom in Egypt has a special flavour all its own, one which can be best summed up in a quotation from the Times correspondent written at a time when optimism about Egypt's economic potential was at its height and there was a feeling in the air that all things were possible:

> An extraordinary revolution is rapidly proceeding in this country. Europe has finally understood the immense future of Egypt and is eager to develop her budding resources. Every steamer is pouring a new population and a golden stream on our shores; energy and capital are taking possession of the land, and urging it forward in the path of civilization and wealth. Not only are the cities of Alexandria and Cairo receiving so great an influx of inhabitants that, although whole quarters are rising on every side, house room is still insufficient, and rents are always increasing, but the inland towns and villages are over-run, and factories with high chimneys and long lines of black smoke cut the clear sky of our flat landscape through the length and breadth of Lower Egypt. . . . The Viceroy has expressed his conviction that, although the cattle murrain has been a grievous present calamity, it will confer a lasting benefit, by compelling the adoption of an improved system, which will civilize his people while enriching them.

. . . New firms came forward to undertake public works contracts; the amounts of money borrowed from Europe became larger and larger; imports remained at a high level. To an Egyptian living in 1875 looking at the changed face of his country, the modern city of Cairo, the railways linking every major Delta town, the harbour works at Alexandria, 1865 must have seemed as far away as 1845 or earlier. The only lasting effect of the boom was the fact that it caused the cultivation of cotton to spread into every corner of Lower Egypt and to remain there, firmly entrenched in the rural rotation of crops in spite of the falling prices and high taxes.

E.R.J. Owen, "Cotton Production and the Development
of the Cotton Economy in 19th Century Egypt"
(thesis, Oxford University, 1965), quoted in Issawi,
The Economic History of the Middle East, pp. 417, 429.

During this period all three countries were engaged in numerous wars, which drained a large part of their resources, but Iran enjoyed a longer period of peace than the other two. Nevertheless, its development was much slower. Its population grew little if at all. Its transport system saw no improvement except for the appearance of a few Russian steamships on the Caspian Sea and an occasional British one in the Gulf and the revival of the ancient Tabriz-Trabzon caravan route that shortened communications with Europe. Only a very small part of its agriculture was commercialized and there was no discernible change in either techniques or land tenure. Its efforts at industrialization, in the 1850s, were very feeble. Its currency depreciated by over half in relation to sterling and its government revenues increased very little. Very few foreigners settled in the country and fewer Iranians went to Europe, with a consequent lack of intellectual stimulus.

26 • The cotton plant

Egypt, by contrast, experienced considerable change. Its population rose to some 5.5 million, or at about 0.8 per cent a year. The cultivated area was considerably extended; more important, large-scale irrigation works (diversion dams, dikes and canals) made it possible to grow more than one crop per annum, including the valuable "summer" crops such as cotton and sugar, and agricultural output greatly expanded, with a corresponding increase in exports and imports. Agriculture had become market-oriented, and tenure had been radically transformed and almost all farmland was privately owned by landlords or peasant proprietors. Navigable canals and roads were built and in 1853 the first section of the Alexandria-Cairo-Suez railway was opened. An adequate port was built at Alexandria. Many foreign technicians and businessmen came to Egypt and hundreds of Egyptians were sent to Europe for study or training; technical and secondary schools were set up and a large-scale program of translation and publishing initiated, thus starting a far-reaching intellectual awakening.

These developments did not proceed smoothly. Muhammad Ali (1805-49) attempted to set up a state-owned and -managed industry and transport, financed by compulsory deliveries of cotton and other crops and a foreign trade monopoly. His success was considerable but after 1841 the system broke down under its own weight and because of foreign pressure. The monopolies were abolished and the factories dismantled. But the improvements in agriculture and transport served as a foundation for future development.

Turkey was engaged in major wars throughout the period, against foreign powers or rebellious subjects. It was not until the 1840s that serious
attempts at industrial development—only partly successful—began, not till
then did foreign trade expand significantly, and Turkey was less integrated
in the international network than Egypt. The commercialization of agriculture and the transformation of land tenure was less advanced than in Egypt
and, in all probability, population growth was slower. But Turkey's educational efforts matched those of Egypt and its intellectual progress was at
least as great.

1913

In the next fifty years the processes described above accelerated. In
real terms Egypt's foreign trade multiplied twelve-fold, Iran's four-fold and
Turkey's almost three-fold; the League of Nations' estimates for 1913 were:
Egypt $291 million, or $24 per capita, Iran $93 million or $9, and Turkey
$273 million or $15. Thanks to improved hygiene and, probably, to greater
food supplies, population about doubled in all three countries, with the
towns growing a little faster. The rise in the labor force, and the availability
of arable land, made it possible to expand cultivation. Output of cash crops
like cotton, tobacco, silk, opium and dried fruits rose very fast and capitalist relations increasingly prevailed in agriculture, Egypt being again in the
lead. This was aided by the adoption, in Egypt and Turkey, of Western-style
agricultural and commercial codes and law courts that made it possible to
sell or mortgage land and facilitate the collection of debts. Numerous foreign banks opened branches in Egypt and quite a few in Turkey but only
two (British and Russian) in Iran; they concentrated heavily on the moving
of the crops for export and the financing of imports. Transport expanded
greatly: in 1913 Egypt had 4300 kilometers of railway and Turkey 3200 but
Iran was still without any; similarly, modern ports had been built at
Alexandria, Port Said, Suez, Istanbul, Izmir and Beirut, but in Iran the only
noteworthy improvement was at Enzeli. Currencies were a little more sta-
ble and the governments were handling their finances somewhat better, on
both the revenue and the expenditure side.

The Middle East received more than its share of the outflow of
European capital in the last third of the nineteenth century. By 1913,
Egypt's foreign debt, public and private, stood at about $1,000 million, and
that of the Ottoman Empire at an equal amount, some 60 per cent of the private capital being in Turkey; Iran's was a little over $100 million. Much of

27 • Port Said, Egypt

the public debt had been spent on wars or wasted by monarchs, but some had been used for railways and other public works. In all three countries the servicing of the debt absorbed a large proportion of government revenues and remittances of interest and profits were a heavy burden on the balance of payments. In Egypt and Turkey a small, but growing, industrial nucleus had come into being, but in Iran there were only a few factories struggling hard to survive. Another hopeful sign was the increasing proportion of capital goods in imports and the rising proportion of GNP devoted to investment—over 10 per cent in Egypt, a little less in Iran and Turkey.[2] Still another was the rapid growth in education and the emergence of an intelligentsia.

A review at this point brings out significant differences between the three countries. By any criterion, economic or social, Iran stood far behind the others. Both Egypt and Turkey had a per capita income of about $50— a figure that was not too low by contemporary standards—but in other respects there were marked contrasts. The level of living of the masses in Turkey seems to have been higher and the distribution of income and wealth—notably land—more equal. Turkey also had a more experienced political and administrative elite. But in purely economic terms Egypt was distinctly more developed. On a per capita basis its foreign trade was considerably greater, its industrial output somewhat larger, its transport system far more serviceable and its financial structure much more elaborate and widespread. Its economy was distinctly more monetized and a much larger proportion of its agricultural output reached the market. Few countries could match its superb irrigation system, which made it possible to intensify agriculture and greatly raise output per acre—but only slightly per man. Its cities enjoyed amenities unrivalled in the Middle East until well after the Second World War. Its debt burden was also heavier and a larger proportion of its national product was absorbed by foreigners, including the 250,000 foreign residents in Egypt—a figure much larger than that of Turkey and many times as great as Iran's.

1950

During the First World War and its aftermath, Turkey suffered more than most belligerents and large parts of Iran were overrun and devastated. Egypt, on the other hand, was unscathed militarily and accumulated large sterling balances; hence its lead over the other two countries lengthened, as is shown in Table 5.1.

TABLE 5.1 Iran, Egypt and Turkey, 1925

	IRAN	EGYPT	TURKEY
Population (millions)	(12.5)	14	13.1
Imports (millions of dollars)[a]	88	250	246
Railways (kilometers)	250	4,555	4,700
Automobiles[b]	4,450	17,740	7,500
Cement output (metric tons)		90,000[c]	59,000[c]
Refined sugar output (metric tons)		109,000[c]	5,000[c]
Students in schools	74,000	635,000	413,000

[a] In this and subsequent tables, only import figures are shown; exports are omitted, since both the inclusion and the exclusion of petroleum would be misleading.
[b] 1926.
[c] 1928.

In the inter-war period the same general forces were at work in the three countries. Like other underdeveloped regions, the Middle East suffered from deteriorating terms of trade, shrinking exports and balance of payments strains in the late 1920s and 1930s. This reinforced the desire to industrialize, which had already been strengthened by the shortages felt during the war, and the recovery of tariff autonomy around 1930 enabled all three governments to protect and foster manufacturing. And in all three an attempt was made—most far-reaching in Turkey—to transfer economic control from foreigners or members of minorities to ethnic Egyptians, Iranians or Turks. But there was also a marked contrast. Egypt essentially maintained its "open," private-enterprise economy and kept its link with sterling, while in Iran and Turkey the government was largely responsible for industrialization, set up various state banks and agencies and conducted most foreign trade under bilateral agreements and blocked accounts. As is shown by Table 5.2, Iran, starting from a very low level, made the greatest relative progress and somewhat reduced the gap between it and the others. Turkey also advanced quite rapidly, overtaking Egypt in several respects and, although no reliable figures are available, probably slightly surpassing it in per capita GNP.

TABLE 5.2 Iran, Egypt and Turkey, 1938

	IRAN	EGYPT	TURKEY
Population (millions)	15	16.4	17.1
Imports (millions of dollars)	55	184	119
Railways (kilometers)	1,700	5,606	7,324
Automobiles	(15,000)	33,700	11,300
Cement output (metric tons)	65,000	375,000	287,000
Refined sugar output (metric tons)	22,000	238,000	247,000
Cereals output (million metric tons)[a]	3.09	3.63	6.46
Cotton output (metric tons)[b]	34,000	400,000	52,000
Energy consumption[c]	1.55	2.05	2.18
Students in schools[d]	234,000	1,309,000	810,000

[a] Wheat, barley, maize, rice - annual average, 1934-38.
[b] Annual average, 1934-38.
[c] Million metric tons of coal equivalent.
[d] 1936/37.

During the Second World War the three countries just escaped becoming a battlefield, but once again the impact was uneven. Iran suffered most, being occupied by British and Soviet troops and experiencing severe disruptions. Turkey remained neutral, trading with both sides, but was forced to keep 500,000 men under arms, with serious effects on its agricultural output. Egypt was a base for British troops and cut off from Europe; this caused shortages and hardships but greatly stimulated industrial growth and once more enabled it to accumulate large sterling balances, which were gradually drawn down after the war. On the whole, however, as Table 5.3 indicates, there were no significant changes in the relative position of the three countries. But after 1950 their growth paths began markedly to diverge. Egypt went through two great upheavals. First, the 1952 Revolution which, following the beneficial land reform of that year, led to the wholesale nationalization of industry, transport, finance and foreign trade of 1957 and 1961; on balance, the latter had an adverse effect on economic development. Secondly, Egypt was involved in successive wars with Israel, suffering increasing damage to its economy; a further drain was the war in Yemen, and more generally, the huge burden of defense expenditures, which in recent years rose above 20 per cent of GNP and, of course, were made possible only by massive outside aid. As a result, growth was rather slow - an average of 4 per cent per annum in 1960-73, or little above the population increase of 2.5 per cent.

TABLE 5.3 Iran, Egypt and Turkey, 1950

	IRAN	EGYPT	TURKEY
Population (millions)	19.3	20.4	20.9
Imports (millions of dollars)	191	564	286
Railways (kilometers)	3,180	6,092	7,634
Automobiles	38,300	77,900	32,600
Cement output (metric tons)	54,000	1,022,000	396,000
Refined sugar output (metric tons)	69,000	218,000	186,000
Cereals output (million metric tons)[a]	3.09	3.72	6.74
Cotton output (metric tons)[b]	26,000	364,000	99,000
Electricity output (million kWh)[c]	200	642	676
Energy consumption[d]	4.51	4.42	5.40
Students in schools (thousands)	743	1,597[e]	1,798

[a] Wheat, barley, maize, rice - annual average, 1947-51.
[b] Annual average, 1947-51.   [d] Million metric tons of coal equivalent.
[c] 948.   [a] 1949.

Turkey got off to a very good start, with Marshall Plan aid, after 1948, but soon developed severe imbalances that slowed down its advance. After 1963, a fresh spurt was made, and progress continued on a broad front, with a rapid increase in industry, trade, finance and infrastructure and a rather slow one in agriculture. The government made a notable contribution but growth was most marked in the private sector, which saw the emergence of a large entrepreneurial class, the expansion of the managerial and technical salaried middle class, and the rapid growth of a skilled labor force; of particular significance was the migration of nearly one million workers to Germany and other parts of Western Europe: not only did their remittances reach a peak of $1.4 billion in 1972, but they brought back skills and attitudes which are bound to have far-reaching effects. In 1960-72 Turkey's rate of growth was 6.4 per cent, compared to a population increase of 2.5 per cent. In social terms it is certainly the most advanced of the three countries, its literacy rate in 1970 being 55 per cent, compared to 40 per cent in Egypt and 35 per cent in Iran, and its crude death rate 1.3 per cent compared to 1.4 and 1.6.

After the dislocations caused by the Soviet occupation of Azerbayjan and the oil nationalization crisis of 1951 and its aftermath, Iran entered a long period of political stability and very rapid economic growth. In 1960-72 GNP increased at 9.6 per cent a year, one of the highest rates recorded, and population at 3.2 per cent. Here too there was a happy mix of public and private endeavor and, like Turkey, Iran has seen the very rapid growth of both an entrepreneurial and a salaried middle class. Here too development was widespread, agriculture being the lagging sector. Over the whole period, Iran received much less foreign aid than either Egypt or Turkey, but by the late 1960s oil was making a large contribution to economic growth and after 1971 the increase in oil revenues was explosive. Table 5.4 shows how, by 1972, Iran had overtaken the other countries by most economic, but not social, criteria. Since then its advance has been extremely, and indeed unsustainably, fast.

TABLE 5.4 Iran, Egypt and Turkey, 1972

	IRAN	EGYPT	TURKEY
Population (millions)	31.2	34.8	37.0
Per capita GNP (dollars)	490	240	370
Per capita energy consumption[a]	954	324	564
Per capita steel consumption (kilograms)	59	30	55
Per capita textile consumption (kilograms)[b]	5.1	4.6	6.7
Per capita sugar consumption (kilograms)	28	16	20
Imports (million dollars)	2,410	899	1,508
Railways (kilometers)	4,944	5,500	8,133
Railway freight (million ton kilometers)	3,693	2,976	6,641
Automobiles (thousands)	481	206	372
Cement output (thousand metric tons)	3,372	3,822	8,424
Refined sugar output (thousand metric tons)	598	550	811
Electricity output (million kWh)	9,100	8,030	11,242
Cereals output (million metric tons)[c]	7.7	6.7	17.1
Cotton output (thousand metric tons)[d]	209	495	536
Students in schools (thousands)[e]	4,820	5,708	6,720

[a] Coal equivalent, kilograms.
[b] 1971-72.
[c] Wheat, barley, maize, and rice, annual average, 1972-74.
[d] Lint, annual average 1972-74.
[e] 1971.

II

Analysis of the factors determining the course of events surveyed above may be carried out under the following headings: location and topography, resources, social structure, political structure, and the interplay of international political forces.

Location and Topography

Location largely explains Egypt's early and Iran's belated start. Egypt was only a few days' journey by steamship from Europe, which made it easy for thousands of foreigners to settle in the country and many more to visit it. At their peak, just before the First World War, Europeans constituted 16 per cent of the population of Cairo, 25 per cent of Alexandria and 28 per cent of Port Said, forging strong economic, social and cultural links between Egypt and Europe. Iran, on the other hand, was inaccessible for European-based steamers until the opening of the Suez Canal in 1869, and remained remote until the air age, being thus deprived of a powerful stimulus. Turkey's location was almost as favorable as that of Egypt; it was further from Western Europe, a handicap that was not offset by proximity to Central Europe until the completion of the Vienna-Istanbul railway in 1888. Turkey received many fewer foreigners than Egypt, and Iran far fewer still.

Location also explains Egypt's head-start in transport. Both the Alexandria-Cairo-Suez railway and the Suez Canal were designed to serve European-Asian trade rather than Egyptian economic needs, but the railway in particular was also very beneficial to Egypt. Iran, by contrast, lay well off the main international trade routes and, except for some chimerical British and Russian railway schemes, was never envisaged as a transit route. The same was true of Turkey. The only alternative to the Suez Canal that was seriously considered was the Syrian-Mesopotamian route. The Istanbul-Baghdad railway was designed mainly to serve Ottoman, not German, political and economic objectives.

Egypt's topography is also much more favorable than that of Iran and Turkey. The flatness of the land and the omnipresence of the Nile and its branches means that the whole country is accessible to water transport, which greatly facilitated the spread of a cash-crop agriculture geared to foreign markets. Neither Turkey nor Iran have any significant stretches of navigable rivers. In Turkey this is partly compensated by the length of the coastline and the concentration of the population on the rims of the peninsula, but it still left large stretches of the country without water or mechanical transport and therefore virtually outside the world market. Iran was far worse off: its coastline on the Gulf is short and inhospitable and the bulk of its population and agriculture lies in the north, cut off from the oceans by formidable mountain ranges and deserts. It was only when regular steam navigation was established on the Caspian Sea and the Russian railways reached Baku in 1884 that Iran was linked to a large and expanding market.

Resources

Egypt had only one major resource, fertile land, but until the First World War this was fully adequate to sustain rapid growth. With the introduction of long-staple cotton in 1821, Egypt had an export staple that was not produced by any industrial country except the United States, that constituted the raw material of the main item in international trade, cotton textiles, and that therefore enjoyed a rising demand. With increasingly elaborate and expensive irrigation works, Egypt could steadily expand its cultivated area and output and between 1848-52 and 1908-12 the volume of cotton exports rose more than twenty-fold. By then, however, the limits of cultivation had been reached, output and exports stagnated and, in addition, the terms of trade deteriorated. Accelerated population growth resulted in a falling land/man ratio and per capita income began to decline. When supplementary resources were sought in industrialization it was too late for speedy relief.

Turkey lacked the counterpart of Egyptian cotton, but it had a much broader and more diversified agricultural and mineral base. For the reasons given above and below, this was developed much more slowly, but when it was, it generated greater momentum. Partly for the same reasons, industry followed the same course and by the 1950s Turkey forged ahead.

Iran's great and at present decisive resource, oil, was not discovered till the eve of the First World War. After that output expanded rapidly but the impact on the economy was slight, partly because the industry had remained relatively small and partly because only a small fraction of oil revenues was devoted to development. It was only in the 1960s that oil tipped the balance of resources in Iran's favor; since then the enormous increase of revenues has pushed it far ahead, and the government is trying to use this windfall capital to create other resources, in agriculture, industry and mining, that can sustain future growth when oil gives out.

Social Structure

The Middle East entered the period of this study with a very unfavorable social structure, which is only now being slowly improved. First, it had experienced neither Renaissance nor Enlightenment, its cultural level was extremely low, its technical and scientific skills almost non-existent and its masses illiterate. But the trouble went even deeper: in contrast to the European, the Middle Eastern entrepreneurial bourgeoisie was too weak to influence policy and make its interests respected; no measures to protect handicrafts, manufactures, agriculture and shipping, like those of Elizabeth, Cromwell, Colbert and other European monarchs and statesmen, are recorded until the nineteenth century. Power lay in the hands of soldiers and bureaucrats whose concern, apart from enriching themselves and increasing state revenues, was to ensure the provisioning of the cities to keep the populace quiet—which explains the strange phenomenon of higher duties being levied on exports than on imports and illustrates the fact that policy was based on "fiscalism", not mercantilism. Hence when economic development came its main agents had to be foreign. In all three countries the large-scale enterprises were established by European capital —British and French, then German and in Iran Russian—and Europeans supplied the requisite entrepreneurial, managerial and technical skills. For the rest, Egypt imported its bourgeoisie en bloc, from Europe or neighboring lands: Lebanese Christians, Armenians and Greeks and Jews. In the inter-war period, and to a greater extent during and after the Second World War, these were gradually squeezed out by a Muslim bourgeoisie, whose development may well have been inhibited by their overwhelming presence. The latter had hardly got into its stride when it was felled in the 1960s. Iran's much feebler development required a correspondingly smaller bourgeoisie; here too, Armenians, and to a much lesser extent Jews, played an important part but there was also a small Muslim trading class which formed the nucleus of the present powerful Iranian bourgeoisie. In Turkey the situation was more complex. From the eighteenth century, or even earlier, an active bourgeoisie had emerged among the Greeks, Armenians, Jews and other non-Muslims, and in the course of the nineteenth century it controlled the greater part of foreign trade, finance and shipping and a considerable part of cash farming. When industry began its promoters, in so far as they were not foreigners, were Greeks or Armenians. Clearly these groups greatly stimulated Turkey's economy but, in view of the rising tensions between them and the Turks, one wonders how long development on that basis could have been sustained. In a series of explosions between 1895 and 1923 Turkeydrove its minorities into exile and then settled down to the task of creating its own bourgeoisie.

Political Structures

Only two questions will be examined under this heading: the governments' ability to promote development and their desire to do so. For a long time Egypt was in far the best position: Muhammad Ali (1805-49) controlled his country much more effectively than any other Middle Eastern monarch and, as noted above, initiated a massive, though only partly successful, development program. Another spurt occurred under Ismail (1863-79) whose extravagance contributed to Egypt's loss of independence but who also greatly developed its infrastructure. Under British rule (1882-1922) Egypt was efficiently administered and much investment took place in irrigation and transport, but with a neglect of such important sectors as industry and education. After that, however, Egypt enjoyed less freedom of action than Iran or Turkey and its government showed less interest in economic development.

The Ottoman government, preoccupied with wars and uprisings, did not seriously attempt to promote economic development until the reign of Abdul Hamid (1876-1908), which witnessed a fairly rapid and broad-based advance in agriculture, mining, transport and foreign trade. The Young Turks paid more attention to economic affairs, and industrialization and railway-building accelerated, but the country was soon engulfed in the Italian, Balkan and First World Wars. Mustafa Kemal (1919-39), renouncing imperial ambitions, carried out a far-reaching social and political revolution and laid the groundwork for subsequent development.

The Iranian government was by far the weakest, and with increasing British and Russian intervention, its authority actually declined in the decade preceding the First World War. It was left to Reza Shah (1925-41) both to re-establish central government control and to initiate economic and social development. After the setbacks caused by the Second World War and its aftermath, his task was taken up, with greater success, by his son, the last Shah, till the Khomeini revolution.

International Forces

The Ottoman Empire was by far the strongest of the three states and, consequently, suffered least from the presence of external forces. The Turks soon mastered the art of playing off the Great Powers against each other, thereby not only preserving their independence but sometimes securing valuable concessions. Thus when Turkey declared bankruptcy, in 1881, its foreign debt was cut by half, in contrast to Egypt which had to accept responsibility for all its outstanding debts. Similarly, there is little doubt that Germany's interest in Turkey, and its massive and beneficial investments in railways and other enterprises, were at least partly due to the desire to draw the Empire to its side. But this multiplicity of outside forces also had disadvantages, best seen in the attempts of the various Powers to block each other's railway projects and in the British refusal to allow the Turks to modify their tariffs, for fear this would benefit the Germans.

Egypt suffered twice from foreign interventions, in 1841 when the Powers forced Muhammad Ali to dismantle his economic system and in 1882 when the British occupied the country. Thereafter, until the Entente Cordiale of 1905, the French and Russians could be relied upon to use their position in the Caisse de la Dette and elsewhere to thwart any British schemes for the development of Egypt.

But in a way the main victim of international rivalry was Iran. After fruitless attempts by Britain and Russia to sway it to their side, both countries tacitly agreed that their interests were best served by keeping Iran underdeveloped. The British were haunted by the nightmare of Cossacks charging on India while the Russians were equally scared of British economic and political penetration of their vulnerable Caucasian flank.[3] Hence, until the Anglo-Russian agreement of 1907, which in effect partitioned Iran into spheres of influence, both Powers opposed railway and other projects, a fact that ranks high among the causes of Iranian lack of development.

One final point may be mentioned—the disadvantage of an early start. For the reasons given above, Egypt's natural resources began to be exploited very early but its human resources were not correspondingly developed, immigration supplying the necessary skills. By contrast Iran—like Iraq, the Sudan and the Arabian peninsula—was almost untouched until the twentieth century. As a result, it did not experience the early and rapid population growth, and the ensuing population pressure, of Egypt. Nor was its development distorted by the presence of large foreign settlements and economic institutions. When it did start building, in the 1920s, it could do so on relatively unencumbered ground.[4]

In 1800 Turkey was somewhat ahead of the other two countries in economic and social development, and Iran may possibly have been a little better off than Egypt. In 1913 the order was: Egypt, Turkey, Iran. In 1978, it was Iran, Turkey, Egypt.

Notes

1. The term "Turkey" designates the area within the borders of the Republic. "Ottoman Empire" refers to the area directly ruled by the Sultans at the given date. This paper draws heavily on my three books: *The Economic History of the Middle East* (Chicago 1966), *The Economic History of Iran* (Chicago, 1971) and *The Economic History of Turkey* (Chicago, 1980), and the sources cited therein.

2. Samir Radwan, *Capital Formation in Egyptian Industry and Agriculture* (London, 1974), p. 236; Julian Bharier, *The Economic Development of Iran* (Oxford, 1971), p. 55; Vedat Eldem, *Osmanli Imparatorlugunun iktisadi sartlari hakkinda bir tetkik* (Istanbul, 1970), p. 309.

3. Both sides had ample justification for their fears; for the Russian see the correspondence, in 1878 and 1885, from the "Comité patriotique", representing "all nationalities in the Caucasus" and headed by various Georgian and Armenian notables, promising an insurrection in case of an Anglo-Russian war—PRO, F078/3902, Trebizond, 1886; British fears of Russian expansionism have often been described and explained.

4. See Charles Issawi, "Asymmetrical Development and Transport in Egypt, 1800-1914," in William R. Polk and Richard L. Chambers (ed.), *Beginnings of Modernization in the Middle East* (Chicago, 1968); idem, "Middle East Economic Development, 1815-1914; the General and the Specific" in M.A. Cook (ed.), *Studies in the Economic Development of the Middle East* (London, 1920).

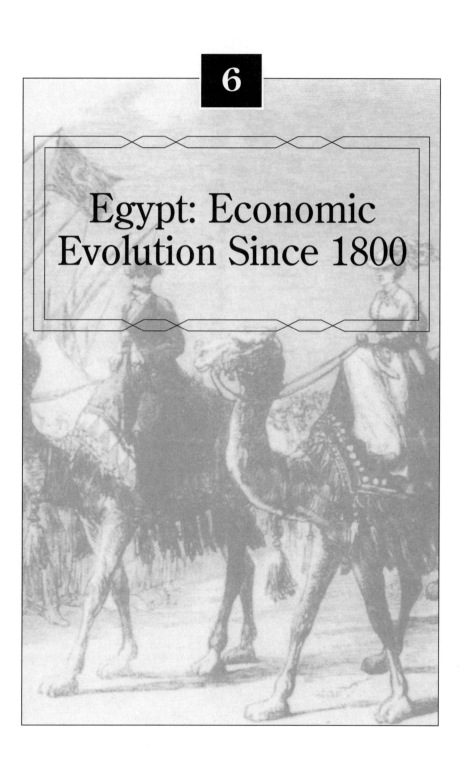

6

Egypt: Economic Evolution Since 1800

gypt is facing economic difficulties due, to a large extent, to the pattern of its evolution in the last two hundred years. I shall examine this under four headings: Egypt's relatively unfavorable position in 1800; its lop-sided growth in the nineteenth century; its accumulating difficulties in 1922-52; and, lastly and briefly, its achievements and failures since the 1952 Revolution.

The Situation in 1800

Partly because of such external shocks as the Black Death and the diversion of the trade routes, partly because of the nature of Mamluk government, and partly because of the cultural stagnation affecting the whole Middle East, Egypt's economic and social condition around 1800 was profoundly unsatisfactory. This is brought out by comparison not only with Western Europe but with such regions as Russia, Japan, China, the Balkans, and Latin America. (See Chapter 2.)

Egypt's agriculture compared very favorably—in yield per acre and, unless my sums are wrong, also per man—with those of most other parts of the world. Its transport system was also adequate, thanks to the magnificent Nile and its branches and canals; I say this although aware that there were no man-made ports, no roads, no carts and only a couple of carriages in the whole country. Technology had shown no improvement since ancient times. The level of the crafts may have actually declined. The tax system was oppressive and inefficient. And there was no remote equivalent of the commercial and financial institutions and devices that had developed in Europe and were also to be found in Russia, Japan and parts of Latin America—banks, insurance, double-entry book-keeping, stock or produce exchanges, and so on.

In the cultural field the gap was still wider. Egypt's literacy rate must have been below 5 percent. Its ancient university, al-Azhar, showed no signs of life that I can discern, though I should immediately add that some scholars whom I respect disagree with me. The official curriculum of al-Azhar did not include the philosophical or scientific works of the great Muslim thinkers, not even al-Ghazzali. Printing had not been introduced. When

Muhammad Ali started his reforms, he could not find a single Egyptian who knew a European language and, as far as I am aware, no one had a clue regarding Western science. This may be contrasted not only with Europe but also with the other regions which I mentioned. See Chapters 1 and 10 in this volume.

One can sum up the situation by saying that, unlike the above-mentioned regions, Egypt had neither a strong and enlightened government that promoted development nor an educated and active bourgeoisie. For thirty years or more, the first deficiency was remedied by the titanic energy of Muhammad Ali, who shifted Egypt's agriculture from basin to perennial irrigation growing cotton, developed transport by building the port of Alexandria and opening the Mahmudiya canal and, starting from scratch, set up an impressive industrial structure. At the same time he revolutionized education by sending students to Europe and opening numerous technical schools.

> Alexandria was too much like a European city to be novel, and we soon tired of it. We took the cars and came up here to ancient Cairo, which *is* an Oriental city and of the completest pattern. There is little about it to disabuse one's mind of the error if he should take it into his head that he was in the heart of Arabia.
>
> Mark Twain, *The Innocents Abroad*, vol. II (New York, 1869), p. 170.

Lop-Sided Development, 1850-1914

The breakdown of Muhammad Ali's system—under foreign pressure but also because of his failing energy—shifted Egypt to another path, indicated by its comparative advantages in agriculture and transport. It became an export-oriented economy, sending out cotton and other agricultural goods and importing practically everything else. Helped by the shortage caused by the American Civil War, cotton exports shot up; between 1848-52 and 1908-12 they increased nearly twenty times in volume and almost as much in value and in purchasing power. This was achieved by a vast expansion in irrigation, crowned by the opening of the Aswan Dam in 1902, at that time the largest in the world. It required the laying down of a vast network

28 • The old Aswan Dam

of railways—and it may be pointed out that Egypt got a railway before Sweden, Central Poland, or the Balkans and long before Japan. It led to the enlargement of the port of Alexandria and the building of new ones at Suez and Port Said. Foreign banks were founded, and they and the foreign-owned cotton export firms financed the movement of the cotton crop and the return flow of imports. Alexandria was recreated, the population rising from 10,000 or 15,000 in 1800 to nearly 450,000 in 1917, and vast new quarters, provided with modern amenities, were built in Cairo and elsewhere. By 1913, Egypt presented many aspects of a developed country. Its per capita income, about $50.00, was higher than that of Japan, twice as high as that of India, and almost one-quarter that of France.[1] Per capita foreign trade (exports plus imports), at $24.30, was higher than in Spain, twice as high as in Japan, Greece, and Bulgaria, and two and a half times as high as in Russia. Its railway network per inhabited square kilometer or per capita was one of the highest in the world.[2] And there are clear indications of an improvement in the level of living of the masses.[3]

However, this development was lop-sided or asymmetrical.[4] On the purely economic side it had two grave defects. First, the large increase in output, income and exports had been dissipated in consumption or remitted abroad. The savings rate remained very low; for 1903-13, it is put at about 3.5 percent by Bent Hansen. To make matters worse, a huge foreign debt—about $1 billion—had been accumulated, making Egypt one of the most highly indebted countries per capita. Secondly, hardly any manufacturing industry had been developed. For this there were many reasons: the small size of the market, the scarcity of raw materials and power, the lack of skilled workers, the shortage of capital, etc. But two political factors were also very important. First, the Egyptian government's hands were tied by the Anglo-Turkish Commercial Convention of 1838, which prevented the lifting of import duties above first 5 and then 8 percent, or the imposition of a differentiated tariff. And secondly, Egypt's British rulers had no great wish—to say the least—to promote its industrialization.[5]

These two economic deficiencies were accompanied by an equally grave social one—the failure to develop Egypt's human resources. The most striking index of this, in addition to poor health conditions, is the extremely low literacy rate—in 1907, only 7 percent overall. This is far below the contemporary figures for the countries used for comparison—whether Greece's 39 percent or Japan's nearly 100 percent. Here too, the British have received most of the blame and there is no doubt that their zeal for education was less than overwhelming. But I cannot help believing that Egyptian society itself bears the greater responsibility, and that much more could have been done if the necessary will had been present. After all, it does not cost much to teach people to read and write, but it does take hard work.

Egypt was able to achieve quite rapid economic growth with a minimum amount of social development because it acquired the skills required to run a modern economy by importing its bourgeoisie en bloc. At the top of the social pyramid—along with the large Egyptian landowners—stood the European capitalists—French, British, Italian, etc. Europeans ran the banks, insurance companies, cotton export firms, mines and factories, railways and public utilities. They also staffed the higher ranks of the professions: physicians, engineers, lawyers (in the mixed courts) and so forth. Below them came other foreigners and members of minority groups—Greeks, Armenians, Jews and Syrian Christians, who performed two main functions, salaried and entrepreneurial. The salaried group provided technical and administrative skills: as journalists, engineers, lawyers, doctors, employees in banks and other businesses, accountants, skilled workers, etc. The entrepreneurial group formed a link between the large European capitalists, concentrated in Alexandria or Cairo, and the farmers and urban masses. They lent money to growers, bought their crops and moved them to Alexandria for shipment abroad, and in return supplied them with imported manufactured goods. This bourgeoisie of foreigners and members of minorities was surely essential for Egypt's development; without it, the machine could not have run. But its presence had two harmful effects.

First, it inhibited the growth of an indigenous bourgeoisie, without which no durable development can take place. Secondly, it imprinted in the Egyptian mind the notion that capitalism was something alien, carried out by, and for the exclusive benefit of, foreigners. This idea was to bear bitter fruit in the 1950s and 1960s.

Accumulating Difficulties, 1922-1952

In this period Egypt began to face increasing difficulties. The development path it had been following for nearly a hundred years had led to a dead end. First of all, the reserves of arable land were running out and expansion of cultivation could be achieved only by increasingly costly irrigation works. In 1912, the cultivated area had been 5.3 million feddans (acres); by 1952 the figure had risen by only 10 percent to 5.8 million. However, various dams had made it possible to convert some acreage from basin irrigation, growing only one crop a year, to perennial irrigation, growing three crops in two years, and the cropped area had risen by 21 percent. Secondly, the price of Egyptian cotton—along with other agricultural prices —fell sharply in world markets in the late 1920s and 1930s, Egypt's terms of trade deteriorated, and the purchasing power of its exports shrank. Thirdly, the growth of the population began to accelerate. From about 3.8 million around 1800, population increased a little over three times to 12.8 million in 1917. But between 1917 and 1960 it more than doubled, and since then has almost doubled again, standing at over 50 million. At present rates of growth, the population should double again in under 30 years. The combined effects of all these factors have been a shrinkage in the amount of cultivable land per head, a decline in per capita GNP and the conversion of Egypt—traditionally a grain exporter—into an ever greater importer.

Until the 1930s, Egypt's successive governments, preoccupied with the struggle for complete independence, showed little awareness of these problems. Measures were taken to intensify agriculture, by using improved seeds and by expanding irrigation and drainage. This helped to raise cotton and grain yields, but also increased the costs of production. In 1930, the commercial treaties that restricted Egypt's tariff autonomy lapsed, and in 1936 the capitulations that restricted its fiscal autonomy were abolished. The government seized this opportunity to embark on an industrialization program, based on tariff protection and aiming at import substitution. The tax system was also reformed, income taxes being imposed for the first time. This program achieved a fair measure of success and created an industrial nucleus that served Egypt well during the Second World War. Like the First World War, the Second caused a great shortage of industrial goods, owing to the cutting off of sources of supply and the increased demand created by the Allied troops stationed in Egypt. However, this time, Egypt had an industrial structure that could seize the opportunity; output rose by over one-half and industrial profits expanded greatly. Much of these profits were reinvested after the war. Helped by further protection, output continued to expand. By 1952 industrial production was about 2.5 times the prewar level.[6]

Another important aspect of this period was the growth of an indigenous bourgeoisie, brought about by three factors. First, the expansion of certain sectors created opportunities which were seized by Egyptian entrepreneurs, e.g., in industry and navigation. Secondly, the expansion of education meant that many more trained Egyptians were available for employment in the urban sectors. Thirdly, the government used what pressure it could to promote "Egyptianization," i.e., the increased hiring of Egyptians in various foreign firms and, wherever possible, the replacement of foreigners by Egyptians. Lastly, tens of thousands of foreigners, seeing the end of their privileges in Egypt and apprehensive about the future, left the country.

However, all these measures—intensification, industrialization, and "Egyptianization"—as well as a slight improvement in the tax structure and an increase in education and other social services—could not offset the effects of a sluggish agriculture and rapid population growth. During the war per capita incomes, and the level of living, had declined sharply and the postwar advance had, by 1952, at best just restored the prewar level, and may actually have not quite reached it.[7] A sense of economic failure was certainly one—though by no means the main—factor behind the 1952 Revolution.

Egypt After 1952

In agriculture, since the 1952 Revolution, three important measures may be noted. The successive land reforms have transformed Egypt's agrarian structure, which in the past had been marked by great inequality. Over 1 million feddans of land, or one-sixth of the cultivated area, was transferred from large landowners to small farmers, and one-tenth of the rural population benefited from this measure; a larger number benefited from the reduction in rents. Most observers agree that the reform did not disrupt production and may indeed have enhanced it. Some maintain that it has not really solved any major problems, having merely replaced a large landowning class by a middling one—but in our very imperfect world, this must surely count as an achievement.

Other important measures in agriculture include the building of the High Dam, extension of cooperatives, further intensification and a shift to more valuable crops. The Dam has come in for a lot of criticism—much of it, I cannot help feeling, arising from the fact that it was built by the Russians. It has certainly provided flood control, additional supplies of water, and vast amounts of electricity, admittedly at an ecological cost. Equally obviously, the vast reclamation of marginal lands envisioned in the plans has not come about,[8] but one can hardly blame the Dam for this. A shift to fruits and vegetables, for which Egypt is ideally suited and which I have been advocating for nearly 50 years, has also taken place.[9] Unfortunately, very little of the increase in production has been exported, going instead to meet the growing demand of the urban population. Intensification has continued but the results have been limited: in 1973-84, agricultural output grew by only 2.5 percent a year, or slightly below the population growth and well below the increase in demand. As a result, the per capita index of food production fell from 100 in 1974-76 to 91 in 1982-84. Concurrently, imports of cereals rose from 3.9 million tons in 1974 to 8.6 million in 1984.[10]

Industrialization has been pursued with much energy since the Revolution. It will be remembered that in 1945-52 private enterprise had produced a rate of growth of over 10 percent in industrial output, but following the revolution this fell sharply. The state therefore stepped in, at first to supplement and then to take over the private sector. Much was undoubtedly achieved; the output of existing industries expanded and new ones were created. Following the 1965 economic crisis, caused by overextension, sectoral imbalance, inadequate savings, shortage of foreign exchange, the war in Yemen, and the increasingly obvious inefficiency of the public sector, the growth rate of industrial output fell sharply, to 3.8 percent a year in 1965-73; however, following Sadat's new policies, this rose again to the very impressive figure of 10.3 in 1973-84.[11] Moreover, there were signs that some industries were becoming competitive and penetrating world markets: in 1965, 46 percent of manufactured exports went to the Soviet Union and Eastern Europe and only 20 percent to industrial market economies; by 1983, the Soviet share had dropped to 40% and the Western had risen to 38%. But when all this has been said it remains that the public sector, which

29 • Nasser

accounts for the bulk of Egyptian industry, is in the main a horror story, in terms of overstaffing, imbalances, low efficiency of investment, and low productivity per worker. I shall not repeat the usual examples but just point out the automobile industry: in the late 1970s the Nasr factory produced one car per man per year, whereas an identical Fiat factory in Spain produced over 8. It is worth adding that the comparable British figure was 17 and the Japanese figures ranged from 30 to 50.[12] John Waterbury, on whom I have freely drawn in his section, has an excellent analytic account of the development, and shortcomings, of the public sector.[13] Some years ago I stated that: "It is difficult to imagine a more cumbersome and inefficient instrument of industrial management than Middle Eastern bureaucracy," a judgment that was quoted approvingly by a reviewer in a Czech journal, who presumably was thinking of his own bureaucrats. I see no reason to revise this estimate, but am fully aware that in Egypt, as elsewhere in the Middle East and most of the world, including the United States, bureaucracy is there not only to stay but to grow. Another of Nasser's objectives was to raise the investment rate, in order to promote overall growth. Indeed, this was surely one of the reasons for the massive nationalizations of the 1950s and 1960s. At first some success was achieved and the gross domestic savings rate rose from 12 percent of GDP to 14 in 1975. But after that it dropped sharply, to a low of 4 in 1975, rising again to 12 by 1984. This was far below the investment rate and in 1984 Egypt's resource balance—i.e., the extent to which it drew on foreign resources to cover its consumption and investment—was no less than 13 percent of its GDP, a figure exceeded only by some very poor countries.[14] The reasons are only too clear. On the one hand, private consumption has grown quite rapidly. The government has not been willing to squeeze the population hard enough to extract greater savings from them—and who shall blame it? On the other, government consumption has shot up at a very high rate. This in turn has been due to the very high military expenditure, caused mainly by the conflicts with Israel—which at one time were absorbing the enormous figure of over 20 percent of GNP—and to the growth of bureaucracy, where numbers have multiplied several fold. In these circumstances there were only two possible outcomes: the elimination of investment, which would have spelled stagnation, or seeking foreign grants and loans. As a result, by 1984, Egypt's gross external liabilities amounted to over $23 billion and its debt service absorbed 34 percent of the value of its exports of goods and services.[15]

One last word about the development of Egypt's human resources. As noted earlier, at independence Egypt had achieved little in the fields of health and education. Since then, and more particularly since the revolution, very much more has been done. Three figures are indicative. Life expectancy at birth has risen from about 31 years in the 1930s and 47 in 1965 to 60 years in 1984; this reflects the massive reductions in the general death rate, and more particularly in infant mortality. Literacy has risen from 18 percent in 1937 and 38 percent in 1957 to close to 50 percent today; this reflects the great expansion of schools, which today provide for practically all children of school age. And, at the level of higher education, there is the great and impressive increase in the number of qualified Egyptian scientists, physicians, agronomists, statisticians, and others. I need hardly add that this includes many women. To one who, like me, can vividly remember conditions prevailing 60 years ago, the change that has taken place is most gratifying.

However, there is no reason for complacency—far from it. For the sad fact remains that in the scale of social development Egypt stands low—lower indeed than in the scale of economic development. The best indicator of this is the Physical Quality of Life Index, compiled around 1980 and based essentially on birth rates, death rates, literacy and education. Egypt scored 52—the highest being Iceland with 98 and the lowest Guinea Bissau with 14. This is low compared to the poorer Asian countries, whose per capita incomes were not too different from those of Egypt: Sri Lanka 81, Thailand 75, Philippines 72, and China 71, though it is higher than India's 43.[16]

Today, technology has become the most important single factor of production and the future of nations is becoming increasingly dependent on how well they can absorb technology, including very advanced branches like computers and biotechnology.[17] Already South Korea, Taiwan, Hong Kong and Singapore, and others, have shown how countries with an educated, adaptive labor force can break into fields which were thought reserved for highly developed ones. In this coming race, Egypt cannot afford to remain behind and its performance will depend on how well it succeeds in developing its human resources.

Notes

1. For figures, sources and qualifications see Charles Issawi, "Asymmetrical Development and Transport in Egypt," in William R. Polk and Richard L. Chambers (eds.), *Beginning of Modernization in the Middle East* (Chicago, 1968), pp. 399-400.

2. See tables in *ibid.,* pp. 384, 394.

3. See Charles Issawi, *An Economic History of the Middle East and North Africa* (New York, 1982), pp. 104-105.

4. On this see Charles Issawi, "Egypt Since 1800: A Study in Lop-Sided Development," *Journal of Economic History* 2, no. 1 (March 1961).

5. See Charles Issawi, "British Policy and Egyptian Industrialization: A Case Study" (forthcoming).

6. See indices in Charles Issawi, *Egypt in Revolution* (London, 1963), pp. 113, 173.

7. *Ibid.,* 290.

8. John Waterbury, *The Egypt of Nasser and Sadat* (Princeton, 1983), pp. 64-65, 297-300.

9. *Ibid.,* 290.

10. World Bank, *World Development Report,* 1986 (New York) Appendix Tables.

11. World Bank, *loc. cit.*

12. Waterbury, *op. cit.,* p. 105, citing Ali al-Gritli.

13. *Ibid.,* chapters 4-6.

14. World Bank, *loc. cit.*

15. *Ibid.*

16. Roger Hansen and V. Kallab, *U.S. Foreign Policy and The Third World* (New York, 1992), pp. 153-61.

17. W. Michael Blumenthal, "The World Economy and Technological Change," *Foreign Affairs* 66, no. 3 (1988).

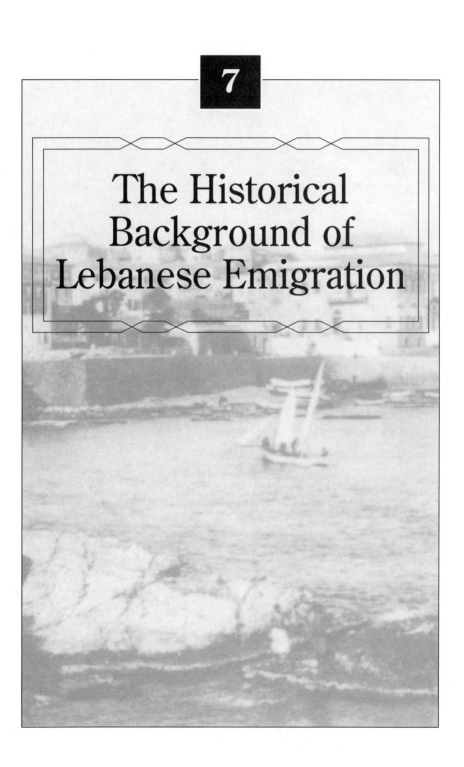

7

The Historical Background of Lebanese Emigration

tudents of migration divide the operating forces into "push" and "pull" factors. My task will be to describe the many factors that pushed the Lebanese out of their homeland. These push factors can be subdivided into political, economic and social forces. I shall often have to look beyond Lebanon's borders, to Syria, Palestine and further.

The Political Background

In the first few decades of the nineteenth century, geographical Syria, including Lebanon, was the scene of many regional and international conflicts; after that it witnessed bitter communal and social strife. The two sets of factors were loosely connected. Both combined to make life miserable for the population and thus to make them ready to consider the possibility of emigration.

These wars and occupations contributed to the ensuing civil strife by helping to undermine the traditional feudal structure of Lebanon and by exacerbating relations between religious communities.

Applied to the Middle East (the Ottoman and Safavi empires) the word "feudal" is a misnomer, but it describes quite accurately conditions in Mount Lebanon in the seventeenth to the mid-nineteenth century.

The main characteristic of this society was its hierarchical character. A person's status as a nobleman or commoner was determined by birth and was hereditary. So was his allegiance: a *muqata'ji* (lord) owed protection to his men and they in turn owed him loyalty, paid him rent and taxes and took his side in the conflicts between the Qaysi and Yamani factions, or their successors, that divided the country. The *amir* (prince) did not exercise direct jurisdiction over his subjects but only through the subject's lord; since he had only a small number of retainers and only exceptionally hired mercenaries, his capacity to impose his will on his subjects was strictly limited. Moreover, although the *amir* was always chosen from the Shihab family, and more often than not was a son of the previous incumbent, no regular principle of succession was recognized. This meant that the *muqata'jis* wielded considerable influence in the selection of an *amir*. Since they often owned a considerable amount of land within their fief, and frequently fought their neighbors over their borders, the *muqata'jis* had great power. By the same token, the *amir* spent much of his time setting one lord against another.

The second characteristic is that loyalties cut across religious lines. Because of the Maronites' southern migration (see below) many of them, as well as other Christians and Shi'is, owed allegiance to a Druze *muqata'ji*. The Qaysi and Yamani factions and their successors transcended religious lines and pitted coreligionists against each other. The *amirs* also took their religion rather lightly and some were even suspected of having secretly embraced another one. For example Fakhr al-Din (1590-1635) was believed to have become a Druze or even to have been baptized, and Sayyid-Ahmad Mulhim (1778) and his sons and Bashir II (1793-1840) almost certainly became Maronites.

The result of all these factors was that, although a poor and stagnant society, Lebanon enjoyed a degree of religious tolerance unknown in other parts of the Middle East. More generally, the Lebanese had much greater security of life and property, a fact commented upon by European observers. Volney's remark has often been quoted:

> "I can discover no other cause [for the density of population] than that ray of liberty which glimmers in this country. Unlike Turks every man lives in a perfect security of life and property. The peasant is not richer than in other countries; but he is free, "he fears not," as I have often heard them say, "that the Aga, the Kaimmakam, or the Pasha, should send their Djendis, to pillage his house, carry off his family, or give him the bastinado . . . "[1]

By the late 1850s northern Lebanon was in turmoil. Peasant uprisings, backed by the clergy, soon dispossessed and expelled Maronite feudal families and seized their property (see below). The movement spread to the south, where it was bound to degenerate into a communal conflict, pitting Maronite peasants against their Druze lords. Fighting soon broke out and the Druzes, being much more disciplined, inflicted great losses on their opponents. "In less than four weeks an estimated total of eleven thousand Christians had been killed, four thousand more had perished of destitution, and nearly a hundred thousand had become homeless refugees. The Druzes had also lost a number of dead, but otherwise their triumph had been amazing." The property damage was put at 15 to 20 million piastres— though one French estimate ran as high as 175 million. The fighting in Lebanon sparked a massacre in Damascus; a Presbyterian missionary estimated the number of Christians killed to be at least 3,000 men, or over one-third of the number of males; Salibi's figure is 5,500 persons. Property losses were put at 150 million piastres, or £1,250,000. Many thousands of Christians fled from the interior to the coast.

These events provoked an international reaction. A French army landed in Beirut and, reluctantly, Britain decided not to oppose it. The Porte sent its Foreign Minister, Fuad Pasha, who dealt severe punishments to responsible Turkish officers and civilians and much lighter ones to the Druze leaders. A règlement organique was promulgated in 1861, under which the country (i.e. the Mountain, excluding coastal areas and plains) was administered until the first world war. The governor (*mutasarrif*) was to be a Catholic, who was an Ottoman but not a Lebanese subject. He was to be assisted by a local administrative council, representing all the religious communities, by paid officials and by a locally raised gendarmerie. Taxes were assessed on the basis of a census and a cadastre and the proceeds were spent within the country; indeed until 1878 the budget showed a deficit which was met by a subsidy from Istanbul. Under this regime Lebanon enjoyed security until the first world war, made considerable progress and was free from communal strife.

Economic Trends[1]

In the course of the hundred years or so before the first world war, Syria witnessed appreciable economic progress; this is in sharp contrast to its experience in the two preceding centuries. However, this development was neither continuous nor even in its impact on various sectors, regions, classes and sects. Hence the overall improvement was accompanied by much discontent. Moreover, the most sustained progress occurred between 1880 and 1914, that is after emigration to the New World had begun to gather momentum. Before that there had been some very difficult periods, such as the 1840s following the Egyptian withdrawal, the 1860s because of the communal clashes, and the 1870s with the fall in world prices of agricultural produce.

The population of geographical Syria grew rapidly, from perhaps 1.2 million in 1800 to around 1.5 million in 1840, 2.5 million in 1878 and 4 million in 1913. The rate of population growth seems to have accelerated, from perhaps 1 percent per annum in the first half of the century to 1.4 percent in 1895-1913.

For Lebanon, numerous population estimates are available, but they

30 • Beirut city and harbor

are inconsistent. In 1840 Bowring quoted two government figures for the Mountain, 154,000 and 192,000, and judged the former nearer the mark.[3] Chevallier, using French and Lebanese sources, has higher figures, but settles for the figure of about 200,000 in 1840.[4] More reliable figures are 210,000 for 1878 and 240,000 for 1895, which would suggest that Bowring's lower estimate is the most acceptable and that the annual rate of growth was between 0.7 and 0.8 per cent, which seems plausible.

As elsewhere in the Middle East, the growth was due to the combination of high birth rates and falling death rates. Birth rates seem to have been particularly high among the Maronites and low among the Druzes, many of whose men were drafted into the army or fled to Hauran.[5] As for the declining death rates, they were due—as elsewhere—to the weakening of the Malthusian checks. Hygienic conditions improved with the introduction of vaccination and with the quarantines set up by the Egyptians, and plagues diminished. And it is noteworthy that the cholera epidemic of 1865, which devastated the coast and the interior, caused very few deaths in the Mountain.[6] Famines were eliminated, thanks to the improvements in transport that made it possible to import wheat easily from abroad and avoid the sharp fluctuations in price characteristic of the interior.[7] Lastly—except of course for the communal clashes of 1841, 1845 and 1860—Lebanon enjoyed peace and security.

In the eighteenth century, as noted by Volney and others, Lebanon was already far more thickly populated than other parts of Syria or the Middle East. In the nineteenth century, the density greatly increased. On the eve of the first world war, Mount Lebanon had 159 inhabitants per square kilometer, compared to 34 in the *vilayet* (province) of Beirut, 25 in Jerusalem, 15 in Aleppo and 13 in Damascus.[8] Basing his estimates on a study made by the Lebanese Ministry of Agriculture, Chevallier puts the density of population around 1840 at 250 per square kilometer of cultivated area (80,000 hectares, or 800 square kilometers out of a total of 3,200 governed by Bashir II).[9] This high density of population must have been one of the main factors pushing the Lebanese to emigrate.

Another very important factor was the integration of Lebanon in the world economy, through trade, transport and communications, and finance.

In the nineteenth century Syria's trade expanded greatly. Between 1833 and 1910, imports, in current prices, rose 8.9 times, exports 7.4 times, and total trade 8.4 times. Deflating by British export and import prices gives a compound rate of growth of 3.5 percent per annum in imports and 3.1 in exports.[10] No figures are available for Lebanon, but the trade of Beirut— which although administratively separate had developed very close economic and social ties with the Mountain—expanded greatly.[11] In the eighteenth century Beirut had been a small and somnolent port but by 1825, thanks to the enterprise of its Christian merchants, it was handling most of the trade of Damascus and its position improved further under Egyptian rule. By the 1850s it was handling about 70 percent of Syria's sea trade, but thereafter its share fell to under 30 percent in 1910-12, when Alexandretta and Jaffa shot forward and Tripoli and Haifa were linked by rail to the interior. Between 1833 and 1871-3, Beirut's imports rose 2.8 times, or 2.7 per cent per annum, and its exports rose 2.56 times, at 2.5 per cent; between 1871-3 and 1910-12, imports rose 1.5 times, or 1.1 per cent, and exports 1.03 or 0.1 per cent.[12]

Beyrout is the seaport of Damascus, from which it is distant about 70 miles. It is little more than a deep roadstead, with good anchorage, the mole being neglected. Its population is estimated at about 15,000, and its bazaars are large, and generally well supplied with merchandise. The consul states in his report, written before the retreat of Ibrahim Pacha,—

Beyrout is certainly, at present, the most flourishing commercial city in Syria in proportion to its size; and, as my personal observations have hitherto been confined to this place, I may be inclined to overrate the general commercial prosperity of the country. A wealthy class of Christians reside here, whose habits, both as regards dress and the consumption of other luxuries of civilized society, exceed those of the generality of their countrymen. This body of Christians were, under the former government, refugees to Mount Lebanon, and have now returned to Beyrout since the Egyptian invasion. If any Christians feel a leaning to the present government, it is those who have found a security to their property under it, which they did not previously enjoy; even these feel that they possess, by a most precarious tenure, their advantage.

John MacGregor, *Commercial Statistics* II (London, 1847), quoted in Issawi, *The Economic History of the Middle East*, p. 224.

Beirut owed its dominance in trade to its pre-eminence in means of transport. In 1863 a modern road—the first in Syria—linked it with Damascus. In 1893 it inaugurated a modern port, the only one of its kind between Izmir and Port Said, and in 1895 a railway—close second to the Jerusalem-Jaffa line of 1892—was opened between Beirut and Damascus. In 1861 the Beirut-Damascus telegraph line was opened; in 1863 Beirut was linked to Istanbul, and shortly thereafter to Alexandria. Early in this century, telephones began to be used.[13]

Beirut was also the financial center of Syria. In 1856 the Ottoman Bank opened a branch in that city and by 1914 it had been joined by the Anglo-Palestine Company, Deutsche-Palästina Bank and Banque de Salonique. Insurance companies also proliferated and by 1910 there were 19 companies representing seven nationalities. Of an estimated 206 million francs of European (mainly French) investments in Syria, some 82 million, or 40 percent, were in Beirut, in the port, road, railways and other utilities. During the period of autonomy starting in 1861, Mount Lebanon built an excellent network of roads: in 1900 415 kilometers and 261 projected, or about 211 per thousand square kilometers and 2.25 per thousand inhabitants.[14]

All these developments transformed the structure of the Lebanese economy. In agriculture the main change was the expansion of silk cultivation and the diffusion of small-scale ownership. Already early in the eighteenth century, exports of silk from Lebanon to France were quite considerable. Parts of the Mountain specialized so heavily in the production of silk and other cash crops that it could meet only about half of its requirements of cereals; the rest had to be imported from the inland parts of Syria. In the late 1840s, a study by Urquhart of a small Lebanese farm showed that it concentrated on mulberry trees (for silkworms) and vines, between which a small amount of grain was sown and vegetables were planted; the grain and vegetables were consumed by the family, whereas wine and floss were almost entirely marketed. The earned income was used to pay taxes and to buy clothing, bread and foodstuffs, since the harvest from the farm did not cover food requirements. Quite clearly this farm was no longer living in a barter economy but was closely tied to the market, and this was true of a large part of the Mountain.[15] From a study by a British consul one can conclude that in 1846 silk accounted for 57 per cent of the value of gross agricultural output and in 1855, when cereals prices were exceptionally high because of the Crimean War, for 44 percent.[16] After 1861, progress was rapid: the ten-year average output of cocoons of the whole of Syria rose from 1,756 tons in the 1860s to 5,337 in 1901-10; of this, about three-quarters came from Lebanon.[17]

Silk growers were not involved in the market merely through their sales of cocoons. From 1840 on, silkworm eggs were imported, from Iran, Italy and elsewhere; after the pébrine disease struck, in the 1870s, eggs were imported from France and from the Silk Institute in Bursa. Farmers also borrowed funds from European and Lebanese merchants. Lastly, they set up a large industry to reel the silk (see below).

The value of the silk produce in the 1880s represents about 3,000,000 okes of cocoons, at about 3 to 5 fr. per oke or 3,000 bales of silk weighing respectively 100 kilog. The whole of this produce is exported to France. The production in the districts of the vilayets adjoining the Lebanon may be estimated at about one-half of the latter.

The cultivation of the mulberry tree is universal throughout the Lebanon, and has in many places supplanted that of the olive and vine.

. . . As is well known, Syria is an important center of silk production. From Tripoli to Saida, and from the coast to the Anti-Lebanon chain of mountains, the Mountain is covered with factories for the raising of silkworms and the reeling of cocoons. These factories are an important source of income for the people of this country, who thanks to this industry grow large mulberry groves on land of low fertility which would otherwise have remained untilled and unproductive.

It is especially since 1850 that the raising of silkworms and reeling of cocoons have remarkably developed; today there are 67 factories, almost all in the hands of natives, whereas between 1840 and 1850 there were only 5, of which 3 belonged to Frenchmen. This rapid expansion is due to various causes. First of all I would mention the undoubted security that the new Administration has introduced in the Mountain and that, by giving the people the assurance that they will not be disturbed in their undertakings, has encouraged them to risk in such enterprises capital which during the previous state of turbulence they were forced to hide.

Reports by the French Consul, quoted in Charles Issawi, *The Fertile Crescent 1800-1914* (New York and Oxford, 1988), pp. 79, 306.

The spread of ownership came about for several reasons. In contrast to other parts of the Middle East, in 1840 Bowring noted:

In Mount Lebanon almost every male inhabitant is a small proprietor of land. In the neighborhood of Beyrout there are also a great number of land-holders who, for the most part, cultivate the wild mulberry tree. Large proprietors there are few, except among the emirs of Mount Lebanon, some of whom have extensive lands, which they either cultivate for their own account, or let out to farming tenants.[18]

The social upheavals of 1840-60 broke up many large estates. Peasants also acquired land from large owners by purchase, using funds sent by emigrants (see below) or through *mugharasa* (co-plantation), a system under which a peasant planted trees on barren land and, when they reached maturity, received part of the land as his share.

As a result of all those developments, the planted area expanded considerably, terraces were built to cultivate hillsides, and forests rapidly dwindled both in the Mountain and in the Beirut *vilayet*. Lebanon was filling up and its inhabitants were immersed in a monetary economy.

The city of Beirout is beautiful, with its bright, new houses nestled among a wilderness of green shrubbery spread abroad over an upland that sloped gently down to the sea; and also at the mountains of Lebanon that environ it; and likewise to bathe in the transparent blue water that rolled its billows about the ship (we did not know there were sharks there). We had also to range up and down through the town and look at the costumes. These are picturesque and fanciful, but not so varied as at Constantinople and Smyrna.

Mark Twain, *The Innocents Abroad* (New York, 1869), p. 153.

In industry, developments in Lebanon were unique. In other parts of the Middle East the inflow of European machine-made goods, carried by improved transport, dealt the local handicrafts a severe blow. Some scholars believe that the distress of the handicraftsmen was an important cause of the communal conflicts in Aleppo and Damascus. In Lebanon however, including Beirut, handicrafts were relatively unimportant, and any decline that may have occurred in them was much more than offset by the rapid growth of silk reeling.[19] A modern industry was started by French and British capital but by the 1860s most of it was owned by Lebanese and by the turn of the century it was almost wholly in Lebanese hands. Its fixed capital was estimated at £100,000 and it employed 10,000 to 20,000 workers, mostly women. Like silk raising, reeling relied on advances from merchants and bankers, in France or Beirut.

Another activity that drew Lebanese villages into the world market was tourism. In addition to catering to European and American tourists visiting the sights, by the beginning of the twentieth century Lebanon was attracting appreciable numbers of summer visitors from Egypt, Syria and Iraq. Their presence no doubt had a marked demonstration effect on the villagers.

> Lebanon is the natural summer resort for Syria, Mesopotamia, Karamania [south Turkey], and Egypt . . .
>
> There are 5 First-Class Hotels, which afford all comfort to their patrons, and 80 Medium Class Hotels, scattered all over the area of the Mountain. Recently, the scope of summer tourism has greatly expanded, tripling the size of such villages as 'Aley, Bhamdun, Sawfar, Bayt Mery, and Dhuhur al-Shuwayr during the last 20 years.
>
> The [direct] income derived by the Mountain from summer tourism is estimated at 20 million piasters. The price of land in some of these villages has risen enormously; 20 years ago a square meter of land was worth 10 *paras* to one piaster, in such places as 'Aley, Bhamdun Station, Sawfar, Bayt Mery, and Dhuhur al-Shuwayr; today it fetches 20 to 100 piasters.
>
> Emigration from Lebanon has helped the development of tourism, for the great attachment of Lebanese to their homeland has led them generally to use their savings to purchase real estate and build houses in their village of origin, which has added to the comfort and amenity of the housing available to tourists.
>
> Among the benefits of travel has been the broadening of the mind of the Lebanese and their awareness of development issues such as that of transport, which plays an important part in the life of Lebanon.

Hence, in the last 30 years or so, we have seen the Lebanese busy building roads and bridges. The scope of their work becomes apparent when we recall that Lebanon is the only Ottoman province that has a network of roads, totaling 1200 kilometers, for an area of only 400 square kilometers of arable land. This was achieved through the funds accumulated by Lebanese abroad, by dint of saving. One can only admire their effort and energy.

Isma'il Bey Haqqi, ed., *Lubnan: mabahith 'ilmiya wa ijtima'iya* (Beirut, 1918), quoted in Issawi, *The Fertile Crescent*, p. 85.

31 • Resort town on Jounieh Bay

An even more powerful reminder of the outside world was the remittances sent home by Lebanese emigrants. By 1900, the annual amount being received by inhabitants of Mount Lebanon was put at £200,000 and around 1910 it was estimated at £800,000.

The peculiar structure of the Lebanese economy—so different from that of other parts of the Middle East—and its extremely high degree of monetization is brought out by a national income estimate (see Table 7.1).

TABLE 7.1: National Income Estimate of Lebanon

SOURCE OF INCOME	MILLION PIASTRES
Remittances from the USA	90
Silkworm breeding	60
Agricultural produce	30
Silk reeling	15
Foreign visitors	15
Industry	10
(tanneries, alcoholic drinks, soap, cigarettes, matches)	
Total	220

Source: A. A. Naccache, Inspector of public works and agriculture, in A. Ruppin, *Syrien als Wirtschaftsgebeit* (Berlin, 1917), pp. 15-16.

One may presume that this monetization of the economy and involvement in the market made the Lebanese more aware of the outside world and its possibilities, and more ready to consider emigrating. Of course Lebanon was to pay a horrendous price for its peculiar economic structure: the famine of 1915-18. The mobilization of farmers and unfavorable weather reduced cereal crops; transport was diverted for military needs; grain found its way to the Arab tribes; the relentless Allied blockade prevented the import of food; the market mechanisms broke down; and the Ottoman authorities were less than eager to supply the coastal regions and the Mountain, whose loyalty was in doubt. Death from starvation and starvation-related diseases in greater Syria probably surpassed 500,000, or one-eighth of the population; of this the greater part was in present-day Lebanon.[20]

Social Factors

The relevant social factors may be briefly considered under four headings: urbanization, education, the formation of a middle class, and conscription.

Urbanization in Lebanon means, of course, Beirut, but it should be noted that other towns also grew. Between 1830 and 1914, the population of Tripoli rose from 15,000 to 30,000, Ba'albak grew to about 25,000 inhabitants and both Sayda and Zahleh to about 15,000. In other words, no Lebanese citizen was more than one or two days' walking distance from a town and most lived within two or three days' travel from Beirut. One would expect the sight of urban living to have had a stimulating effect on country people and to have opened their minds to the possibility of emigration to far bigger cities overseas.

Beirut grew very slowly until the late 1830s, from some 6,000 around 1800 to about 10,000, but after that its growth accelerated. It became the commercial and transport and communications center of the Levant, and it also became an administrative center. Protestant and Catholic missionaries and other foreigners began to settle in the cities. During the communal upheavals of 1845 and 1860, thousands of Christian refugees came to Beirut from the Mountain and the interior and Christians became a majority of the population. By 1860 the total population may have been about 60,000 and by 1914 it was 150,000. By 1914 Beirut was well provided with amenities: waterworks installed in 1875, gasworks in 1888, electricity in 1909 and electric streetcars in 1908. The city lights of Beirut, so clearly visible from the Mountain, were beckoning people to migrate to more exciting places.

In education Lebanon had a head start over other parts of the Middle East, thanks to its contacts with the Catholic church. As early as 1584 the Maronite College in Rome was opened and its graduates returned to spread education in the Mountain. In 1610 a Syriac press was introduced and in 1624 a school was opened. By the middle of the eighteenth century there were five presses, serving the various Christian sects, and many more schools, and the Jesuits were also active in education.[21] In the nineteenth century, thanks to the efforts of both foreign missions and local clergy, education expanded very rapidly. The Americans opened their first school in Beirut in 1834 and established their press, which was to render such great service to Lebanon and the Arab world. The Jesuits returned in 1831, set up their equally good press in 1853 and founded many schools. The British were also active and, from the 1880s, so were the Russians. In 1869 a US consular dispatch stated: "Previous to 1860, in Beirut, there were but 4 girls' schools and 15 boys' schools, while from 1860 to 1869 there were established 23 girls' and 29 boys' schools . . . a grand total of 75 schools with 5,150 pupils or 6 per cent of the whole population."[22] By 1913 Mount Lebanon had 330 schools, with perhaps over 20,000 pupils.[23] As for Syria as a whole, it had about 100,000 pupils, or some 15 per cent of the school-age population. Two institutes of higher education had been founded in Beirut, the Syrian Protestant College in 1866 and the Jesuit St. Joseph University in

1875, as well as a government Medical College in Damascus in 1903.

The press was very highly developed by Middle Eastern standards. Between 1851 and 1914, 143 periodicals were founded in Beirut and Lebanon. Most proved ephemeral but, in 1914, in the whole of Syria there were 50 dailies, 15 weeklies and 20 monthlies or quarterlies; of these, a large number were in Beirut. In the Mountain, in 1900, there were four weeklies. As for books, Touma lists 338 new titles up to 1914, and believes that the actual figure was about twice as great. Of the authors, the enormous majority were Christians, with only a few Muslims or Druzes.[24]

In 1845 an American missionary had already observed that in Kisrawan "from one-fourth to one-third of adult males can read," though far fewer women had received any education. By 1914 the overall literacy rate in Mount Lebanon for those ten years old or over may have been around 50 per cent—an exceptionally high figure for a country outside Europe and North America.[25] This high level of education and exposure to the press must surely have stimulated emigration.

All these developments facilitated, and were facilitated by, the emergence of a middle class, first mainly entrepreneurial then salaried as well: prosperous farmers growing cash crops; merchants engaged in internal, regional and international trade; agents of foreign shipping lines; employees of the road, railway and port companies, of banks and of the above-mentioned public utilities; owners of silk-reeling factories and a few minor industries; hotel keepers; teachers; newspaper publishers and editors; officials of the Beirut *vilayet* and the autonomous Mountain administration— all this constituted a bourgeois nucleus which had no counterpart in other Arab countries, and in Turkey only among the minorities. This middle class was aware of developments in the outside world. One may also presume that some of its members were periodically ruined by the world-wide economic and political crises and would have been tempted to seek their fortune elsewhere.

Conscription

Traditionally, in the Ottoman Empire, non-Muslims were exempt (or excluded) from military service, paying instead a poll tax. As noted above, under Egyptian rule the Druzes were drafted, and the Christians came to believe that their turn would follow, an important contributory cause to the uprising against Ibrahim. In the Hatti Humayun decree of 1856, full equality was promised to non-Muslims, and this eventually led to their being required to serve in the armed forces. The draft was gradually introduced and in 1871 was formalized in a law. Under its autonomous regime, Lebanon remained exempt, but in the adjacent parts of the vilayets of Beirut and Damascus fear of conscription seems to have been an important factor stimulating emigration and it may well have had some effect in the Mountain too.

A question may be raised here: how did the Lebanese villages get the message that there were opportunities abroad? Personal contacts probably played the main part—an occasional returnee, coming home to get married, for a visit, or for retirement. Letters and telegrams reached the villagers through the expanding postal networks. In addition, there were brokers (*simsar*) employed by the shipping lines. Through these contacts the villagers formed a picture of an outside world rich in opportunities if inaccurate in its geographical outlines: for instance, until quite recently "Amerka" covered Australia and West Africa as well as the Americas. Here are some examples: "I am emigrating to that part of Amerka that is under French rule; it is very hot there and the people are black," I was told in the 1940's about Senegal. On the other hand "Nayurk" meant the United States —"it is just like Lebanon, consisting of a capital and villages and I am going to join my brother in one of the villages", i.e. Chicago.

The Course of Emigration

Emigration from Lebanon to adjacent or nearby areas has a long history: Maronites to the Tripoli and Latakia regions, to Palestine and to the coastlands; Druzes to Jabal al-Duruz, and so on. Very little can be said on this subject, for lack of data.

The trail-blazers of overseas emigration from Syria were the Greek Catholics (Melkites) of Sayda who, in the eighteenth century, came to control a substantial segment of Syrian maritime trade with Egypt and to operate most of the vessels (French owned) engaged in that trade.[26] Some of them settled in Damietta and elsewhere, and extended their businesses when the French establishments were ruined by the Revolutionary wars. Under Muhammad Ali the number of Syrians increased, some—like the Bahris mentioned earlier—playing a significant part in the administration. Egypt's rapid expansion in the nineteenth century drew many emigrants from Lebanon and other parts of Syria and by the 1900s they numbered some 50,000. They played a leading part in the Egyptian press and a significant part in trade and the professions. Most of them had been educated in French or American schools and had acquired a foreign language.[27]

The communal clashes and upheavals of the 1840s and 1850s provided the stimulus for large-scale emigration from Lebanon. In 1848, a company was founded, with a capital of 200,000 francs, to promote the emigration of Maronites to Algeria; fortunately, the scheme was not successful.[28] In 1858 an estimated 5,000 emigrants had left from five Maronite villages alone.[29] After 1860 emigration accelerated and by 1900 an estimated 120,000 had left Syria, the vast majority from Lebanon, at first for the United States and soon after to Brazil and other Latin American countries.[30] By 1896 emigration from Syria was running at 5,500 people a year; by then the Christians had been joined by Druzes. In 1900 the American consul put the number of Syrians in the United States at over 50,000, and in 1902 the British consul stated that "emigration is always on the increase and has now extended from the Lebanon and Anti-Lebanon to all districts of Syria." In 1900-14, some 225,000 "Syrians" or "Turks" (these were the designations used for Syrians and Lebanese in both the United States and Latin America) had emigrated. In 1911 the U.S. Immigration Commission pointed out that Syrian immigrants had higher levels of skills than other immigrants: 22.7 per cent were in skilled occupations and 20.3 per cent were in trade.[31] However, a 1904 report by the U.S. consul in Beirut shows that most of those engaged in trade were small peddlers; of 842 graduates to date of the American College (University), only 37 had left for the United States,[32] but a much larger number had gone to Egypt, Sudan and other parts of the Middle East.

The average Syrian in America seems to live as cheaply and meanly as possible in order to accumulate money to send or bring back to his native land. Judging by the number who return to their former homes to build houses and purchase land it would seem that the height of their ambition is to become land proprietors in their native haunts. It is a commonplace observation among Syrians and foreigners that all houses built with tiled roofs in the Lebanon districts from which the emigration flows have been built with American money. When it is considered that there is hardly a village in the most remote parts of the Lebanon that has not at least 2 or 3 new houses with tiled roofs and that even whole villages have been thus constructed—the amount of money diverted from America and permanently invested in Syria can be easily recognized. Some slight clue as to the amount of money sent home by Syrians residing abroad can be gathered from the department of the Imperial Ottoman Bank that between £400,000 and 500,000 come annually from said sources. All this shows the general tendency of the Syrians to withdraw money from the countries in which they are sojourning. How large a proportion of this amount comes from the United States I cannot say, but I have reason to believe it is large.

In regard to their protestations of patriotism I regret to report that a very large number of these naturalized citizens cast aside the cloak of American citizenship when they sail from the United States for the purpose of visiting Syria. They provide themselves with Turkish passports in New York or Marseilles presumably for the reason that the Turkish consuls acting on the instructions of the home Government refuse to acknowledge the validity of their citizenship certified to by such passports and therefore decline to grant the visas. The acceptance of a Turkish passport may therefore be due to the ignorant belief that American consuls in Syria "either will not or have not the power to protect them."

> Magelssen to Loomis, September 12, 1904, US GR 84,
> Miscellaneous Correspondence, Beirut, quoted in Issawi,
> *The Fertile Crescent*, pp. 71-72.

By 1914, emigration was running at 15,000-20,000 a year. Overall, it is estimated that some 350,000 Syrians had left, two-thirds to the United States and most of the rest to South America. The number of Lebanese abroad, estimated at over 100,000, equalled at least a quarter, and in some districts a half, of the population.[33] There is the story of the man who, when asked what was the population of his village, replied: "Five thousand abroad and one thousand at home, for purposes of reproduction." The contribution of the emigrants to the national income of Lebanon has been noted, and their remittances have been a major item in the balance of payments. Their intellectual and social contributions are incalculable.

Notes

1. C. F. Volney, *Travels Through Syria and Egypt in the Years 1783, 1784, and 1785,* 2 vols. (London, 1788), vol. II, p. 73. This section has been mainly based on Adel Ismail, *Histoire du Liban* (Paris, 1955), vol. I; Kamal Salibi, *The Modern History of Lebanon* (London, 1965); Iliya Harik, *Politics and Change in a Traditional Society, Lebanon 1711-1843* (Princeton, N.J., 1968); Dominique Chevallier, *La Société du Mont Liban* (Paris, 1971); and Toufic Touma, *Paysans et institutions féodales chez les Druzes et les Maronites du Liban* (Beirut, 1986).

2. Except where otherwise specified, the information in this section is derived from Issawi, *Fertile Crescent.*

3. John Bowring, *Report on the Commercial Statistics of Syria* (London, 1840, repr. New York, 1973), p. 4.

4. Chevallier, *op. cit.,* pp. 33-42.

5. *Ibid.,* pp. 46-7.

6. Issawi, *Fertile Crescent,* pp. 51-4.

7. *Ibid.*

8. A. Ruppin, *Syrien als Wirtschaftsgebeit* (Berlin, 1917), p. 10.

9. Chevallier, *op. cit.,* p. 41.

10. Issawi, *Fertile Crescent,* pp. 129-31.

11. Leila Fawaz, *Merchants and Migrants in Nineteenth Century Beirut* (Cambridge, Mass., 1983), passim.

12. For further figures and details see Issawi, *Fertile Crescent,* pp. 127-51 and Boutros Labaki, *Introduction à l'histoire économique du Liban* (Beirut, 1984), chapter 5.

13. For details, Issawi, *Fertile Crescent,* pp. 203-24.

14. *Ibid.,* pp. 410-14, 135, 82; Ruppin, *op. cit.,* p. 267.

15. I.M. Smilyanskaya, "Razlozhenie feodalnikh otnoshenii v Sirii i Livane ..." tr. in Charles Issawi, *Economic History of the Middle East* (Chicago, 1966), p. 228.

16. See tables in Issawi, *Fertile Crescent,* pp. 290-2.

17. See table in *ibid.,* p. 321; Labaki, *op. cit.,* pp. 136-7.

18. Bowring, *op. cit.,* p. 102.

19. See list of crafts in Issawi, *Fertile Crescent,* p. 382; and figures on silk reeling, *ibid.,* p. 378.

20. See forthcoming article by L.S. Schilcher.

21. For these and other developments see Harik, *op. cit.,* pp. 159-66 and Hitti, *op. cit.,* pp. 675-7; see list in Touma, *op. cit.,* pp. 348-60.

22. See dispatch in Issawi, *Fertile Crescent,* p. 54.

23. Touma, *op. cit.,* p. 353, basing himself on Cuinet, gives a figure of 120,000, which seems much too high.

24. *Idem,* pp. 358-60; Issawi, *op. cit.,* p. 32.

25. *Ibid.,* pp. 30-3, 81.

26. Robert M. Haddad, *Syrian Christians in a Muslim Society* (Princeton, N.J., 1970) p. 40.

27. A.H. Hourani, "The Syrians in Egypt ... " *Colloque international sur l'histoire du Caire* (Cairo, 1964), pp. 226-7; Thomas Philipp, *The Syrians in Egypt, 1725-1975* (Stuttgart, 1985); Charles Issawi, "The transformation," *op. cit.*

28. Ismail, *op. cit.,* vol. IV, pp. 305-7.

29. I.M. Smilyanskaya, *Krestyanskoe dvizhenie v Livane,* tr. in Issawi, *Fertile Crescent,* p. 49.

30. For breakdowns, see Elie Safa, *L'Émigration libanaise* (Beirut, 1960), pp. 188-91.

31. K. Karpat, "The Ottoman emigration to America, 1860-1914," *International Journal of Middle Eastern Studies,* May 1985.

32. See report in Issawi, *The Fertile Crescent,* pp. 71-2.

33. Ruppin, *op. cit.,* p. 14.

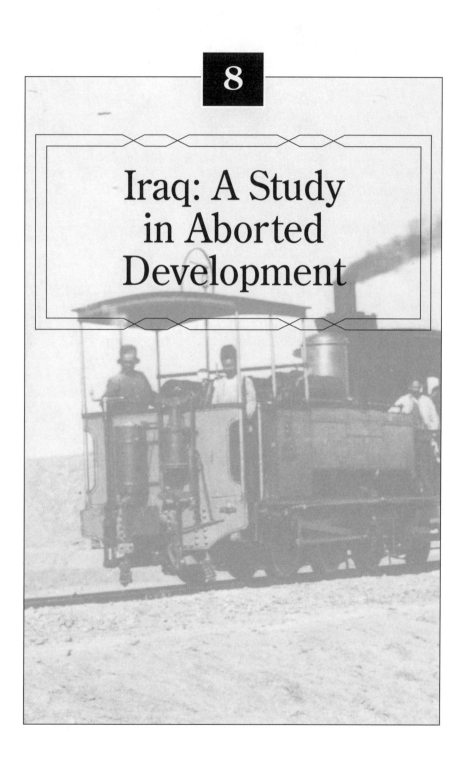

8

Iraq: A Study in Aborted Development

t has been said that "Brazil is the land of the future; but, then, it has been for the last three hundred years." In the same way, Iraq has been the land of the future for the last hundred and fifty years.

Travellers to Iraq in the nineteenth century were almost unanimous in their assessment of the country's potentialities. Iraq had all the resources necessary for development: navigable rivers (the only ones in the Middle East apart from the Nile); abundance of fertile and easily irrigable land; minerals, including, it soon became clear, oil; proximity to such large markets as India, Turkey, and Iran; control of old and valuable trade routes; and access to the ocean. All that was needed to ensure rapid economic growth was the establishment of law and order, an injection of small amounts of foreign capital and enterprise, and the provision of some mechanical transport, such as a railway to the Mediterranean or steam navigation on the Tigris and Euphrates to export the anticipated surplus of grain and other produce.

1800-1914[1]

The course of development did not turn out to be quite so simple. In fact, Iraq's history over the last two centuries consists of long periods of very slow growth punctuated by short bursts of rapid development, all of which were abruptly ended by some catastrophe brought on either by an outside factor or by forces originating within the country itself.

For almost the whole of the nineteenth century, there were powerful forces impeding development. First and foremost, Iraq has always been subject to devastating floods—it is no coincidence that the story of the Deluge and Ark first appears in a Sumerian text of the third millennium B.C. The great engineer Sir William Willcocks, who built major works in India, Egypt, and Iraq, said that of all rivers the Nile was the most gentlemanly. He was too polite to add that the Tigris and Euphrates are among the most villainous. Sweeping down from the Turkish mountains when the snows melt in the spring, they swiftly rise to great heights (the Tigris by an average of 18 feet and the Euphrates by 11), overflow their banks, spread

32 • Crossing the Euphrates

havoc in the surrounding villages and fields, and, abandoning their usual channels, cut new ones or create swamps. In addition, they have a high salt content, and, time and again in its millennial history, Iraq has seen its soil suffer from salinization and its production decrease, with a corresponding decline in civilization. The rivers also have a high content of silt, which chokes irrigation works. During the period from 1840 to 1907, no less than twenty major floods occurred with devastating results. In 1894, the American consul in Baghdad reported: "The water reached several feet up on the wall of the house I occupy, the outer wall of which was partially destroyed and threatened to fall, my Sardab (cellar) filled, and I would sit at my office window with hook and line and catch all the fish I wanted."[2] As late as 1954, Baghdad had to be protected with a wall of sandbags against a flood that swept away the main highway to Mosul.

Only slightly less devastating were the epidemics that swept over the country. As in previous centuries, there were major outbreaks of the plague in 1799, 1802, 1822, and, most terrible, 1831, which was followed by a major flood; between them the latter carried off some 50,000 to 70,000 of Baghdad's estimated population of 150,000. There were further outbreaks in 1867, 1877, and 1881, but they were relatively mild. Furthermore, cholera, which first came to the Middle East from India in 1821, grew in virulence until the end of the century.

In April the plague reached Baghdad, and by the 10th of that month 7000 persons had died of it. What made matters worse was the scarcity of food and the refusal of the water-carriers to deliver water to the inhabitants, causing general misery. In addition, the flood struck Baghdad on April 21st, surrounding the city, drowning thousands of persons, and making it impossible to transport food to the people. Five days later the city's northern dyke and part of the fortress broke and the waters rushed in and submerged 2000 houses in one hour; within 24 hours the palace and 7000 houses had been reduced to ruins and Daud pasha's thoroughbred horses were seen to be wandering in the city. After two days the waters began subsiding and by the end of the first week in May the threat of the plague and flood had disappeared and the survivors began to bury the dead . . . and Daud pasha recovered from his attack of plague.

Ahmad Susa, *Fayadanat Baghdad fi al-tarikh*, vol. 2, Baghdad, 1965, quoted in Issawi, *The Fertile Crescent,* p. 103.

Except for a not-too-effective system of quarantines, modern medicine had almost no impact, but by the beginning of this century a few foreign physicians were practicing and a few small hospitals had been opened by missionaries; their salubrious effect was, however, confined to the major cities.

Insecurity continued to prevent development in most of the country. Most governors were incompetent, and some were venal. Their main objective was to bring Iraq under control, increase revenue, and impose conscription. This was naturally resisted by the tribesmen, especially in the southern part of the country, which was predominantly Shi'i while the government was Sunni. Repeated expeditions to assert government authority and collect taxes resulted only in the destruction of crops and livestock and the further alienation of the people. And, until 1914, piracy in the Gulf took its toll on merchant shipping, and the great tribes in the Syrian desert continued to pillage the caravans on the Damascus and Aleppo routes.

Complaints have been made to me on this head by Masters of the merchant ships and the HCC [Honourable Company's Cruiser] Psyche once succeeded in taking a pirate boat but the crew deserted her and swam naked to the shore, the boat was detained and when the owners came forward to claim her, their property was delivered to them at the particular intercession of the *Musallim* [Governor] and on a promise of their future good behaviour.

Similar acts have nevertheless since been repeated by others and among these the event herein described.

I have used every endeavour to discover the perpetrators and to recover the plunder, but hitherto without effect, which has at length induced me to address the Moontifik Shaikh whose control extends over almost every tribe on both banks of the river except the Chaab Arabs . . . There is little doubt that the Moontifik Shaikh encourages these piracies, by neglecting to punish them and by directly participating in their gains. If therefore he continues to tolerate them nothing will secure our shipping in the river from further attacks but the severe public example of burning every boat of this description, which three or four cruisers would effect with ease. . .

Taylor to Rich, November 20-21, 1820, IOPS Bombay, 385/1, quoted in Issawi, *The Fertile Crescent,* p. 106.

However, in the second half of the nineteenth century, worldwide forces were bringing about important changes in the economy and society of Iraq. Demand for Iraqi produce, notably wheat, barley, dates, and livestock products, was growing rapidly. Lower freights, due to improvements in shipping and the opening of the Suez Canal in 1869—which brought the Gulf within reach of Europe by steamers-made these products much more competitive in world markets. Between 1869-1870 and 1912-1913, seaborne exports rose twelve-fold and imports even faster, by 22 times. Since both export and import prices fell by about 20 percent in this period, the increase in real terms was correspondingly greater.

The effects of this expansion in exports were far-reaching. This expansion made it profitable greatly to increase production, and cultivation began to be rapidly extended by means of very simple irrigation works. A need was felt for more manpower, and this, together with the virtual elimination of famines and the reduction in epidemic diseases, may have stimulated population growth. The expansion in exports also led to the sedentarization of nomads, since the demand for agricultural produce rose far more rapidly than that for pastoral products. In turn, these developments transformed Iraqi rural society. Hitherto, land had been owned and operated by the whole tribe or clan; now, it began to be appropriated by the shaykh, with the other members working as sharecroppers. The process was accelerated by the application of the Ottoman Land Code of 1858 realized by the reforming governor Midhat Pasha. This aimed at encouraging private property and increasing government revenue and stipulated that all land should be registered in individual ownership. The result was the alienation of almost all tribal land to shaykhs or, occasionally, city merchants or money-lenders. The application of the Law was therefore suspended, leaving a large amount of land without a clear title. Henceforth, and until the 1958 revolution, Iraqi rural society was to consist of two classes: a small number of very large and powerful landowners and a mass of landless peasants.[3]

The expansion of foreign trade was achieved with hardly any improvement in the infrastructure. Grain was floated downstream in traditional craft, but steam navigation was introduced in the 1840s by a small British firm, which was soon followed by others; this led to a considerable decrease in time and a smaller one in freights. The port of Basra, however, remained totally unimproved, and no roads or railways were built. Only a few, small banks were opened, and they confined their operations to trade and foreign exchange. The monetary system was as confused as elsewhere in the Ottoman Empire, several currencies circulating side by side, at widely fluctuating rates, and trade being hampered by a shortage of means of payment. No modern industries were built, and handicrafts suffered from the competition of imported machine-made goods and the shift in tastes. Education made very little progress. The government opened a few schools in the main towns, as did foreign missions. The total number of pupils in modern (as distinct from traditional mosque) schools, however, was about 7,500 for a population of about 2,500,000. Literacy was put at 5 to 10 percent of the townsmen, or say 2 to 3 percent of the total population. "Of publishing, book production, or generally readable literary output there was nothing save the dull official newspaper."[4] None of the cities had electricity or purified water.

At the beginning of this century, Iraq was, even by Middle Eastern standards, a very backward country. Egypt, Turkey, and Syria were far ahead of it in such indices of development as foreign trade, transportation, industrialization, education, and availability of urban amenities. Only Iran stood at a comparable level.

In the decade preceding World War I, however, progress accelerated noticeably.[5] The Ottoman government became much more interested in development and had somewhat more funds available. Foreign interest in Iraq also grew: the Germans began building the Berlin-Baghdad railway, which was planned to reach Basra; they also saw Iraq as a potential supplier of petroleum and cotton. The British shared the craving for oil and had growing commercial and other interests. In 1914, "Bargains were struck"

33 • A third class coach in the Baghdad Railways

(to quote E. M. Earle), and implementation of major plans began. A railway was built between Baghdad and Samarra, to join the Anatolian-Syrian line. The river fleet was expanded. The Hindiyya barrage was built on the Euphrates, and work started on other schemes under a master plan drawn up by Sir William Willcocks. An Anglo-German Oil Company was formed and awaited only the granting of a concession to begin exploration. Iraq seemed poised to leap forward, but its movement was halted by the outbreak of war.

Just as German Near East policy, with the Baghdad Railway and its extension to the Persian Gulf, cut to pieces the English idea of an overland connection from the eastern basin of the Mediterranean Sea to India, in like manner the Mesopotamian oil interests of the Deutsche-Bank group concerned with the Baghdad Railway came into conflict with British oil strategy. The following time considerations are important: in the year 1903 the Baghdad Railways document was signed, and the next year, 1904, the realization of the English encirclement policy began in a systematic way and Lord Fisher produced his new program of support for an oil burning fleet . . .

The Mesopotamian interests of the Deutsch-Bank-Petroleum A.G. group were based partly on the above-mentioned special treaty of 1904 of the Anatolian Railway Company and partly on Article 22, Section I, of the concession document dated March 5, 1903, of the Baghdad Railway Company. There it was stated that "the concessionaire may exploit mineral deposits discovered in a zone 20 kilometers wide on either side of the roadbed; in the agreement of the Anatolian Railway Company, in 1904 with the Turkish civil list, i.e., with Sultan Abdul Hamid. In this agreement, the Deutsche-Bank group was granted special privileges, including, for one, the right to explore the oil fields in the *vilayet's* of Mosul and Baghdad and, for another, the right to an option for their exploitation. Whether or not this agreement constituted a monopoly, it certainly created the constitutive preconditions for one.

At that time the English had no designs of any kind regarding oil concessions in Mesopotamia. At the outset the English had been satisfied with blocking a possible penetration of the Deutsche-Bank into southern Persia. . . .

Under the at least "moral" cover of the Admiralty, there followed in 1909 the founding of the Anglo-Persian Oil Company, so that now the cross-blows [*Querstösse*] from the southeast, with powerful support in the Persian Gulf, were considered all the more lasting. [William Knox] D'Arcy [Board of Admiralty] then maintained that he had obtained a promise from two Turkish grand vizirs that he would be given the concession for Mesopotamia after 1912. . . .

But the British, in pinning their hope on the Young Turk regime, had been thoroughly mistaken. Instead of separating themselves from us, the Young Turks stuck to the earlier foreign-policy direction of their empire. In the Mesopotamian oil question they seemed to prefer a compromise between the German and English interests to bringing the conflict to a head, and in the period of 1912 to 1914 there was Bethmann-Hollweg's policy of German-English understanding with its aim for a "Baghdad peace." Under the influence of this policy, or making use of it, Sir Ernest Cassel in particular worked for a unification of English and German interests in the Mesopotamian oil question. Out of this arose the "Turkish Petroleum Company," which was to become world-famous after the war.

In 1913, when Churchill sent his "research committee" under Sir Edmund Slade to South Persia, the statutory entry of the government into the Anglo-Persian Oil Company seems already to have been a certainty, so that its interest was immediately carried over to the Turkish Petroleum Company.

On March 19, 1914, a "reconstitution" of the Turkish Petroleum Company ensued, which mainly involved a withdrawal by the National Bank of Turkey of its 50 per cent share of the total capital, at the once more increased level of £160,000, in favor of the Anglo-Persian Oil Company. The pertinent document was signed not only by representatives of the two companies, but also by representatives of the two governments, Sir Eyre A. Crowe for the government of His Britannic Majesty and Herr von Kühlmann for the imperial German government.

With this the Turkish Petroleum Company, with a 75 per cent majority shared by two British groups, was turned into a tool of British oil policy and, because of its "simple majority" 50 per cent of the Anglo-Persian Oil Company, into a branch of the British government concern. Its concession for the *vilayet's* of Mosul and Badhdad in Mesopotamia, which subsumed the "right of option" of the Anatolian Railway Company of 1904, was confirmed anew, granted once more, or recognized, as a "German-English concession" through an *iradeh* of June 28, 1914, of which the English ambassador, Sir Louis Mallet, handled the distribution to interested European quarters. To the extent that the Germans had a voice in this "reorganization," the transaction was connected in a vague way with the initially secret agreements of the "Baghdad peace" which were reached by Prince Lichnowsky and Sir Edward Grey in July, 1914, and could no longer be ratified. The Deutsche-Bank group was allegedly promised participation in the British shipping monopoly on the Shatt al Arab (mouth of the Tigris-Euphrates), as well as in shipping in the interior on the Tigris and the Euphrates.

. . . Turkey, after her entry into the war in November, 1914, notified the Anglo-Persian Oil Company that she viewed as void the permission given earlier.

Long before this notification, England had removed the German share of 25 per cent and transferred it to loyal hands, to the administration of Launcelot Grey Hugh Smith, chairman of the Turkish Petroleum Company, so that England, from its own point of view, had obtained full ownership. And in August, 1914, long before the entry of Turkey into the war, the British Empire had already begun military operations in Mesopotamian districts, had continued these operations with tenacity until the conquest of Baghdad in March, 1917, and in November, 1918, after the cessation of hostilities had occupied Mosul as well. Under her own power Great Britain, even before the signing of the Versailles treaty, discussions with France having become pressing, disposed of the participation relationship and, by taking up Berenger's ideas, gave up or offered to give up 25 per cent to France.

Along with the situation based on military power there was a legal situation which was juridically opaque. For that reason Mesopotamia became the main arena of conflict in this hemisphere, while Mexico remained the main arena of conflict in the Western Hemisphere; and with the objections of North America, the "Mosul question" which arose took on a world-wide political scope and fame. . . .

Karl Hoffmann, *Oelpolitik und angelsächsischer Imperialismus* (Berlin, 1927), quoted in Issawi, *The Economic History of the Middle East*, pp. 199-201.

1914-1958

During the whole of the First World War, Iraq was a major battlefield and suffered much loss of life and property. However its infrastructure, such as it was, was not destroyed and indeed emerged greatly improved. The British army set up port facilities in Basra, laid a railway from that town to Baghdad, and built many roads. But the cessation of hostilities was soon followed by local clashes with various elements of the population. In 1920, a large-scale insurrection, covering about a third of the country, broke out. Its suppression cost the British hundreds of lives and some £40 million. Iraqi casualties were far higher and were accompanied by much destruction of property.

By 1921, order had been reestablished, Faysal, a member of the Hashemite family from Mecca and ally of Britain, had been set on the throne, and economic growth could be resumed.[6] During the next two decades, much progress was made in two critical areas: transport and agriculture.

Railways were built over the whole length of the country, for a total of 1,300 kilometers in 1938. In 1939, they were connected with the Syrian and Turkish railways, and the Berlin-Baghdad dream was realized. Thousands of kilometers of improved roads were constructed. Numerous bridges carried railways and roads across the rivers. The port of Basra was greatly improved. Telecommunications were established with the outside world. Airports were built, and Baghdad became a major stop in international aviation. An Iraqi airline also served internal and regional traffic. Altogether,

34 • Train in Iraq in the 1920s

although the transport system was still defective, it served the country's needs more or less adequately.

There was practically no progress in agriculture in the way of diversifying crops or improving methods. Conservatism, poverty, and ignorance were major obstacles, but no less important was the land tenure system. The British, whose power was based on the *shaykhs,* confirmed and consolidated the prevailing agrarian system, and the landlord-dominated Iraqi parliament was not about to change it. Hence, a large proportion of the land continued to be without clear title, and almost all the remainder was held by absentee landlords. In these circumstances, almost no one had an incentive to improve and invest; tools remained primitive, no chemical fertilizer was used, and yields were extremely low.[7]

However, the expansion of irrigation led to a large extension of cultivation. The Kut barrage was built on the Tigris in 1937, as were various minor projects. More important was the extension of pump irrigation, which by 1939 watered nearly 2,500,000 acres. The cultivated area increased from 900,000 acres in 1913 to over 4,000,000 in 1943. Between 1926, when figures first became available, and 1938, output of wheat about doubled and of barley more than doubled, and the volume of cereals exported also rose twofold.

In other fields, where the country started from scratch, progress was much more rapid. A sound currency, based on sterling, was established, and several banks, mainly foreign, opened branches all over the country. A few factories were built for textiles, leatherware, food-processing, tobacco products, and other simple consumer goods; a government-owned agricultural and industrial bank was founded to promote development. The cities were provided with such amenities as electricity, purified water, paved streets, and public transport. The number of school children rose from under 10,000 in 1920 to 110,000 in 1937; colleges of law, medicine, and teacher training were established or expanded; and hundreds of students were sent abroad for higher education. Health conditions showed some improvement.[8]

A landmark was the beginning of large-scale oil production in 1934, with the opening of a pipeline to the Mediterranean. Annual output rose to 80,000 barrels a day and government receipts to nearly $10 million, or over a quarter of total public revenue; this was used mainly for development. It has been estimated that annual gross investment (excluding private buildings) rose from £800,000 in 1922-30 to £2.1 million in 1930-39;[9] this represents a savings and investment rate of perhaps 7-8 percent.

35 • Oil Field

Once more this rapid growth was aborted. During the Second World War and its aftermath there was a marked slowing down of the economy. The flow of oil through the pipeline was considerably reduced, and in 1948 the branch to Haifa, now a city in the enemy state of Israel, was shut off, decreasing revenue. Inflation was rampant, the cost of living index showed a six-fold rise, and shortages were felt by the population. The uprising against the British in 1941 caused some disruption, and the continued post-war agitation considerably more. The exodus of the Jewish community, who handled a large part of Iraq's trade, also represented a serious economic loss. However, in the 1950s, the pace of development picked up again. Thanks to the laying down of a new and larger pipeline to Baniyas, oil production rose to nearly 700,000 barrels a day. At the same time, following the Iranian nationalization crisis, new agreements were negotiated, raising the government's "take" per barrel from about 22 cents to 70 cents. As a result, total government receipts from oil rose by 1953 to over $160 million. In addition, thanks partly to government pressure and partly to a more far-sighted attitude on the part of the companies, steps were taken to hire more Iraqi technical and managerial personnel and to integrate more closely the industry in the national economy; hitherto, it had been a self-contained enclave.[10]

The government used the additional funds to launch a vast and far-reaching development program. First of all came flood-control and irrigation. Under a master plan drawn up by foreign experts a series of huge dams was built on the Tigris and its tributaries (the Diyala and the two Zabs) and on the Euphrates. These works, whose combined cost was to total hundreds of millions of dollars, diverted flood water to large depressions such as Habbaniya and Wadi Tharthar. By 1958, Iraq was, for the first time in its long history, secure against floods.[11] The dams also provided irrigation for an estimated eventual total of 3,750,000 acres. This permitted the expansion of the cultivated area, in spite of the loss of much land to salinization because of the failure to install drains. Hence, although yields seem to have fallen quite sharply, total production increased considerably. From 1934 to 1938, output of wheat averaged 480,000 metric tons and of barley 580,000, during the years 1948 to 1952, they rose to 936,000 and 934,000 tons, respectively; and between 1954 and 1958, to 1,423,000 and 1,172,000. This increase of nearly 150 percent may be compared with a population growth that almost certainly did not exceed 60 percent. However, poor methods of cultivation and the land tenure system continued to depress the peasant's condition. As before, the government did not attempt to carry out a land reform, but it did set up several model settlements on government-owned land, of which the best known was the Dujayla scheme. But these benefitted only a tiny fraction of the rural population. Hence, large numbers of landless peasants left the countryside and flocked to Baghdad and other cities, swelling the turbulent urban populace.

There was also a certain amount of industrial development. Laws passed in 1929, 1950, and 1955 gave increasing tax exemption to new industrial firms, and loans were advanced by the Industrial Bank. Between 1948 and 1954, investment in industries other than petroleum rose from 3 million Iraqi dinars to about 20 million; between 1950 and 1958, value added, in current prices, doubled. At the latter date, nearly 80,000 persons worked in industry, which consisted mainly of the usual branches to be found at an early stage of development: textiles, food-processing, building materials, and metalworking. In 1957, a Six-Year Plan, aggregating some $120 million, was adopted and was being implemented.[12]

Railway transport showed little development, but, in 1955, the government allocated £15 million for extension and improvements. The road system was greatly extended and improved; by 1956, there were 2,900 kilometers of surfaced roads and 8,000 of dirt roads, and several hundreds more were under construction. Airports and telecommunication were also extended and improved, as were financial and banking systems.

All these developments show up in the national income figures, which now became available. One series puts annual growth between 1950 and 1956 at 11 percent and another at 7 percent between 1953 and 1958. Some estimates give higher figures. The increase in oil revenues and higher government expenditure account for the greater part of the increase, but the other sectors also made a contribution. The few available data on levels of living show an improvement in the consumption of staple products.[13]

There was also a distinct improvement in social conditions. This was the result of strenuous government efforts, stimulated by Lord Salter's report of 1955, pointing to the economic and political implications of the gap between the water control and irrigation projects and the living conditions of the people.[14] A beginning was made on providing public housing in the cities. Public health measures, including a campaign against malaria (the number of cases reported dropped from 500,000 in 1950 to 10,000 in 1959), began to reach the villages. By 1958, there were 123 hospitals, with over 9,000 beds and over 500 dispensaries, and 1,200 physicians, of whom, however, over half were in Baghdad. The number of children in primary schools rose from 196,000 in 1949 to 527,000 in 1958 and in secondary schools from 23,000 to 99,000. Baghdad University increased the number of its constituent colleges, and the number of its students rose from 1,200 in 1940 to 8,600 in 1958; it also began to include distinguished scholars among its faculty. The position of women showed some improvement, especially with regard to education and employment.[15]

1958-1991[16]

All this came too late to save the monarchy, which was, appropriately, overthrown on July 14, 1958. The causes of the revolution were numerous: general hatred of the government for its pro-Western policy (especially after the Suez attack in 1956), middle class resentment of political repression, rural poverty, urban misery, and the ambition of army officers inspired by Nasser's example.

The revolution was not unusually bloody, though much more so than the Egyptian, which, like the Nile, was very gentlemanly. Its aftermath, however, was highly disruptive. Communist, Ba'thist, and Nasserite groups fought street battles and terrorized the population. A televised people's court struck fear in the upper and middle classes. Civil strife pitted Kurd against Arab, Communist against Ba'thist, Nasserite against Iraqi nationalist. Soon a large proportion of Iraq's intelligentsia, administrators, entrepreneurs, and technicians left the country.

The adverse effect of all these events was aggravated by various economic measures taken by the government. In 1958, a Land Reform was initiated, modelled on the successful Egyptian one of 1952, but far more sweeping in scope. Its effect was highly disruptive. Civil disorder, lack of records, and the inadequacy of the bureaucracy impeded implementation. So did the persistence of tribal structures and the lack of adequate roads, drains, and storage facilities. The functions of management and provision of credit, formerly performed, however harshly, by the landlords and merchants, were to be taken over by government-sponsored cooperatives and other agencies, but those proved few in number and inefficient in operation. Later attempts to set up collectives had their usual negative effect. A series of droughts hit the country, sharply reducing yields, and total output fell considerably. Drainage was neglected and salinization increased markedly, making much land unfit for cultivation.[17] A further adverse factor should be noted.

In Egypt, the land expropriated was soon handed over to the beneficiaries, whose secure title to their plot ensured that they would farm it efficiently. In Iraq, however, for reasons noted earlier, distribution was very slow; by the time the dictator Qasim was overthrown, in 1963, only 40 percent of the expropriated land had been distributed. A pause followed until 1970, when a new law drastically reduced ceilings and, unlike the 1958 law, did not pay the landlords compensation. This brought up the amount of land held by the state to 6,500,000 acres—or 46 percent of the agricultural area—in addition to the 2,500,000 previously held or otherwise acquired by it. Of this, 4,000,000 acres, or under half, had been distributed by 1975, the balance being held by the Ministry of Agrarian Reform.

Once again, a highly promising development had been cut short; by the end of the 1970s, however, there were signs of improvement. Almost all the rural population now owned land and had an incentive to farm it better. The great dams completed or started under the monarchy were providing more water, though drainage was still neglected. The government began paying more attention to agriculture, providing more and better inputs and allowing more private initiative. As a result, yields and production began to rise slowly. But by now Iraq, formerly an exporter of grain, had become a large importer; it could afford to do so because of its rising oil revenues.

Drastic measures were also taken in the urban sector, but their effect was less disruptive. From the very beginning, the revolutionary government put much greater emphasis on industry and allocated larger sums for investment in it. Available figures show almost a doubling of industrial "value added" between 1958 and 1963 and a fifty percent rise in investment. In July 1964, however, practically all large-scale factories were nationalized, and limits were placed on individual holdings in other companies. Here, too, the mechanisms set up by the government to replace private initiative proved inadequate. Available figures show a distinct, though not considerable, fall in output following the takeover. Recovery, however, was relatively swift, and, aided by continued large investments, output resumed its upward trend. However, in almost all industries for which figures are available, the rate of growth between 1964 and 1969 was lower than it had been from 1960 to 1964. In the 1970s, massive investments were made, and numerous petrochemical, engineering, electronic, and metal industries were established, many of them for military purposes. Naturally, this rapid industrialization was accompanied by numerous problems arising from faulty planning, political interference, bureaucratic mismanagement, and shortages of technicians, skilled workmen, and raw materials. Efficiency remained low, but the progress achieved was undeniable. The same July 1964 law also nationalized banks, insurance companies, and trading companies; these firms, together with industry, were grouped under four public organizations.

The mainstay of the economy continued to be petroleum, and here, too, drastic changes took place. Output continued to rise, and so did oil revenues but at a slower rate, owing to price reductions in 1959 and 1960. The government was dissatisfied with existing conditions, and negotiations began with the oil companies for better terms. These stalled, and, in December 1960, Law 80 expropriated, without compensation, 99.5 percent of the original concession areas. Negotiations dragged on, being later complicated by a dispute with Syria over the pipeline carrying Iraqi oil to the Mediterranean. In 1967, the government began developing, with Soviet help, the southern field of Rumaila. In June 1972, Iraq nationalized the Iraq Petroleum Company and, later, the Basra Petroleum Company, bringing all oil production under government control.[18]

As a result of this controversy, Iraq's output of oil grew much more slowly than that of other Middle Eastern countries; between 1960 and 1973 it just doubled—to 2,000,000 barrels a day, compared to a fourfold rise in the region as a whole. As late as 1974, total oil revenues were only $575 million; but, after that, thanks to the price rises of 1973 and 1979, they shot up to $7.5 billion in 1975 and peaked at $26 billion in 1982, after which they fluctuated around a level of $10 billion.

This huge inflow of funds naturally sent GNP soaring. According to the World Bank, GNP in 1979 stood at $2,410 per capita (it had grown by an annual average of about 8 percent since 1960). There is no doubt that the level of living rose significantly in this period.

The postrevolutionary governments did much to provide social services. Low income houses were built in large numbers. Hospitals and other health facilities expanded greatly. By 1983, the number of children in primary schools had risen to 2,700,000, of whom 46 percent were girls; in secondary and other schools, 1,068,000; and in higher education, 127,000, of whom 85,000 were in college, with thousands more abroad. The literacy rate rose to over 60 percent. All signs pointed to a continued rapid expansion and rise in economic and social levels.

At this point, Saddam Hussein, who had been ruling the country with an iron and bloody hand since 1968, made his first great mistake: he invaded Iran in 1980. This may have been motivated by fear of Iranian subversion, but he was probably lured—as others were before him, for example in 1792 and 1918—by the prospect of an easy victory over a neighbor supposedly laid prostrate by a revolution. Instead, he found himself engaged in a nine-year war, with hundreds of thousands of casualties, a drop in oil production to 700,000 barrels a day—with some recovery after 1984—and a huge amount of destruction in Basra and other areas of combat. From 1980 through 1989, Iraq received some $120 billion in oil revenues and over $80 billion in loans. It is safe to say that the bulk of this money was spent on prosecuting the war and buying arms.

With United States help, Saddam managed to avert defeat and, for a few months, set about repairing the war damage. But he was desperate for more revenues and made his second, and greatest, mistake by invading Kuwait on 2 August 1990, and refusing to withdraw after being repeatedly summoned to do so. He had obviously not read his Shelley:[19]

Rome was, and young Atlantis shall become
The wonder, or the terror, or the tomb
Of all whose step wakes power lulled in her savage lair.

The results are vividly described in the two following paragraphs taken from the report submitted by United Nations Under-Secretary-General Martti Ahtisaari:

> The recent conflict has brought near-apocalyptic results upon the economic infrastructure of what had been, until January 1991, a rather highly urbanized and mechanized society. Now, most means of modern life support have been destroyed or rendered tenuous. Iraq has, for some time to come, been relegated to a preindustrial age, but with all the disabilities of postindustrial dependency on an intensive use of energy and technology. . . . Underlying each analysis is the inexorable reality that, as a result of war, virtually all previously viable sources of fuel and power (apart from a limited number of mobile generators) and modern means of communications are now essentially defunct.

This was followed by the great loss of life and destruction caused by the Shi'i and Kurdish uprisings and their suppression. A study by a Western group of experts from August to September 1991 found that the mortality rate for children had risen to 80 per thousand, from 20 to 30 before the war. One million children, or 29 percent of the population under 5, suffered from malnutrition, and nearly 120,000 were severely malnourished. Farm output had dropped by 75 to 80 percent because of the breakdown of irrigation systems and the shortage of inputs.[20] The country is also saddled with heavy reparations. In the course of the last eighty years, Iraq has been beset by repeated setbacks, from which it has recovered. This time it will take longer.

Notes

1. For a detailed account of the period 1800-1914, see Charles Issawi, *The Fertile Crescent, 1800-1914: A Documentary Economic History* (New York, 1988).

2. Sundberg to Ubl, 10 May 1894, United States National Archives, Group 84, Baghdad, Miscellaneous Correspondence.

3. On land tenure in Iraq see Saleh Haider, "Land Problems of Iraq," thesis, London University, 1942 (partially reproduced in Charles Issawi, *The Economic History of the Middle East* (Chicago, 1966), pp. 163-78; E. Dowson, *Enquiry into Land Tenure* (Letchworth, 1931); Doreen Warriner, *Land and Poverty in the Middle East* (London, 1948); idem, "Land Tenure Problems in the Fertile Crescent" in Issawi, *Economic History,* op. cit., pp. 71-78; Albertine Jwaideh, "Midhat Pasha and the Land System of Lower Iraq," *St. Antony's Papers,* 3, 1963; idem, "Aspects of Land Tenure and Social Change in Lower Iraq," in Tarif Khalidi (ed.), *Land and Social Transformation in the Middle East* (Beirut, 1983).

4. S. H. Longrigg, *Iraq, 1900 to 1950* (London, 1955), p. 21.

5. On this period, see ibid. and Issawi, *Fertile Crescent,* op. cit.

6. For the period 1918-1940, see Longrigg, op. cit.; Joseph Sassoon, *Economic Policy in Iraq, 1932-1950* (London, 1987); Sa'id Himadeh, *al-nizam al-iqtisadi fi al-'iraq* (Beirut, 1938).

7. On agrarian conditions, see Hanna Batatu, *The Old Social Classes and the Revolutionary Movements of Iraq* (Princeton, 1978); Abdel Salih Alwan, "The Process of Economic Development in Iraq," thesis, University of Wisconsin, 1956.

8. On education, see Matta Akrawi and Roderick Matthews, *Education in the Arab Countries of the Near East* (Washington, D.C., 1949).

9. Ribhi Abu El-Haj, "Capital Formation in Iraq, 1922-1957," *Economic Development and Cultural Change,* July 1961.

10 On oil and oil revenues, see Charles Issawi and Mohammed Yeganeh, *The Economics of Middle Eastern Oil* (New York, 1962); Abbas Alnasrawi, *Financing Economic Development in Iraq* (New York, 1967).

11. Knappen, Tippets, Abbott and McCarthy, *Report on the Development of the Tigris and Euphrates River Systems* (Baghdad, 1954); F. F. Haigh, *Report on the Control of the Rivers of Iraq* (Baghdad, 1952).

12. Kathleen Langley, *The Industrialization of Iraq* (Cambridge, Mass., 1961); F. Jalal, *The Role of Government in the Industrialization of Iraq, 1950-1965* (London, 1971).

13. K. G. Fenelon, *Iraq: National Income and Expenditure, 1950-56* (Baghdad, 1958); Khair al-din Haseeb, *The National Income of Iraq, 1953-61* (London, 1964).

14. Lord Salter, *The Development of Iraq: A Plan of Action,* Iraq Development Board, Baghdad, 1955; see also International Bank for Reconstruction and Development, *The Economic Development of Iraq* (Baltimore, Maryland, 1952).

15. Fahim Qubain, *Reconstruction of Iraq, 1950-1957* (New York, 1958); Doris Adams, *Iraq's People and Resources* (Los Angeles, 1958).

16. For this period see Edith and E. F. Penrose, *Iraq: International Relations and National Development* (London, 1978); Marion Farouk-Sluglett and Peter Sluglett, *Iraq since 1958* (London, 1987); Abbas Kelidar (ed.), *The Integration of Modern Iraq* (London, 1979); and the annual statistical publications of the World Bank, United Nations and UNESCO.

17. Robert Fernea, "Land Reform and Ecology in Post-revolutionary Iraq," *Economic Development and Cultural Change,* April 1969.

18. See Oles and Bettie Smolansky, *The USSR and Iraq* (Durham, N.C., 1991), chapter 2.

19. *Hellas, a Lyrical Drama* (1821).

20. *New York Times,* 22 October 1991.

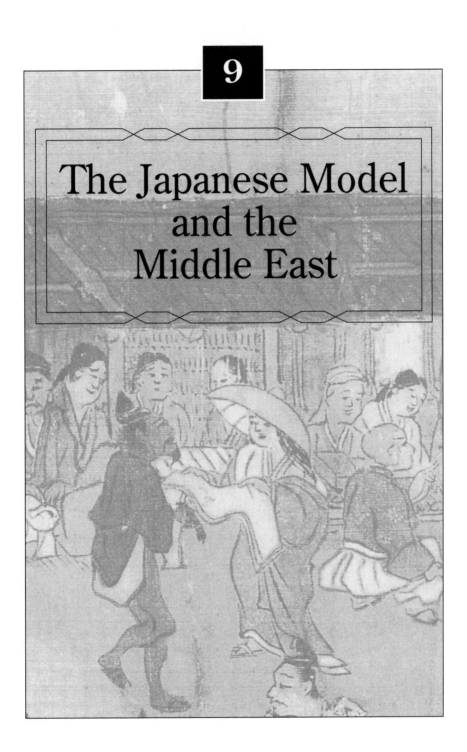

9

The Japanese Model and the Middle East

hy did Japan alone among the countries of Asia, Africa, and Latin America "make it" in the nineteenth and early twentieth centuries? Why not the Arabs? Why not, for instance, Iraq, whose potential was, and still is, so great? It has been said that "Brazil is the land of the future, but then it has been for the last 300 years." And so has Iraq: one could cite numerous accounts written during the last 150 years that are ecstatic about Iraq's economic possibilities, because of its combination of fertile soil, mineral wealth, navigable rivers, and proximity to India, Turkey, Iran, and other economic centers.

Or why not Egypt, which was the Arab country that, all things considered, was the best placed for modernization? This question has been raised before. In 1952, at the end of a discussion of the course of Egyptian history in the second half of the nineteenth century and of possible alternatives, this author wrote: "If during that time she had had a government that was both national and enlightened . . . Egypt might have emerged into the twentieth century as a small scale Japan."[1] As Manon and Des Grieux sang wistfully about their dream house, "Qui n'a pas fait des rêves?" Some fifteen years later, Roger Owen took the matter up much more thoroughly and discussed the numerous factors that enabled Japan to achieve rapid all-round development.[2] This chapter will follow in his footsteps, but will continue a little further, and point out some other features of the landscape.

A few scattered indicators taken at various times in the nineteenth century might have suggested that Egypt was, in fact, doing rather better than Japan. Take, for instance, the two countries' understanding of what was happening in Europe. In the eighteenth century, the Japanese had a much deeper interest in and clearer notion of European science and technology than did the Arabs (or Turks), but by the 1830s, thanks to Muhammad Ali's educational missions and the foreign schools established in Lebanon and Egypt, the position was reversed. Al-Tahtawi's *Takhlis al-Ibriz fi Talkhis Baris,* published in 1834, shows a firm grasp of French society and politics, and in particular of the 1830 Revolution. The Armenian Yusuf Hekekyan, who was put in charge of the Egyptian Engineering School in 1830, was, as his delightful and instructive papers show, as Anglicized as it was possible for a foreigner to be.[3] In contrast, in Japan "Fujita Toko, a prominent but poorly informed nationalist, concluded in 1826 on the basis of similarities in clothing styles that Holland had lost its independence to Russia and that Japan was now threatened by a monolithic Roman Catholic West."[4]

Or consider the following western judgment on Japan, exactly one hundred years ago, in 1881. "Wealthy we do not think it will ever become: the advantages conferred by Nature, with the exception of the climate, and the love of indolence and pleasure of the people themselves forbid it. The Japanese are a happy race, and being content with little are not likely to achieve much."[5]

Or this one: "The national banking system of Japan is but another example of the futility of trying to transfer Western growth to an Oriental habitat. In this part of the world principles, established and recognized in the West, appear to lose whatever virtue and vitality they originally possessed and tend fatally towards weediness and corruption."[6] And, according to Marius Jansen, around 1900 Kipling declared "the Japanese should have no concern with business. The Jap has no business savvy." This surely offsets the numerous disobliging remarks about the Arabs and Egyptians, of which here is one example by Lord Cromer:[7] "The mind of the Oriental, on the other hand, like his picturesque streets, is eminently wanting in symmetry. His reasoning is of the most slipshod description. Although the ancient Arabs acquired in a somewhat high degree the science of dialectics, their descendants are singularly deficient in the logical faculty. They are often incapable of drawing the most obvious conclusions from any simple premises of which they may admit the truth." Or even better, this gem: "The Oriental has a remarkable capacity for assimilating to himself the worst and rejecting the best parts of any European civilization with which he may be brought in contact."[8]

But why dwell on what the Egyptians and Japanese thought of Europe, or what Europe thought of them? For a social scientist, there are other, more objective, indicators of economic development. In 1913, Egypt's per capita gross domestic product was slightly higher than that of Japan, and its foreign trade (imports plus exports) per head of population was twice as high. In relation to both its inhabited area and population, Egypt's railway network was also far more extensive than that of Japan.[9] Surely all that means something.

It does, but other figures tell a different story, notably those on education, health, birth and death rates, industrial production, capital formation, and the development of various economic institutions. It was the latter that were to prove decisive. Before analyzing them more closely in trying to understand the nature of the "Japanese miracle," however, let us once more consider which of the prerequisites of modernization existed in Egypt in the nineteenth century.

There was, first, Egypt's extraordinary homogeneity. Egypt had no ethnic or linguistic minorities and only a small, and thoroughly assimilated, religious minority. Its population was almost totally sedentary and, in addition, very homogeneous in its social characteristics. The contrast between Egypt and other parts of the Middle East and North Africa in this respect is immense, but Egypt also compares very favorably with most countries in other parts of the world, including many in Europe.

Second, due in part to its compactness, its sedentariness, its river transport, its irrigation system, and its bureaucratic tradition, Egypt has for over 5,000 years been under centralized government control. This control broke down in the eighteenth century, but was swiftly reestablished by Muhammad Ali and has continued to increase to our day. Here again, one cannot overstress the contrast between Egypt and Syria, Iraq, and the Maghreb. Egypt is a governable country, and that is surely an indispensable condition of modernization.

Third, Egypt had a substantial agricultural surplus. In 1844, long before any rise had been registered in wheat yield, the latter was an estimated 1,000 kilograms per hectare. This figure was about equal to those for France and Germany, and well above those for northern, central, and eastern Europe.[10] It was perhaps twice as high as yields in other parts of the Arab world. Output per farm worker must also have been fairly high, since population was sparse and land abundant. Egypt's cultivated area was about 3,000,000 acres and the number of male farm workers may have been around 1,000,000, implying that each worker had an average of some 3 acres of land at his disposal. With the introduction of cotton, which led to perennial irrigation and double-cropping, both output per acre and output per man increased severalfold. Patrick O'Brien has studied this question in depth, and we can summarize his conclusions as follows: Between 1821 and the end of the century, farm output per acre rose nearly 12 1/2 times, and per head of rural population over 6 1/2 times.[11] This represents a very large surplus which, if it had been used, could have provided the capital required for quite rapid development.

Fourth, Egypt had an advantage that was almost unique in the Middle East and North Africa, though fairly common in more humid regions: excellent internal waterways. The Nile, with its branches and irrigation canals, penetrates every part of the inhabited area. Moreover, the prevailing winds are northerly, which means that boats can sail upstream and float downstream. Thus, it has always been possible cheaply to transport agricultural produce to the towns (Alexandria, Cairo, and others), and to export the surplus. Furthermore, Egypt was quick to modernize its transport. The port of Alexandria, connected to the Nile by the Mahmudiyya canal in 1819, was by far the best in the Middle East and North Africa and one of the two or three leading ports in the Mediterranean. Other good ports were soon built at Suez and Port Said. Egypt had a railway before Sweden or central Poland, and long before Japan. By the end of the nineteenth century its rail network, whether measured relative to inhabited area or population, was one of the densest in the world.

Fifth, thanks to its bureaucracy, its long-established fiscal traditions, and its numerous agricultural cadastres and surveys, repeated over the centuries, the Egyptian government was able to extract a large proportion of the agricultural surplus. In the eighteenth century, taxes were rather high on both agricultural and commercial incomes, and under Muhammad Ali they rose steeply. Indeed, Muhammad Ali's methods were very close to those of the Soviet government in the 1930s: they consisted of compulsory purchase of farm produce at low prices and resale to urban consumers or foreign exporters at much higher prices, the government pocketing the difference. Like the Soviets, Muhammad Ali used most of the funds thus obtained for armaments, but also like them he invested large amounts in transport, industry, education, and other economic activities. His example shows what could have been done in the field of development.

Finally, in 1800 Egypt was, by contemporary standards, a highly urbanized country. Cairo had over 200,000 inhabitants, a large figure for that time, and other towns of 5,000 inhabitants or more had a total population of about 150,000. In other words, some 10 percent of Egypt's population lived in towns.[12] This percentage was at least equal to that for France in 1800 and higher than that for other European countries with the exception of Great Britain and the Netherlands.[13] All students of modernization agree that a large urban base is an indispensable precondition of the process.

At this point, one may be tempted to ask the question freshmen students of economics sometimes put to their professor: "if you are so smart, why aren't you rich?" Why didn't Egypt become rich? One can best answer this by seeing why Japan did. Japan had five major advantages denied to Egypt as well as one minor one—somewhat more abundant and varied natural resources. The latter point can be dealt with briefly. In absolute terms,

36 • Cairo Mameluk monuments

Japan is poor in resources, and its man-land ratio was far higher than that of Egypt, but it had small reserves of coal, iron, and copper, on which it relied heavily for many decades. It has abundant water power, which it harnessed at an early stage, supplying electricity not only to the factories and railways but also to the village craftsmen. Some rivers were navigable, though improvement was often necessary. And its long shoreline offered great opportunities for coastal navigation, of which the Japanese have always taken full advantage. This enabled Japan to save on railways, which require such heavy capital investment; it was only at the very close of the nineteenth century that Japan's total railway mileage exceeded that of Egypt, with its far smaller inhabited area and population. As for the major factors, they were a favorable location that reduced the danger of foreign interference; a social cohesion unmatched in the world; far more developed human resources; an early orientation toward economic growth and a much greater sense of curiosity; and an extraordinarily wise leadership, which seems to have had an uncanny knack for taking the right economic measures. These topics are discussed in more detail below.

Whereas Egypt is at the very center of the world—at least the Old World, which is what has counted—Japan is at the very edge. This means that the aggressive imperialisms of the nineteenth century—British, French, and Russian—could reach Japan only at the end of a very long line of communications, where their impact was greatly attenuated. If Japan had been situated, like Egypt, at the junction of three continents, would it have been able to preserve its independence and shape its own destiny? Perhaps —after all Turkey succeeded (albeit just barely) in preserving its political independence, though certainly not its economic freedom of action, and 30 million tough Japanese would have given any imperialist pause. Even as it was, though, the Japanese had to accept the "Unequal Treaties" with the West. This meant that until the late 1890s Japanese customs duties could not be raised above a nominal 5 percent, and full autonomy was not achieved until 1911; moreover, until the late 1890s foreigners had the right to be judged in their own consular courts and not in the Japanese tribunals. But, being Japanese, they managed to carry out an amazing economic and social transformation even with that handicap. Egypt, on the other hand, had to wait until 1930 for the lapse of the Commercial Treaties which deprived it of tariff autonomy and until 1937 for the abolition of the Capitulations, which severely restricted its fiscal, administrative, and judicial freedom of action. Egypt experienced forty years of British occupation, a period that saw many real improvements but, on balance, gave an unhealthy twist to economic and social developments.

Another advantage of Japan's location should also be mentioned. Japan enjoyed three centuries of peace and, until it started its own form of rather profitable imperialism in the 1890s, its expenditure on armaments was low. In contrast, under both Muhammad Ali and Ismail, Egypt spent large amounts on defense, leaving that much less for development. Ottoman expenditure on armaments and war was immense.[14]

Some readers may feel that the external factor is sufficient to explain Japan's superior performance, Indeed, Galal Amin claims in his very interesting recent book *Al-Mashriq al-'Arabi wa al-Gharb* that foreign pressure fully explains the failure of both the Arab developmental initiative of the 1820s through 1840s, led by Muhammad Ali, and the one of the 1950s and 1960s, led by Gamal Abd al-Nasir. I do not agree. Indeed, in almost every respect except the technological, Japan had largely been modernized before it was "opened up" by the United States and Europe, in the 1850s and 1860s, and this, above all, explains its unique performance. In Bertrand Russell's apt phrase, Japan was an "economically but not culturally backward" country.[15]

First and foremost, Japan exhibited *cohesion*, to a degree unmatched in the world. Japan's ethnic, linguistic, and religious homogeneity is probably greater than that of any other country. The only threat posed to this homogeneity—the rapid spread of Christianity in the sixteenth century—was summarily and brutally dealt with by the Tokugawa government and, for good measure, Japan retreated into strict isolation for some 250 years, and had to be pried out by warships. But Japan had, and still has, more than homogeneity. Again to an unparalleled degree, it has social cohesion—what that amazing man Ibn Khaldun called *'asabiyya,* i.e. social solidarity. He saw, what so many Anglo-Saxon social scientists are still determined not to see, that *'asabiyya* is the foundation of a country's greatness and prosperity, and Japan would have struck him as a textbook example.

Asabiyya: Social solidarity is found only in groups related by blood ties or by other ties which fulfill the same functions. This is because blood ties have a force binding on most men, which makes them concerned with any injury inflicted on their next of kin. Men resent the oppression of their relatives, and the impulse to ward off any harm that may befall those relatives is natural and deep rooted in men.

If the degree of kinship between two persons helping each other is very close, it is obviously the blood tie, which, by its very evidence, leads to the required solidarity. If the degree of kinship is distant, the blood tie is somewhat weakened but in its place there exists a family feeling based on the widespread knowledge of kinship. Hence each will help the other for fear of the dishonour which would arise if he failed in his duties towards one who is known by all to be related to him.

The clients and allies of a great nobleman often stand in the same relationship towards him as his kinsmen. Patron and client are ready to help each other because of the feeling of indignation which arises when the rights of a neighbour, a kinsman, or a friend are violated. In fact, the ties of clientship are almost as powerful as those of blood.

This explains the saying of the Prophet Mohammad, "Learn your genealogies to know who are your near of kin", meaning that kinship only serves a function when blood ties lead to actual co-operation and mutual aid in danger—other degrees of kinship being insignificant. The fact is that such relationship is more of an emotional than an objective fact in that it acts only by bringing together the hearts and affections of men. If the kinship is evident it acts as a natural urge leading to solidarity; if it is based on the mere knowledge of descent from a common ancestor it is weakened and has little influence on the sentiments and hence little practical effect.

Ibn Khaldun, *An Arab Philosophy of History,* pp. 103-4.

It also struck another genius, Thorstein Veblen, who in 1915 wrote a most perceptive essay on "The Opportunity of Japan,"[16] placing its bid for world power a generation away—close enough, as it turned out. Japanese history is full of examples of self-sacrifice and devotion to duty proclaimed by this cohesion, from the *samurai* and *kamikaze* warriors to the Toyota and Sony workers. Cohesion also explains both the sense of obligation felt by firms toward their staff, which results in the so-called "life employment" system, and the consensus sought, at many levels, before decisions are taken. But there is one more thing to say on this subject. Not only was the nineteenth-century Japanese population cohesive and obedient, but the oligarchy that carried out the Meiji transformation in the 1870s and 1880s was very homogeneous, having a common geographic and social origin, similar ages and backgrounds, and similar values.[17]

Let us now turn to Japan's human resources. These may be studied under four headings: education, health, birth control, and the education and employment of women. In the eighteenth century and the first half of the nineteenth century Japan made enormous strides in educating its commoners, by founding thousands of schools throughout the land. By the 1850s "an estimated 40 percent of the male population and 10 percent of the female had achieved some degree of literacy." In the cities the figures were much higher, being put at 75 to 85 percent. At this point it is worth noting that, in contrast to many other countries, the nobility not only did not oppose, but seems to have encouraged the spread of education among commoners. One result was a very large publishing industry; in the 1780s some 3,000 titles were being published each year, editions of over 10,000 were not uncommon, books were cheap, and both free and commercial lending libraries were active.[18] These figures compare very favorably with Western Europe. With the Meiji Restoration and the beginning of rapid modernization, education surged forward. By 1907 over 97 percent of children of school age were attending primary school, and illiteracy had been to all intents and purposes wiped out.

One hardly needs to point out the contrast between this record and that of the Arab countries. In 1907, 93 percent of Egyptians were illiterate and, except in Lebanon and Syria, the situation in the other Arab countries was even worse. And even today, the Arab countries have not reached the degree of elementary schooling achieved by Japan eighty years ago. The rapid development of natural resources that took place in the Arab world has not been accompanied by a proportionate development of human resources. Egypt imported its middle class *en bloc,* in the form of

Europeans, Greeks, Syro-Lebanese, Jews, and Armenians. In North Africa the dichotomy was even sharper, since the French or Italians supplied not only the middle class but also the skilled working class. The oil countries of the Gulf are witnessing a similar process today. Only Lebanon and Syria experienced a development of human resources that matched their rather slow economic growth.

Japanese education was based on state schools, but it is worth noting that half the universities were private. Also worth noting is the heavy emphasis on practical and technical subjects.[19] In contrast, except under Muhammad Ali, Arab education has stressed the humanities and law.[20]

Health may be dealt with very briefly. In the nineteenth century, conditions of hygiene in Japan seem to have been distinctly superior to those prevailing in the Middle East or other developing regions, and the death rate was around 25 per 1,000, compared to over 40 in the Middle East and North Africa. This implies much less wastage, in both human and economic terms. By the 1920s Japan's death rate had fallen below 20—a figure not reached in the Arab world until the 1950s—and in the early 1950s the Japanese rate fell below 10, a figure typical of advanced countries.

The matter of birth rates is more interesting. For some 150 years Japan managed to keep its population constant at 30 million, partly because of the usual Malthusian checks of war, pestilence, and famine but also because of deliberate control by means of abortion and infanticide. In the second half of the nineteenth century birth rates seem to have risen slightly, but at their highest they were well below those in the Arab world, about 35-40 per 1,000 compared to, say, 45-50, and fell slowly to about 30 in the late 1930s. After World War II Japan's birth rate plunged more precipitously than that of any country on record and soon settled at the European level of 15, whereas Arab rates have remained at 40-50, producing an explosive population growth.

As regards the position of women, no one would claim that Japanese women were, or are, among the most emancipated. It is, however, a fact that at an early date the Japanese began to make good use of their womanpower—or, if one prefers, to exploit their women. "By the 1890s, women outnumbered men workers in the factories" and were employed, in substantial numbers, "as office workers, telephone operators, teachers and receptionists . . . Girls' primary school attendance rates began to equal boys'." Progress at the middle and higher school level came a decade or two later.[21]

It was not only social development that had long roots in Japan's history. The same was true of economic development. Two different aspects should be distinguished: Japan's early interest in and quick absorption of western science and technology; and the purely indigenous, spontaneous development of the Japanese economy in the seventeenth and eighteenth centuries.

As early as the sixteenth century, European visitors to Japan "usually reported lively curiosity about Western civilization on the part of the Japanese."[22] After foreigners had been excluded, a peephole on the outside world was provided by the small, isolated Dutch colony on the island of Deshima. Late in the seventeenth century some Japanese started learning Dutch and in the eighteenth century they began systematically to study Western technology, science, and painting; soon a small number of Japanese had become familiar with the Copernican and Newtonian theories, as well as with anatomical science, including the theory of the circulation of the blood. At the same time, some artists began to draw and paint in perspective. By 1811, a Japanese scholar was urging his countrymen to study all kinds of learning. "Foreign though they are, they can help Japan if Japanese study them and select their good points. It is thus quite proper to speak of Chinese learning, and even of Indian and Dutch learning, as Japanese learning."[23]

As the nineteenth century wore on, western learning was adopted wholesale, and at first very indiscriminately. Western textbooks were translated and used in schools, not always with good results, foreign advisers and teachers were imported in large numbers, and in the universities many subjects were taught in foreign languages. But in the 1880s a reaction set in, new textbooks were provided, Japanese teachers replaced foreigners, and Japanese became the language of instruction.[24] Meanwhile, the numerous Japanese who travelled abroad were as observant as their present-day descendants; for lack of Nikon cameras they brought with them sketch books, and sketched almost everything they saw. By contrast, this author does not know of a single reported case of a Middle Easterner drawing anything he saw in Europe or America in the nineteenth century.

Japanese economic development was not wholly dependent on the impetus provided by contact with foreigners. Even before the latter became important, the Japanese achieved great success in certain important fields. Take handicrafts: as anyone who has been to a museum knows, Japanese crafts were highly sophisticated, and they were widespread not only in the cities but in the countryside. Moreover, because of Japan's isolation, these crafts were exposed to the devastating competition of European machine-

37 • Japanese market

made goods far later than were those of the Middle East, India, or Latin America. They also survived much longer because of the peculiar pattern of Japanese development. The Japanese soon picked up European production methods but retained their traditional consumption habits until very recently, whereas the people of the Middle East soon learned to consume *alla franga* but are only just beginning to adopt western production methods. As a result, many Arab handicrafts soon lost their domestic markets, whereas their Japanese counterparts did not. But there is another point: to an unequalled degree, Japan made use of its handicrafts and village industries in its industrialization. Particularly in silk and cotton textiles, which for a long time accounted for the bulk of industrial employment and output, but also in many other areas, including machinery and equipment, a large part of the work was done by subcontracting to small workshops in villages or towns or even to peasant households.[25] One need hardly point out how beneficial was this type of industrialization in terms of employment, saving of capital, and conservation of skills. Unfortunately, there has been little like it in the Arab world.

Still more favorable for development was traditional Japanese agriculture. In view of Japan's very exiguous area and its large population, for centuries sustained efforts had been made to raise output per acre by using better methods, selecting seeds, experimenting with various types of organic fertilizers, introducing new cash crops, and so forth. One book on sericulture had a first printing of 3,000 copies, and many books on various agricultural subjects went through several editions. The spread of literacy through rural Japan, without which the technical literature on farming could not have flourished, is a fascinating story not yet fully known.[26] As a result, Japanese yields were among the very highest in the world and rose steadily; indeed, they were well above those prevailing in most developing countries today. When Japan began its modern development, after a few misguided efforts to introduce western agricultural machinery and farm practices it was found possible to increase output, steadily and appreciably, by continuing along the traditional lines and incorporating the findings of contemporary agricultural research.[27]

Tokugawa Japan was a highly urbanized country. By 1720 Tokyo had about 1,000,000 inhabitants (Peking and London being the only other cities of that size in the eighteenth century), Osaka and Kyoto had about 400,000 each, and some 12 percent of the total population lived in towns of over 10,000 inhabitants, a figure higher than that for all but three or four European countries.[28] Moreover, the nobility was forced to reside in the capital, which further increased urban purchasing power. As a result, a large proportion of the agricultural and handicraft produce of the villages had to move to the cities, in payment of rent and taxes. This greatly stimulated the commercialization of the economy and gave rise to a large class of merchants and financiers. Double entry bookkeeping, some of it on a very high level, was practiced and what was probably the world's first department store was established by the Mitsui family in Tokyo in 1683; the late Ivan Morris told me that their promotional devices included the distribution of free umbrellas. In finance there were "exceptionally highly developed" credit institutions and instruments including paper money, checks, and even "futures transactions in rice" in Osaka in 1730.[29]

Let us touch once more on the matter of attitudes. The *samurai* shared a military ethic which proved highly effective on the battlefield. But in a larger part of the Japanese population a different ethic prevailed, a work and profit ethic. The titles of some of the children's books used in schools are eloquent: in the towns, *Commercial Reader,* 1693; *Wholesaler's Reader,* 1772; *Navigation and Shipping Reader,* 1823; *Good Business for the Clothier,* 1825; in the villages, *Agricultural Reader,* 1762; *Farmer's Reader,* 1766; *Increased Profits for Farmers,* 1811; *Bumper Crops,* 1836.[30] No wonder, after all this, that (like parts of Europe and unlike the Middle East and North

Africa) Japan experienced overall economic growth, estimated at somewhat less than 1 percent a year between the early 1700s and 1860, despite a virtually constant population.[31]

We now come to our last topic: Japan's extraordinarily sound economic strategy when it did decide to modernize, in the 1870s. Three closely related aspects may be distinguished: sparing use of capital and local generation of investment funds; the optimum utilization of the factor mix; and the right sequence of processes and stages.

First of all, by the end of the 1880s Japan's investment rate was over 11 percent of GNP, and the ratio rose steadily to over 20 percent by 1920 and to 40 percent by 1960.[32] These figures are staggering and have no counterpart anywhere in the world except for the Soviet Union under Stalin. By contrast, in Egypt the rate in 1913 was distinctly under 10 percent and in the 1950s and 1960s averaged well under 15 percent. Except for the oil countries during or after the 1950s, the figures for the other Middle Eastern countries were no higher.[33] However, the matter does not end there. By the 1870s Egypt had accumulated a foreign debt of $500 million and by 1913 the figure had doubled. Japan began borrowing much later, but by 1913 it too had a foreign debt of $1 billion. But, first, its population was four times as large as that of Egypt and its economy was more developed; second, whereas the bulk of Egypt's public borrowings had been wasted, and a significant part of its private borrowings misinvested, the Japanese had used almost all their borrowings for highly productive purposes. Turkey and Iran were in much the same situation as Egypt. And, coming to the last few decades, in the non-oil-producing countries of the Middle East a large proportion of investment funds has come from foreign aid.[34]

As regards the factor mix, Japan has always been short of land and, until the last few years, capital was also scarce. Its one asset was good but cheap labor, and of that it made the fullest use. In agriculture, after the previously mentioned brief and unsuccessful experiments with American and European machinery and techniques, Japan reverted to its labor-intensive methods, using huge inputs of labor per acre but also taking the fullest advantage of the discoveries of western and indigenous agricultural research. The result was the highest output per acre in the world, even higher than Egypt's. As in Egypt, output per man remained low but total agricultural production rose rather quickly, and, because of the rise in population, millions of workers were released for employment in other sectors. For many decades agriculture was able to fulfill the role demanded of it: to feed the growing population and to provide the exports needed to earn the foreign exchange required for industrialization.

Industry also developed in a peculiar way. First, as noted earlier, great use was made of existing handicraft skills in the villages and small towns by means of an extensive system of subcontracting. Second, there was the predominance of small workshops equipped with electric and other motors but using labor-intensive methods and having a relatively low output per man. As late as 1934, shops with less than 5 workers accounted for 42 percent of factory output, and among factories those with 5-9 operatives represented 57 percent of the total.[35] Third, for a long time the emphasis was on industries that required little capital but employed many workers, chiefly textiles. To illustrate, at the turn of the century an up-to-date steel plant cost the relatively huge sum of $28-30 million, whereas a modern cotton spinning factory cost $250,000, and small silk filatures or cotton mills cost far less.[36] Hence the initial concentration on silk and cotton textiles, which were soon exported in large quantities; by 1913, half the cotton processed in Japan was being sold abroad, as yarn or cloth.[37] Until the last couple of decades, Japanese industries had lower capital, lower horsepower, and lower output per man than European, not to mention American, industries but that was precisely what the factor mix required.[38]

As regards sequence, Japan at first relied heavily on foreign trade, exporting silk and other raw materials to earn the badly needed foreign exchange. Until the turn of the century, foreign enterprise in Japan was discouraged and foreigners were not allowed to own land or mines. But foreign experts were employed, in large numbers, and Japanese went abroad to study. More important, foreign trade became, in Lockwood's apt phrase, "a Highway of Learning."[39] The Japanese imported textiles, copied them, and soon exported large quantities. They then imported machinery, and copied the machines. They realized the importance of shipping, built a fleet of 1,500,000 tons by 1913—a figure just being attained by a few Middle Eastern countries—and started building steamships. At the turn of the century they started encouraging high-technology foreign firms like General Electric, Armstrong-Vickers, Siemens, Ford, and others to come in and learned from them, but saw to it that foreigners did not control too large a sector of the economy. By the 1930s they had built up a large heavy industrial base, which was put to effective use in World War II.[40] After 1945 they resumed their educational process, this time concentrating on high technology products and giving up armaments at the very moment when the Arabs became fascinated with them and began to devote huge sums to defense. One cannot but contrast this assiduity and persistence with all the lost opportunities in the Middle East in the last 150 years.

Finally, a word about the role of the government in economic development. Government intervention included both overall direction and help in specific fields. A good early example of the former is the Matsukata deflation of 1881, which ended the inflation and monetary disorders that had followed the opening up of Japan and established the financial basis for the country's take-off.[41] Government accounted for some 30 percent of total investment in the period 1887-1936.[42] In addition to building railways, providing other overheads, and subsidizing important branches of activity, the government itself pioneered many industries, setting up model factories which it then turned over to private enterprise.[43] All this is not unusual; it has been practiced, at various times, in both Europe and the developing countries. What is unique, however, is the relation between state and business. Whereas in the United States this is thought of primarily in adversarial terms, resulting in that country's present situation of stalemate and drift, and whereas in most developing countries, including those in the Middle East, the state soon rushes and takes over the private sector, in Japan there exists that amazing symbiosis enviously referred to by its discomfited rivals as "Japan Inc." This brings us to our starting point, Japanese 'asabiyya.

Can one point to more general causes of Japan's success? I myself am inclined to attach much importance to the fact that Japan was perhaps the only country outside Europe to have had genuine feudalism, and that, as Marx saw so clearly, feudalism seems to be a very good preparation for capitalism. The only country approaching this in the Middle East is Lebanon, and perhaps it is no coincidence that Lebanon took to capitalism like a duck to water.

Another interesting observation has been made by Roy Mottahedeh on the contrast between the curiosity shown by Europeans and Japanese about foreign cultures (first Islam and then the Orient for Europe, first China and then the West for Japan) and the lack of curiosity on the part of the Arabs, Turks, and Chinese about European or other cultures. His explanation was that such a curiosity was the result of a combination of a sense of moral superiority and intellectual inferiority, while the Muslims and Chinese, in contrast, had not only a sense of moral superiority but also a mistaken one of intellectual superiority.

In any case, the Arabs missed the nineteenth century capitalist bus which the Japanese boarded so successfully. But there are other buses, and today the Arabs have opportunities that neither the Japanese nor anyone else could have imagined. One hopes that they will make good use of them and find their own roads to development. In doing so, they would be well advised to ponder the experience of Japan and to take some of its lessons to heart.

Notes

1. Charles Issawi, *Egypt at Mid-Century* (London, 1954), pp. 19-20.

2. E.R.J. Owen, *Cotton and the Egyptian Economy* (Oxford, 1969), pp. 356-64.

3. Ahmed Abdel-Rahim Mustafa, "The Hekekyan Papers," in P.M. Holt, ed., *Political and Social Change in Modern Egypt* (London, 1968), pp. 69-75.

4. C. E. Black *et al.*, *The Modernization of Japan and Russia* (New York, 1975), p. 27.

5. Quoted in G.C. Allen, *A Short Economic History of Modern Japan* (London, 1946), p. 2.

6. *Ibid.*

7. Earl of Cromer, *Modern Egypt,* vol. 2 (New York, 1908), pp. 146-47.

8. *Ibid.,* vol. 2, p. 239.

9. For figures see Charles Issawi, "Asymmetrical Development and Transport in Egypt, 1800-1914," in William Polk and Richard Chambers, eds., *Beginnings of Modernization in the Middle East* (Chicago, 1968).

10. Helen Rivlin, *The Agricultural Policy of Muhammad Ali* (Cambridge, Massachusetts, 1961), p. 262; Jerome Blum, *The End of the Old Order in Europe* (Princeton, 1978), pp. 144-45.

11. P. O'Brien, "The Long-Term Growth of Agricultural Production in Egypt: 1821-1962," in Holt, *op. cit.,* pp. 162-95.

12. For a recent and exhaustive study see Justin McCarthy, "Nineteenth Century Egyptian Population," in Elie Kedourie, ed., *The Middle Eastern Economy* (London, 1976), pp. 1-39.

13. For a discussion see Charles Issawi, "Economic Change and Urbanization in the Middle East," in Ira Lapidus, ed., *Middle Eastern Cities* (Berkeley and Los Angeles, 1969), pp. 102-19, reprinted in *idem, The Arab Legacy* (Princeton, 1981).

14. See figures in Charles Issawi, *The Economic History of Turkey, 1800-1914* (Chicago, 1980), pp. 3-4, 324.

15. Quoted by Herbert Passin, *Society and Education in Japan* (New York, 1965), p. 6.

16. Thorstein Veblen, *Essays in Our Changing Order* (New York, 1943).

17. Black *et al., op. cit.,* p. 149.

18. *Ibid.,* pp. 106-9; Passin, *op. cit.,* pp. 11-61; Nan (Ivan) Morris, *The Life of an Amorous Woman* (London, 1964), pp. 26-27.

19. Black, *op. cit.* pp. 219-20, 239.

20. For a breakdown of Egyptian educational missions, see Charles Issawi, *Egypt at Mid-Century* (London, 1954), p. 51.

21. Passin, *op. cit.* p. 97.

22. Black, *op. cit.,* p. 34.

23. Donald Keene, *The Japanese Discovery of Europe, 1720-1830* (Stanford, California, 1969), p. 159 and *passim.*

24. Passin, *op. cit.,* pp. 69-95.

25. William Lockwood, *The Economic Development of Japan* (Princeton, 1954), pp. 480-90.

26. Thomas C. Smith, "Okura Nagatsune and the Technologists," in A.M. Craig and D.H. Shively, eds., *Personality in Japanese History* (Berkeley, 1970).

27. Thomas C. Smith, *Agrarian Origins of Modern Japan* (Stanford, California, 1959); James I. Nakamura, *Agricultural Production and the Economic Development of Japan* (Princeton, 1966).

28. Black, *op. cit.,* pp. 82-85.

29. M. Miyamoto *et al.,* "Economic Development in Pre-historical Japan," *Journal of Economic History,* December 1965; E. S. Crawcour, "Changes in Japanese Commerce in the Tokugawa Period," in John Hall and Marius Jansen, eds., *Studies in the Institutional History of Early Modern Japan* (Princeton, 1968), pp. 198-202; *idem,* "The Tokugawa Heritage," in William Lockwood, ed., *The State and Economic Enterprise in Japan* (Princeton, 1965), pp. 17-44.

30. Passin, *op. cit.,* p. 32.

31. Black, *op. cit.,* p. 60.

32. K. Ohkawa and H. Rosovsky, "A Century of Japanese Economic Growth," in Lockwood, *The State,* p. 90.

33. Charles Issawi, *Economic History of the Middle East and North Africa* (New York, 1982), Chapter IX.

34. *Ibid.*

35. Lockwood, *Economic Development,* pp. 2-178, 202.

36. *Ibid.,* p. 33.

37. *Ibid.,* p. 31.

38. See figures for 1934 in *ibid.,* p. 178-81.

39. *Ibid.,* pp. 320-34.

40. "Japan thus entered the war with an aircraft industry 50 percent equipped with foreign-built tools, and staffed with technicians trained in American plants and engineering schools," *ibid.,* p. 331.

41. Ohkawa and Rosovsky, *op. cit.,* pp. 65-66.

42. David Landes, "Japan and Europe: Contrasts in Industrialization," in Lockwood, *The State,* p. 100.

43. *Ibid.,* also Lockwood, *Economic Development,* p. 326.

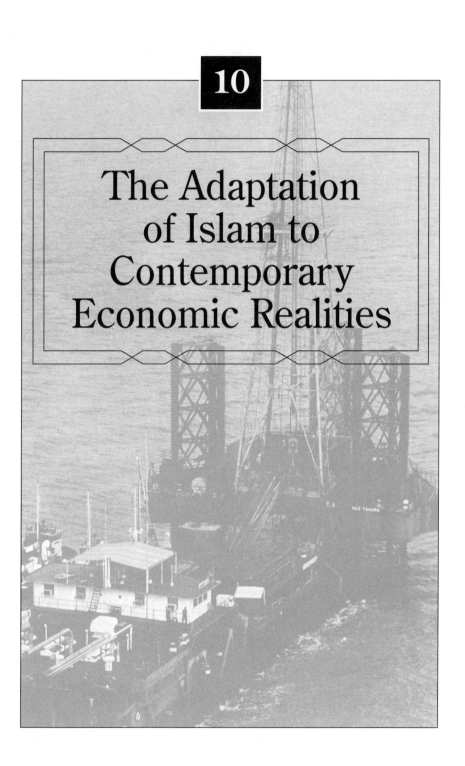

10

The Adaptation of Islam to Contemporary Economic Realities

his chapter will address four broad questions. First, what are the causes of the present discontent, or why were the Middle Easterners and North Africans dissatisfied with the economic evolution which their countries experienced in the nineteenth and early twentieth centuries under Western rule? What were the factors that enabled them to do something about their discontents in the 1960s and 1970s? What was the stock of Muslim economic and social ideas, ideals, and practices on which they could draw when reshaping their societies? And finally, what institutional changes have they actually carried out?

Discontents

To a detached outsider who compares the present state of the Middle East and North Africa with what it was in 1800, or even 1914, the progress achieved is overwhelming. Where camel caravans moved at under three miles an hour, trains, cars, and planes now speed passengers and goods to their destinations. Great harbors and airports have been built. An impressive and ever widening array of factories has been established. And the region has become the center of the world's oil industry and the largest depository of liquid funds in the international money market.

Nor is the progress purely economic. In 1914 only Turkey enjoyed independence; today all the countries of the region do. In 1914 about five to ten percent of children of primary school age attended school; today the figure is more than 70 percent; similarly, literacy has risen from 5 percent to nearly 50. Life expectancy has risen from under thirty years to fifty-five or sixty. Levels of living have distinctly improved. For the first time in several centuries, Middle Easterners are making a significant contribution to world science, literature, and art.

Middle Easterners, however, dwell much more on their misfortunes than on their blessings. Two features of the process of development that took place in the last 150 to 200 years have caused it to appear flawed in their eyes. First, a disproportionate share of the fruits of progress has accrued to foreigners and members of minority groups. Secondly, the social bonds that held the Middle Eastern society together were loosened or snapped. Regarding the fruits, Europeans (French, British, Belgians, Italians and others) and members of minority groups (Armenians, Greeks, Jews and Arab Christians) controlled practically all the urban activities: banking, insurance, foreign trade, industry, transport, etc. In North Africa and Palestine they also owned a large amount of land. Until the 1920s in Turkey, Iran, and Egypt and until the 1950s in North Africa, Muslims felt excluded from modern economic activities and could not but regard capitalism as an alien and exploitative process. By the time a small Muslim bourgeoisie had come into being it was too late; shortly after its foreign or minority counterparts, it was swept away by radical upheavals.

Regarding social bonds, traditional Muslim society, with all its shortcomings, was a tightly knit fabric. Tribal and communal ties of kinship and ownership held together the rural and nomadic populations, who made up more than 80 percent of the total. Guilds and religious fraternities performed the same function for urban craftsmen and merchants, and kinship and neighborhood ties were also strong in the towns. Finally, traditional Muslim ideology, expounded by the Ulema, the learned, religious leaders, was accepted by all and cemented the whole society.

The absorption of the region in the world capitalist market broke or loosened all these bonds. Private property in land soon resulted in social differentiation in the villages and, conjoined with the rapid population growth due to better hygiene, resulted in a large and increasing landless proletariat. The crafts were gradually eliminated by the competition of foreign goods but until very recently little modern industry rose to replace them; this too meant a growing urban proletariat. As already mentioned, the bourgeoisie was overwhelmingly of foreign origin or from minority groups. With the increasing secularization of society the Ulema were replaced by a new, Western-trained intelligentsia of lawyers, journalists, and teachers who, like their Western counterparts, were critical of traditional society and sought radical solutions. The outcome has been the revolutions of the 1950s to 1970s, most of which were led by the army.

FACTORS THAT MADE CHANGE POSSIBLE

Decolonization

European (mainly British and French) imperialism in the Middle East and North Africa reached its apogee just before the First World War with the occupation of Morocco by France and Spain and Libya by Italy, and the partition of Iran between Britain and Russia.

In the previous hundred years, the French had occupied the rest of North Africa, the British had established their rule over Egypt, the Sudan, and large parts of the Arabian Peninsula, and the Russians had conquered Central Asia and Transcaucasia.

Following the First World War, there was a further extension of foreign rule: Britain received League of Nations mandates over Iraq and Palestine and France over Syria and Lebanon. Other potential rivals—notably Russia and Germany—had been eliminated, while British hegemony in the Middle East, and French in North Africa, seemed assured; in fact their position had weakened. Turkey, Iran, Saudi Arabia, and Yemen had become fully independent, and in the interwar period large concessions had to be made to rising nationalism in Egypt and Iraq.

The Second World War completely undermined the Western position in the Middle East and North Africa; by the 1960s all the countries of the region had achieved independence. This process was greatly helped by the United States and Soviet Union, both of whom were anxious, but for different reasons, to eliminate British and French political and economic hegemony in the region. Concurrently, or a little later, the peoples of the region were able to take advantage of the Cold War to eliminate the United States position of strength in, for instance, Iraq, Syria, and Libya and Soviet positions in Egypt. This freedom of movement enabled them to effect sweeping changes in their economy; in particular, they were able to take over practically all foreign investments and businesses in the region.

Accompanying these political changes was an important socio-economic shift: an exodus of some 2,000,000 European settlers from Algeria, Tunisia, Morocco, Libya, and Egypt. A similar exodus took place among the minority groups in these and other countries such as Iraq, Yemen, and Syria.

Oil

Exportation of oil started just before the First World War, but the industry began to yield large revenues to the governments of the region only in the late 1930s. By 1960, the Middle East and North Africa were receiving some $1.5 billion a year in oil revenues and by 1970 $5.5 billion. The oil price revolution of 1973, and the subsequent sharp rises in price, multiplied the revenues many times over. In 1979 the region received the unbelievable

38 • Offshore oil well

sum of $163 billion, and in 1980 the figure was more than $220 billion.

But it was not only a question of revenues. In the course of the 1970s, the governments of the oil-producing countries took over control of the industry. Now, it is they who determine how much shall be produced, not the companies. It is they, at OPEC meetings, who set the price. And, when the occasion arises, it is the governments who specify the countries to which oil will be sold and which will be denied, e.g., in 1973 the United States and the Netherlands.

And the oil revenues have, in turn, created another form of power. OPEC, and in particular its Arab component, was for years almost the only segment in the world economy that enjoyed a large surplus in its foreign trade and balance of payments. The funds that have thus accrued to the Middle Eastern countries have been invested in various international money markets-New York, London, Frankfurt, Zurich, and Paris—and the wishes of their owners have to be taken into account. The foreign exchange reserves of the Saudi Arabian government were, for many years, greater than those of any government in the world, and some of the other Middle

Eastern governments also have huge reserves. In 1980, Saudi Arabia's foreign exchange holdings were officially, and probably conservatively, put at $110 billion. Recently, its financial quota in the International Monetary Fund has been greatly increased and with it its voting rights. All of this naturally generated power, which was used for purposes deemed desirable by the society.

TRADITIONAL IDEALS, IDEAS, AND PRACTICES

Islam, like Christianity or any other great religion, is a vast and complex entity containing many divergent, and sometimes even incompatible, elements.

Dominant themes which have formed the minds and policies of the Muslim Middle East are (1) property; (2) community and state; (3) equality; and (4) the charging of interest, which takes us to the center of economic theory and ideology.[2]

Property

Here we encounter a strange paradox. On the one hand, Islam lays great stress on the right to property. Indeed the notion of the property contract is so central to Islamic law that many other social relations are assimilated to it. Thus in Islam marriage is a civil contract, an essential part of which is the payment by the bridegroom of a stipulated sum of money to the bride's family. Again, much of the medieval Islamic discussion of birth control centers on the notion of property rights; some schools of jurisprudence insisted that if a man wanted to practice certain forms of birth control he had to pay his wife a monetary compensation.

Yet at the same time there is no doubt that, in the Islamic Middle East, ownership of property was a far more precarious matter than in Christian Europe. From the early caliphate on, the history of the Middle East is replete with accounts of the confiscation of the property of merchants, officials, and others. The property basis of Middle Eastern "feudalism" was also much weaker than that of European: Landed estates (or more strictly rents or taxes levied on them) were usually grants made by the monarch in return for military or other services and, in principle, lapsed at the death of the grantee. In practice some were inherited, but estates seldom remained in the same family for many generations. And Middle Eastern "feudalists" usually lived in cities, not on their estates, further weakening the tie between them and their property.

It is not too far-fetched to say that the property basis of the Middle Eastern family structure was weaker than that of the European. This is not to ignore the fact that family feeling and solidarity is very strong indeed in the Middle East. But, with few exceptions, Muslim families do not show the durability and continuity of European families. We do not see the phenomenon described by Schumpeter: "The bourgeoisie worked primarily to invest and it was not so much a standard of consumption as a standard of accumulation that the bourgeoisie struggled for and tried to defend against governments that took the short run view."[3]

Many reasons may be suggested for this difference in family structure. One is the general fluidity of society and the less marked lines of social stratification to be discussed later. Another is polygamy, accompanied by the absence of discrimination between children of wives and those of slaves. Another may be the retention of property rights by Muslim women after marriage, in contrast to European women until quite recently. Still another is inheritance laws: unlike Europe, Islam did not practice primogeniture; all children inherit, females receiving half the share of males, though in practice women were sometimes excluded; moreover, parents could not disinherit their children and could will only a small part of their estate. While this may be socially more desirable, it does not promote capital accumulation or strengthen a business-minded bourgeoisie.

The Middle East thus does not have the equivalent of a strong bourgeoisie, secure in its property rights, which could generate the equivalent of European capitalism. Perhaps the most striking example is the different history of the Hansa merchants in northern Europe and the Karimi merchants in the Indian Ocean area. The commerce of the Karimis extended from China to North Africa and, considering the high price of the spices and other articles in which they traded, their turnover may have been equal to or greater than that of the Hansa. Yet whereas the Hansa dominated the politics of northern Europe for several centuries, the Karimis seem to have had very little power against the Muslim states and the fact that they vanished, leaving no records and only scattered references in contemporary histories, perhaps best illustrates their weaknesses.[4]

Muslims have, then, in principle a deep respect for property but in practice a strong tradition of insecurity and expropriation. This tradition surfaced again in the 1950s.

Community and State

From the very beginning Islam has had a very strong sense of community. It has sought to provide for the needs of its poorer members through the *zakat,* or charity tax, imposed on all forms of wealth. This principle remains very strong and the duty of the community to provide for the needy is taken for granted. It is used to justify some of the nationalizations and sequestrations carried out in various Arab countries and Iran.

> Take care of the poor, the windows and the orphans; pay them special pensions from your Treasury . . . do the same to the blind and to those who can recite the Koran. . . . And, provided this does not overburden the Treasury, build hospitals for sick Muslims, with a staff of physicians and attendants who will cure them and minister to their needs. . . .
>
> Ibn Khaldun, *An Arab Philosophy of History*, p. 89.

Another important aspect is the relation between wealth and power. At the risk of oversimplification, one can say that in the West, during the modern capitalist period, wealth generated power. But in the Middle East the opposite has been true. The great fourteenth century Arab historian and social scientist, Ibn Khaldun, pointed out that rank and prestige made it possible to accumulate wealth.[5] A contemporary Turkish sociologist, Serif Mardin, develops the idea as follows:

> Imagine a society where the central value, the most effective—and more avidly sought after—social lever, is political power—a system where political power affects economics not only directly through the government's control of the market mechanism but where a very large proportion of the arable land is controlled by the state. Imagine a society where status is the primary determinant of income rather than the reverse, as has been the case in Western "capitalistic" society; where "prebendal" rewards are one of the main sources of wealth, but every type of wealth is legitimate only if the state recognizes it to be so. This is a society where the social mechanisms for the perpetuation of private property, such as corporate personality, are

extremely limited, where law is not an adjunct of market transactions but has grown primarily from criminal law, where officials receive extraordinarily generous salaries although their
life earnings are confiscated at their death.[6]

The incomes of those who entirely lack prestige, on the other hand,
will be determined solely by the amount of their capital and the efforts
they put forth. This is the position of most traders, and that is why those
traders who enjoy prestige are more opulent than others.

The same can be observed in many jurists and theologians. Once
their fame has spread, the masses come to believe that helping them is
an act agreeable to God; hence they help them in their worldly affairs
and interests, so that these theologians soon become rich without having acquired any wealth other than the value of the services rendered to
them by their followers. We have seen many such, in towns, villages or
countryside, sitting still in their houses and accumulating a large fortune, while others plough and trade for them.

An Arab Philosophy of History, p. 86.

The social structure of the Middle East state, from the late Middle
Ages on—that is, in the Mamluk and Ottoman periods—had some important economic consequences. Until about the twelfth century, the Middle
Eastern governments were predominantly civilian and did not seek to inter-
fere in the economy but let traders and craftsmen pursue their occupations.
As a result, the economy flourished. But after that, to the accompaniment
of numerous disasters, such as the Crusader and Mongol invasions and the
Black Death, power passed on to the military who relied on the bureaucracy. The result was an economic policy that ignored the interests of the producers—craftsmen, farmers, traders—and concentrated on raising taxes
and seeing to it that cities were supplied with food and other provisions
(since the urban mob would otherwise be troublesome) even if the long-
term interests of the producers suffered. This meant heavy taxation, confiscation, forced deliveries, and the overregulation of producers.

Thus, once more, we do not have in the Middle East the counterpart of
the European bourgeoisie, which, by the late Middle Ages, was in a position
to make its voice heard and its interests safeguarded not only in the city-
states of Italy and the Netherlands but also in the national monarchies of

England and France.[7] In the Middle East the functions of a middle class were for long performed by foreigners and members of minorities; the bourgeoisie was therefore regarded as alien and exploitative, and was easily crushed—together with its Muslim elements—by the military regimes in the 1950s and '60s.

Equality

This subject can be dealt with very briefly. Ideologically, Islam is a highly egalitarian religion. It does, of course, contain some basic discriminations and inequalities between Muslims and unbelievers, between freemen and slaves, between men and women. Within the community of free Muslim males, distinctions were light and blurred. There were no castes as in India, no social estates as in Europe, no consecrated priesthood as in Christianity, no hereditary nobility as in most parts of the world. At most, one can say that the Ashraf (descendants of the prophet Mohammad) enjoyed a certain dignity and prestige.

Moreover, Muslim society was very fluid. As anyone reading the Arabian Nights soon finds out, a porter or fisherman can, by a stroke of fortune or through the whim of the ruler, be elevated to the highest degree of honor and wealth. By the same token yesterday's all-powerful vizier or opulent merchant can equally rapidly be stripped of his position and cast in jail. And history records, down to the nineteenth century, many examples of social mobility which are at least as fantastic as those of the *Arabian Nights.* For example, the Persian reforming prime minister Mirza Taqi Khan, 1848-51, known as Amir-i Kabir, was the son of a cook; his downfall and murder were even swifter than his rise.[8]

The egalitarian ideal was not translated into social practice. Little was done to help the poor, and the contrasts in wealth and power remained very large. Moreover, many jurists justified inequality as socially beneficial. Of course in this respect Middle Eastern society was no worse than others. But the yearning for equality remained strong and was to find expression in the 1950s.

The Charging of Interest

The Islamic attitude toward the charging of interest sprang from the same roots as, and was almost identical with, the early Christian scholastic attitude.

Like the Scholastics, Muslim theologians and jurists started from the

Judeo-Christian and Aristotelian idea that usury was wicked. Unlike sheep or trees, money does not breed, and therefore the charging of interest for a loan is wrong. There has been much discussion as to whether the Arabic word *riba* designated every kind of interest or only usurious interest, but the evidence points to the former, broader, interpretation.

However, interest has been a fact of life for thousands of years, and every society has had to accommodate itself to it. For example, Hammurabi's code (paragraph 88) sets a rate of 20 percent for loans of grain or silver money.[9] In Europe, a partial and temporary way out was to leave moneylending to the Jews. But Christians also wanted to participate and did engage in moneylending, which was highly profitable, and the growing volume of commercial and financial transactions necessitated the development of some form of banking and money market.

Hence, by the fifteenth and sixteenth centuries, we find an important distinction being made between money and money capital. Coins may be sterile, but money capital can be used to expand production and earn profits. Therefore, it was only fair that the lender should be compensated for the profit he could have made on the capital: what a modern economist would call the opportunity cost of the capital.[10]

Something very similar happened in Islam. In principle, moneylending was left to Christians and Jews, but the historical evidence is clear that at all times many Muslims also engaged in it.[11] Moreover, by the early Middle Ages Islamic trade had reached very large proportions, stretching from China to West Africa and covering a great variety of objects.

All this necessitated development of credit: to finance the circulation of goods, to provide means of payment across vast areas by means of bills, letters of credit, and checks, and to supply capital for setting up or expanding business firms. As Avram Udovitch has shown, this was accomplished by various forms of partnership. If A sells B goods on credit, A is entitled to charge a higher price, that is, to make a profit. Or if A invests money in a partnership with B under which B carries out various transactions, A is entitled to part of the profit.[12]

These examples bring out one very important point. A is entitled to a profit—or what we would in some cases prefer to call interest—because he is sharing in the risk incurred by B. Risk-taking is entitled to a reward. We shall now see the use to which this concept is being put in modern times.

PRESENT-DAY INSTITUTIONAL CHANGES

Two main types of change may be distinguished: what we may call the statist and the private property approach.

Over the greater part of the Middle East and North Africa the state has, since around 1960, taken over the bulk of economic activity: banking, insurance, land and sea transport, communications, and large scale manufacturing and mining. Banking and insurance—the greater part of which had been in foreign hands—have been nationalized and are now run by the state. Most railways had either been built by the state (as in Egypt, the Sudan, Iraq, Iran, and Saudi Arabia) or had been taken over in the interwar period; the remaining ones were nationalized after the Second World War. So was maritime navigation and river shipping. Telephones, telegraphs, and radio and television broadcasting have always been government activities.

In the Middle East and North Africa manufacturing and mining were usually started by foreigners, with some help from minority groups. In Turkey and Iran a substantial public sector was developed in the 1930s, accounting for nearly half of total output and employment. But in the 1950s and '60s practically all large scale factories and mines were nationalized in Egypt, Iraq, Syria, Algeria, South Yemen, Libya and, very recently, also in Iran.

The government also exercises control over foreign trade and has many instruments with which to direct agriculture, e.g. price setting, compulsory deliveries, credit allocation, sale of fertilizers and machinery, etc. Internal trade is also closely regulated by the government.

One can, therefore, say that by now only Israel, Lebanon, Turkey, Kuwait, Tunisia, Saudi Arabia, and Jordan have a large private sector. And even in them, particularly in the oil countries where the state has huge revenues, the public sector is growing rapidly.

The roots of this shift are three-fold: socialism, nationalism, and the Islamic or Middle Eastern tradition.

Socialism

In the Middle East and North Africa, as almost everywhere in the world, socialism has had a great appeal to large sections of the population, for reasons good and bad. It is enough to say that while "socialism" continues to be a term of praise, "capitalism" has become a dirty word over most of the region and that "Arab socialism," whatever that may mean, is in vogue. Of course, most Marxists deny that Algeria or Egypt or Iraq are socialist at all and call them "state capitalist" regimes, whatever that may mean.

Nationalism

Nationalism is even more powerful and elemental. In the course of the nineteenth and early twentieth centuries, the greater part of the "modern" sector—foreign trade, finance, mechanical transport, industry, etc.—belonged to foreigners or members of minority groups. Resentment against such people built up and when the opportunity came, their property was nationalized or sequestrated. The impetus thus generated continued, and the property of the fledgling Muslim bourgeoisie was soon taken over too.

Islamic or Middle Eastern Tradition

The claims of the Muslim community on the individual are very great indeed, and the Middle East has no equivalent of the Western tradition of individual rights, protected by an array of legal and political institutions, against the encroachment of the state.

Similarly, there is the old Islamic notion of equity and egalitarianism, which stresses the claim of the poor on society, and condemns the ostentation of the rich. But in the Middle East and North Africa in the last hundred years or so there has been a great amount of conspicuous consumption by the rich, and since, to make matters worse, ostentation took a Western form, including alcohol and the mixing of the sexes, the wrath of devout Muslims against the rich has been very great indeed. Recent events in Iran provide a striking example, but similar attitudes prevail among the Muslim Brotherhood in Syria, Egypt, and elsewhere, and new, even more fundamentalist, groups are springing up in Egypt, the Sudan, Algeria, and other countries, for example, the Mujahidin in Iran and the Takfir wa Hijra group in Egypt. But even among more moderate Muslims "there is a desire for reversion to a simpler morality and to what is conceived to be traditional Islamic conduct."[13] The economic views of all these groups are usually very radical.

The old tradition of the Middle Eastern military and bureaucracy has also helped. As in the past, soldiers and bureaucrats run the state, and pay little attention to the needs of producers. The result has been a cumbrous and over-regulated economy. Middle Easterners are fully aware of the arbitrariness, inefficiency and corruption of their bureaucracy. But, as in

Western Europe and the United States, nothing seems able to stop its inexorable growth. "In the Shah's Iran, merchants saw in Islam protection for traditional business and the rights of private property against a predatory government and the modern industrial sector," which they opposed with the more zest because it was secular and Western oriented.[14] But, as usual, revolution proved no remedy in this respect. However, even the most inefficient engine will sputter along, if injected with a sufficient amount of fuel. Thanks to massive infusions of oil money and foreign aid, the economy has kept going and has even succeeded in ameliorating the condition of at least the urban masses. This kind of socialism is probably there to stay for quite a long time.

The Private Property Approach

Opposition to Arab socialism—which has a secular as well as a Muslim face—sprang from two main sources: the governments of the oil rich Arabian countries, notably Saudi Arabia; and the Muslim Brotherhood and similar groups. A formulation of their ideals was provided in 1977 by a professor at Kuwait University:

1. Complete respect for private ownership.
2. Elimination of wealth centralization and accumulation and emphasis on medium-sized economic units in order to avoid painful roles of capital.
3. Islamic legislations to protect capital of individuals and wealth of nations.
4. Special care for poor and needy social classes.
5. Complete harmony between labor and capital to provide optimal solutions leading to peace on earth for all mankind.
6. An economic policy based on Islamic devices.[15]

Putting the matter in more general terms, Islamic economics has the following characteristics:

First, there is an urge to redistribute wealth. Quite a bit has been accomplished in this direction since the early 1950s: the expropriation of foreign wealth in Egypt, Algeria, and elsewhere, including oil; land reform in Egypt, Syria, Iraq, Iran and Algeria; the sequestration and confiscation of large firms and of shares and bonds in almost every branch of business; and in some countries, notably Iran and Libya, the handing over of private dwellings to homeless people. But, as reformers since the time of Solon and the Gracchi have found out, inequality is a very stubborn animal to deal with. Somehow or other, a new class always seems to emerge; some people somehow manage to live well. And, if nothing else, population growth on the order of 3 percent a year is enough to ensure that a large number of young, restless, and destitute people are thrown on the market each year. Hence, the call for equality is bound to become increasingly strident.

Second, there is the call for industrialization. In this there is nothing peculiarly Muslim. All over the developing world, industrialization is seen as the panacea that will cure all of society's economic, social, and political ills. Indeed, in the long run, industry offers the best hope for these countries. But two remarks are in order. First, in their zeal for industry, Middle Easterners—again in large if not good company—have overlooked the equally urgent need for agricultural development. As a result, agriculture has in many countries failed even to help keep pace with population growth, much less with the rapidly rising demand for food caused by growing incomes. Hence, the Middle East and North Africa—which until the Second World War and even after was a net exporter of cereals—has become the largest importer, per capita, in the world. In 1978 imports of grain amounted to nearly 23 million tons, costing over $4.2 billion; by now only Turkey is a significant exporter.

The second remark is a repetition of the good Arabic saying: "Praise be to God who changes [things] but who [himself] does not change." Until very recently, anyone who hinted that the industrialization policies were ill considered and were being carried out at the expense of agriculture and the food supply was classified as a reactionary and arch-imperialist, in the tradition of Lords Cromer and Curzon. But now it is the radicals who continue, with increasing virulence, bringing these accusations against westernized rulers as they did against the Shah and Sadat.

The third characteristic of Islamic economics is a certain wariness of and hostility to private consumption and individualism. It is not that Islam is inherently averse to consumption and enjoyment. The Quran (Rodwell's translation) says: "O children of Adam! Wear your goodly apparel when ye repair to any mosque and eat ye and drink; but exceed not, for He loveth not those who exceed. Say: who hath prohibited God's goodly raiment, and the healthful viands which He hath provided for his servants?" (S. 7:29) and again, in verse 160 of the same Surah, "Eat of the good things with which we have supplied you."

Indeed Muslims have often criticized Christianity as an otherworldly, ascetic religion, "too heavenly minded to be any earthly good," and contrasted it unfavorably with their own. But a zealous Muslim today would argue that, given all the unfulfilled needs in the world in general and in the Muslim community in particular, and given the scarcity of resources, luxury consumption should be strictly limited. Similarly there is a wariness of men's greed and acquisitiveness and the feeling that individualism should be kept on a tight rein, if necessary by curtailing what are regarded in the West as essential liberties. It is in these respects that contemporary Islam is most critical of the West in general, and the United States in particular, regarding them as indulging and pampering individual desires well beyond the permissible limits, and at the same time stimulating desires with an endless barrage of advertising.

But hostility to the West does not necessarily mean receptivity to the East, though Marxism does exert a certain appeal because of its emphasis on equality and community. For if the basic Islamic category is not the individual, neither is it the class but, to repeat, the community. The whole concept of class struggle is regarded as a mischievous misdirection of attention and energy. Equality and justice must be sought and achieved by, for, and within the Islamic community, whether defined as roughly corresponding with some of the present states or including the whole Muslim world.

After all these generalities, it may be desirable to give a few concrete examples of how Islamic principles are being applied in some countries, notably the oil-rich states of Arabia. Two fields may be singled out—fiscal policy and banking.

In fiscal matters, vast state revenues have been channelled to the private sector in the form of subsidies of foodstuffs and essential goods, a large array of social services, generous advances for houses and setting up businesses, and in Kuwait the purchase by the government of real estate from individuals at very high prices and its resale or leasing to them together with funds to erect a house or other building.

Thus we have a unique phenomenon in history. In the past, all over the world, the chief concern of the state was to transfer resources from the private sector to the public. Here we have the public sector transferring resources to the private.

Another form of transfer may be briefly noted: from the oil-rich countries to poorer areas. Here the record is quite impressive. In 1980 net Arab OPEC aid totalled $6.8 billion, or 2 percent of the combined GNP of the Arab oil states. The main disbursing agencies are the Islamic Development Bank, with headquarters in Saudi Arabia, which finances trade; the OPEC

39 • Offshore drilling

fund, which lends for balance of payments purposes; and the various national funds (Kuwait Fund, Saudi Arabian Fund, Abu Dhabi Fund) which lend for infrastructure development.[16]

The aid has been disbursed in concentric circles. Proportionally, by far the greater part has been given to the poorer Arab countries: Syria, Jordan, Sudan, Egypt, Tunisia, Morocco, Somalia, Yemen, etc. The next circle consists of non-Arab Muslim countries, notably Pakistan, Turkey and some African states. Finally, a small amount has been extended outside the Muslim community, for example to India. Large amounts have also been given, or loaned, to various international organizations, such as the World Bank, International Monetary Fund, and United Nations agencies.

As regards banking, one should distinguish sharply between the rapid growth of what one might call "ordinary," or Western-type, banks belonging to Muslim states and strictly Islamic banks. Until the First World War, all the banks operating in the Middle East and North Africa were either branches of foreign banks—like Barclay's and Crédit Lyonnais—or foreign owned and managed, like the Ottoman Bank and the National Bank of Egypt. In the 1920s and '30s a few banks, owned and staffed by nationals and using the national language, were established, like Bank Misr in Egypt, Ish Bank in Turkey, Bank Melli in Iran, and the Arab Bank in Palestine. In the 1960s, with the sharp increase in oil money, there was a large expansion of banking, especially in the Gulf. New banks were founded, such as the National Bank of Kuwait, the National Commercial Bank of Libya, the Qatar National Bank, the Bank of Oman, and the National Bank of Dubai. Many of these and other banks began to participate actively in world finance, and Beirut and Kuwait emerged as major financial centers.

The explosion of oil revenues in 1973, and again in 1980, greatly accelerated the development of banking. International banking markets evolved in Kuwait, Bahrain and the United Arab Emirates. Joint ventures were set up with foreign banks, for example the Union des Banques Arabes et Françaises and the Banque Arabe et Internationale d'Investissements, both based in Paris; the European Arab Bank in Brussels; the Saudi International Bank in London; and the Arab Latin American Bank operating out of Peru. In Paris there were, in 1981, 35 wholly or partly Arab-owned banks and in London 29, and an entry has been made in other centers such as New York, Singapore, and Tokyo.

Altogether, Arab banks now represent a truly impressive set of institutions. A recent list made by *The Banker* shows that 17 of the 500 largest banks in the world are Arab. The combined assets of the 50 top Arab banks exceed $150 billion; not surprisingly, almost all are domiciled in oil producing countries. Many of them are consortia, in which other Arab or Western banks participate, and their own governments supply a substantial share of capital.[17] These banks play a very active part in the international money market. They are estimated to have supplied 10 percent of all syndicated international bank credits in 1980 and about 27 percent in 1981.[18] Their customers include a wide variety of countries, from the most advanced to the least developed.

The strictly "Islamic banks" developed in the 1970s; in Egypt (Nasir Social Bank), Saudi Arabia (Islamic Development Bank), Kuwait (Kuwait Finance House), Sudan (Faisal Islamic Bank), Bahrain, Dubai, Jordan and elsewhere. There is even one in Calvinist Geneva—Bahrain-registered Dar al-Mal al-Islami. Their combined assets run into the billions of dollars and are growing rapidly.

All of these banks provide, on a fee basis, many of the services available at a Western bank, such as travelers' cheques, foreign exchange transactions, demand deposits, etc. Their peculiarity is that they neither pay nor charge interest. As for payment, neither depositors nor shareholders receive interest; instead they share in the profits made by the bank, receiving a "dividend." As we have seen, this is in line with Muslim medieval theory and practice. It is also quite a profitable business for depositors. For example, in Kuwait in 1980 the dividend paid to depositors was equivalent to an interest rate of 11.25 percent, which compared favorably with current rates on deposits in that capital-soaked country.

Regarding loans and advances, the guiding principle is risk-sharing. For example, both the bank and the borrower may provide capital and share the profits. Or the bank provides all the capital to an agent-manager, who receives a share of profits and may be authorized eventually to buy out the bank. Or the bank finances trade by actually buying the commodity, transporting it to the customer and selling it to him at a mark-up. The profit, not being interest, is legitimate. Or finally, in case of need, consumption loans may be made. For these an administrative fee may be charged, which again is not regarded as interest.

Here is a rather amusing example of the way Islamic injunctions can be turned against Muslim authorities. Starting a long time ago as money changers the Al Rajhi family built up the third largest financial institution in Saudi Arabia. They are very willing to accept interest-free deposits from pious Muslim customers. Not unnaturally, the Saudi Arabian Monetary Agency considers that Al-Rajhi Company for Currency Exchange and Commerce is a bank and, therefore, should be under its jurisdiction and keep reserves with it. "Not so," says Al Rajhi, "we make profits, not interest and therefore cannot be considered as a bank." This is because the company engages in operations that yield a profit, not interest, e.g. buying a tankerload of oil for a customer, holding it for a few days and selling it to the customer with payment delayed until the goods are received.[19]

I may conclude with a somewhat unexpected phenomenon, also in Saudi Arabia: Banks for Women. Under Muslim law women have always had the right to own property and some estimates put women's share of the private wealth of Saudi Arabia as high as 30 to 40 percent. As a result, some thirteen banks catering exclusively to women—and run entirely by women—have sprung up and their business is thriving. A somewhat jaundiced male explanation given by a Saudi Arabian is: "I think the real purpose of the ladies' banks is not to provide any services they did not have before in the existing banks. It is to give all these smart women something to do!" But it is certainly a fact that women feel free to use these banks whereas few if any deal with the ordinary ones, asking their male relatives or servants to do their banking.[20]

In conclusion, there are some very interesting experiments under way in the region. They have been made possible only by the abundance of oil money. But since, barring an earth-shaking cataclysm, oil money will continue to flow into the region for several decades, we can expect to see further attempts to adapt Islam to contemporary economic realities or, as a Muslim might prefer to put it, further attempts to fit contemporary economic institutions into an Islamic mold.

Notes

1. See Charles Issawi, *The Arab Legacy* (Princeton, N.J., 1981) and Charles Issawi, *An Economic History of the Middle East and North Africa* (New York, 1982).

2. The most thorough and comprehensive account of both traditional and contemporary Islamic views is Khurshid Ahmad, ed., *Studies in Islamic Economics* (Jeddah, 1976).

3. Joseph Schumpeter, *Capitalism, Socialism and Democracy* (London, 1950), pp. 160-61.

4. See *Encyclopaedia of Islam,* 2nd ed., s.v. "Karimi," and references cited.

5. Ibn Khaldun, *al-Muqaddimah,* ed. M. Quatremère (Paris, 1858), II: 284; translation in Charles Issawi, *An Arab Philosophy of History* (London, 1950), p. 86, and Franz Rosenthal, *The Muqaddimah* (New York, 1958), II: 326-28.

6. Serif Mardin, "Turkey: The Transformation of an Economic Code," in Ergun Ozbudun and Aydin Ulusan, eds., *The Political Economy of Income Distribution in Turkey* (New York, 1980).

7. This point is developed in "Europe, the Middle East and the Shift in Power," in Charles Issawi, *Arab Legacy,* pp. 111-32.

8. See Feridun Adamiyyat, *Amir-i Kabir wa Iran* (Tehran, 1334); Carter Findley, *Bureaucratic Reform in the Ottoman Empire* (Princeton, N.J., 1980), p. 37.

9. James Pritchard, ed., *The Ancient Near East* (Princeton, N.J., 1958), I: 147-48.

10. Joseph Schumpeter, *History of Economic Analysis* (New York, 1954), pp. 64-65, 101-107, and references cited. To this day the taking of interest disturbs the conscience of a few Christians—see C. S. Lewis, *Mere Christianity* (New York, 1960), p. 81.

11. For evidence on the activity of Muslims in moneylending in the sixteenth-eighteenth centuries see, for Turkey, Halil Inalcik, "Capital Formation in the Ottoman Empire," *Journal of Economic History* (March 1969), and Ronald Jennings, "Loans and Credit in the Early Seventeenth Century Ottoman Judicial Records," *Journal of the Economic and Social History of the Orient* (April 1973); for Iran, J. Chardin, quoted in Maxime Rodinson, *Islam et Capitalisme* (Paris, 1966), p. 57; for Egypt, see Stanford Shaw, *The Financial and Administrative Organization and Development of Ottoman Egypt* (Princeton, 1962), pp. 56-57; for Syria, A. N. Poliak, *Feudalism in Egypt, Syria, Palestine and Lebanon* (London, 1939), pp. 68-69, and Abdul Karim Rafeq, "Economic Relations between Damascus and the Dependent Countryside," in A. L. Udovitch, ed., *The Islamic Middle East* (Princeton, 1981), pp. 674-75.

12. A. L. Udovitch, *Partnership and Profit in Medieval Islam* (Princeton, 1970); Hammurabi's code has a provision (paragraph 98) that investors in trade ventures should share losses and not just receive a fixed profit—see Joan Oakes, *Babylon* (London, 1979), pp. 58-59.

13. Shaul Bakhash, "Reformulating Islam," *New York Times,* October 22, 1981.

14. *Ibid.*

15. Fareed El Naggar, "The Methodology of Islamic Economics and Systems Theory Model," *Middle East Management Review* (January 1977).

16. *The Economist,* November 21, 1981; supplement on Middle East Banking.

17. *The Banker* (December 1981); International Monetary Fund, *IMF Survey,* February 3, 1982.

18. *IMF Survey,* February 3, 1982, and *Economist,* November 21, 1981.

19. *The Economist,* November 14, 1981, p. 108.

20. "Saudi Banks for Women Thriving," *New York Times,* January 27, 1982.

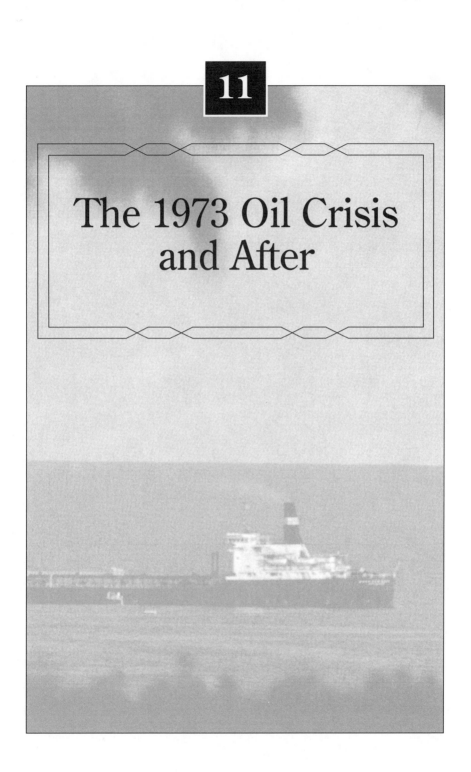

11

The 1973 Oil Crisis and After

The 1973 Crisis

uring October-December 1973, a highly dramatic and momentous event occurred: a group of small, economically underdeveloped, socially less advanced, and militarily weak nations, acting through the Organization of Petroleum Exporting Countries (OPEC), imposed their will on the industrialized world—and on the nonindustrialized world as well. Their action was highly profitable: it is netting them, at present, some $130 billion a year. It was also completely unforeseen, even by those who, like the present writer, expected oil prices to go on rising "steadily and appreciably, over the next decade or two"[1]—let alone by others who asserted that it would tend to fall toward its marginal cost of 10 cents a barrel. What made the psychological impact of the shock even greater was the fact that the Western world had weathered four storms over the previous quarter of a century, some very serious.

In 1948-49, during the first Arab-Israeli war, the pipeline carrying Iraqi oil to Haifa had been shut off[2] and approval of the Trans-Arabian pipeline from the newly developed Saudi fields to the Mediterranean through Jordan, Syria, and Lebanon had been delayed. But no serious repercussions had ensued. The only losers were the Iraqis, whose output and revenues were cut in half; the Israelis, who had to import oil from Venezuela and other distant places; and, to a lesser extent, the Saudis, who had to forgo for about a year the revenues they would have received from oil exports through the Trans-Arabian pipeline.

The second crisis, which followed very shortly after in 1951-53, was caused by the nationalization of the Iranian oil industry by Dr. Mossadegh, and its subsequent shutdown. There were fears of serious shortages, for Iran was by far the largest producer of crude in the Middle East and Abadan was the biggest refinery in the world; moreover, the Korean War had greatly increased the demand for aviation gasoline and certain other products. But the crisis was overcome by considerably expanding output in Saudi Arabia, Kuwait, and Iraq and rerouting tankers on all the main routes. The only major inconvenience was the loss of revenue by the Iranians. On the other hand, Western expectations that Iran would collapse economically as a consequence proved baseless: agriculture showed some increase, industry expanded appreciably due to protection forced by lack of foreign exchange, and exports rose considerably;[3] it took a coup, assisted by the CIA, to overthrow Mossadegh. Conversely, Iranian expectations that the Anglo-Iranian Oil Company would collapse proved even more erroneous: the company, renamed British Petroleum, drew on its fields in Kuwait and elsewhere, and in fact showed record profits. The widespread Iranian belief that Britain's economy would be severely shaken without its profits from Iranian oil proved somewhat premature.

The third crisis came in 1956, during the second Arab-Israeli war. During the attack on Egypt, the Suez Canal was blocked and, to show their solidarity, the Syrians blew up the Iraqi pipelines. This led to fears of a grave shortage in Europe. But the crisis was overcome, partly by rerouting Persian Gulf oil around the Cape of Good Hope, and partly by expanding exports to Europe from the United States and Venezuela, both of which had abundant spare capacity. By the spring of 1957 matters had returned to normal and the opening of the canal shortly after further eased the situation. The shock did lead to some contingency planning in Europe, including recommendations for stockpiling, but the practical results were negligible.[4] The most tangible of these was the stimulus given to supertankers, which could deliver Persian Gulf oil to Europe more cheaply than smaller tankers using the canal.

Supertankers played a critical role in surmounting the fourth crisis in 1967. The canal was blocked at the outbreak of the third Arab-Israeli war and remained so for nine years. No one particularly missed it, however, for by then the bulk of the world's tanker fleet consisted of very large ships. An embargo was imposed by some of the Arab producers but was lifted by the end of the summer because it was not achieving its purpose. Its failure was due partly to the acute disunity prevailing among the Arab states; Egypt was at loggerheads with Saudi Arabia, Iraq, Syria, and Libya, and Syria and Iraq were having a feud of their own—all of which made a coordination of policy impossible. Much more important, there was still spare capacity in the United States and Venezuela that could be drawn upon if needed, and Iran was eager to expand production and regain the position it had lost in 1951—which it did. Lastly, Libya's output could be greatly expanded, and in fact this was accomplished; this sowed the seeds of the next crisis, described below.

To understand the success of oil producers in 1973 following their repeated previous failures, it is necessary to review the fundamental

40 • Supertanker

changes that had occurred in the meantime. A strange concatenation of circumstances had come about. Many strands, several unconnected, had come together to form a strong cable capable of fettering the mightiest industrial powers.

Erosion of the Western Position

From its inception, the Middle Eastern oil industry had rested on two pillars: Anglo-American hegemony in the Middle East and North Africa, and the overwhelming predominance of American and British companies in the world petroleum market.

The hegemony was firmly based. Parts of the area, for example, Sudan and South Yemen, were under direct British rule (or French, in North Africa); others were under friendly governments which, in case of recalcitrance, could be coerced or intimidated as were Iraq and Iran in 1941, Egypt in 1942, and Jordan and Lebanon in 1958. This political control was buttressed by British and American military bases in Libya, Egypt, Iraq, Bahrain, and Saudi Arabia, as well as large French forces in North Africa. Economic ties were a further reinforcement: almost all the region's trade was with Western Europe and the United States; practically all investment was American, British, or, in North Africa, French.[5] So were ideological ties: the ruling groups—landowners, merchants, and others—were favorable to the West and readily proclaimed the virtues—if they did not always follow the spirit—of bourgeois liberalism.

By 1970 all that had changed. The colonial powers had gradually withdrawn, and the bases were successively shut down. Revolutionary regimes had overthrown the monarchies in Egypt, Iraq, Tunisia, Yemen, and Libya, and replaced the foreign rulers in Syria, Algeria, Sudan, and South Yemen. These regimes either were hostile to the West from the beginning or soon became so. This process was reinforced by the arms they received from the Soviet bloc and the ideology they picked up at Bandung and succeeding Third World meetings. It was further encouraged by the large amounts of economic aid some of them—notably Egypt, Syria, Algeria, and Iraq— received from the Soviet bloc and the reorientation of part of their nonoil exports to that bloc. Still another cause of growing hostility to the West was the increasing support given to Israel by the United States and some other Western states in the wake of Israel's escalating wars with its Arab neighbors.

It need hardly be pointed out that this erosion of the Western position is part of a worldwide shift in power away from Western Europe and the United States. In the military sphere it is signaled by the Soviet Union's achievement of parity with the United States; in the economic sphere, by the vast growth in the Soviet bloc and Chinese economies, which has turned them into alternative markets for raw materials and sources of capital goods and arms; and in the political sphere, by the growing nationalism of the Europeans, which makes them increasingly unwilling to cooperate either with the United States (e.g., the breakdown of the Bretton Woods system of fixed exchange rates and its aftermath) or with each other (e.g., the loss of momentum for European integration).

The hegemony of the American and British companies also went back a long way. In 1928 the three largest—Standard Oil (New Jersey), Shell, and Anglo-Persian—were powerful enough to draw up the "As Is" agreement regulating world markets outside the United States and the Soviet Union. By the Second World War, oil discoveries in Texas and Arabia had raised the number of majors to seven (adding Gulf, Texaco, Socal, and Mobil)— eight, if the Compagnie Française des Pétroles is included. The Seven Sisters controlled and developed the oil fields of Venezuela, Indonesia, the Middle East, North Africa, and Nigeria, as well as smaller ones in other parts of the world, and also had important holdings in the United States. In 1952, they accounted for nearly 90 percent of world crude output outside the United States, the Soviet bloc, and China, marketed 75 percent of refined products, owned or chartered two-thirds of the world tanker fleet, and owned all the major pipelines.[6] But in 1953-72, no less than 350 firms invested in oil outside the United States, Soviet Union, and China, many of them in the Middle East and North Africa; by 1968 the share of the Seven had fallen to 75 percent for crude and 50 percent for products.[7] The balance came from "independents" (some of them very large), firms backed by European governments or Japan (such as the Italian Ente Nazionale Idrocarburi, French Compagnie Française des Pétroles and Entreprise de Recherches et d'Activités Pétrolières, and Japanese Arabian Oil Co.), and the state-owned enterprises set up by the Middle Eastern and North African governments (for example, the National Iranian Oil Company and Iraq National Oil Company). The latter played a role that was much more important than their size would indicate, training managers and technicians, exploring new markets, and in general greatly increasing the Middle Eastern governments' understanding of the forces at work in the petroleum world.

This multiplicity of firms greatly weakened the industry as against the producing governments. A system of bilateral monopoly, in which the company was in a much stronger financial position than the host government and in addition could draw on worldwide oil reserves and refineries (as, for example, Anglo-Iranian had done in 1951-53), was replaced by a situation in which the government faced several companies that it could play off against each other. The independents and foreign state companies were willing to grant better terms than the majors, since they were anxious to obtain a foothold in the region—many examples can be cited from the Persian Gulf and Libya. Once in, they were eager to produce as much as possible, without too much care about the possible effect on world supply and prices, since their share of total production was very small. And, once established, they were far more vulnerable to government pressure, since most of them were wholly or largely dependent on production in a single country.

The Rise of OPEC, 1960-73

The Organization of Petroleum Exporting Countries was formed on September 14, 1960, by the heads of the Iranian, Iraqi, Kuwaiti, Saudi Arabian, and Venezuelan delegations meeting in Baghdad. The ground had been prepared a year earlier in April 1959, when Perez Alfonso of Venezuela and Abdullah Tariki of Saudi Arabia had drawn up a gentlemen's agreement signed by the heads of delegations attending the Arab Petroleum Congress in Cairo. The immediate cause was the reduction by the oil companies of the posted prices for crude oil in 1959 and 1960, owing to a glut in world markets caused by increased output by the independents, the Soviet Union, and the majors themselves. These reductions, aggregating about 10 percent, were the first since 1949 and came at a time when the governments were becoming concerned about the price of their oil. For until the "fifty-fifty" profit-sharing agreements of 1950-54, they had received a specified royalty per unit of output amounting to about 20 to 22 cents a barrel; hence, their revenues were in no way dependent on price, and indeed the governments would have tended to favor a low price since that presumably would have meant larger sales and output. After the profit-sharing agreements, however, price became the major variable affecting revenues (now averaging 75 to 80 cents a barrel), since costs of production—at the extremely low figure of 10 to 20 cents a barrel—could hardly be compressed further. Thus the Middle Eastern governments had become increasingly receptive to the overtures for common action which Venezuela—concerned over the lowness of its reserves and loss of markets to cheaper Middle Eastern oil—had been making since 1947. In addition, at the 1959 conference, a resolution had been passed stating that future changes in posted prices should be discussed with the government of the producing country.

OPEC's first ten years can best be considered by analogy with a newly formed labor union. The first task is to organize the workers, accustom them to working together, and develop mutual trust. After that, the union can use its collective power to bargain for higher income. The 1960s were the period of consolidation. Although OPEC failed in its original aim of getting the price cuts rescinded, it succeeded in enlarging its membership to an eventual total of thirteen countries, controlling over 85 percent of world exports; in forming a staff with considerable expertise; in accustoming the governments to working together and giving them a better understanding of the oil market; and in securing from the companies several minor but cumulatively important concessions. The consolidation of OPEC was aided by such events as the disputes between the governments of Iraq (from 1961 on) and Algeria (from 1969) with their respective companies.

In June 1968, OPEC issued a Declaratory Statement asserting that changing circumstances justified the revision of existing as well as future contracts, that the governments had a right to participation in ownership, that posted prices should be determined by the governments and should ensure that these prices suffered no deterioration relative to the price of industrial products, and that the "excessively high net earnings" of the companies should be paid to the governments.[9] Little attention was given to this statement, but in retrospect it is clear that it marked a change in the atmosphere. The following year Iran received higher payments by threatening to demand 50 percent participation, and the Saudi oil minister, while declaring his opposition to nationalization, urged participation. A committee was set up by OPEC to study participation.

The Role of Libya, 1970-71

A new and very dynamic factor intervened at this point—Libya. The closure of the Suez Canal in 1967 had led to a more than doubling of oil production in Libya, whose freight advantage over the Persian Gulf producers had greatly increased—and correspondingly augmented Europe's dependence on Libya. In 1969 a military coup put in power Colonel Qaddafi, a bold, dedicated, fanatical young man who rushed in where angels had feared to tread. In 1970, taking advantage of the high demand for oil, the tanker shortage, which almost tripled spot rates, and the not fortuitous damaging of Tapline in Syria, Qaddafi demanded higher revenues, ordered cuts in production in the name of conservation, and threatened to shut down any recalcitrant companies. He concentrated on the independents because of their great dependence on Libyan supplies. Soon Occidental gave in—reportedly after having asked Esso to replace the oil it would have forgone, which Esso agreed to do only at market prices. The other companies had to follow suit, posted prices were raised by 30 cents, and the tax rate (government's share) was increased from 50 to 55 percent. The crisis had shown quite clearly that the oil companies would not necessarily act in concert and that they did not enjoy the full support of the United States government, whereas Libya was strongly backed by OPEC.

The lesson was not lost on OPEC; at its Caracas meeting in December 1970, it set 55 percent as the industrywide minimum. A meeting was scheduled for Tehran, in which the Persian Gulf countries as a group, led by the Shah, negotiated with the companies as a group. On the advice of the State Department, the companies agreed in February 1971 to a rise in price from $1.80 to $2.18 and an increase in the tax rate from 50 to 55 percent. This was followed in April by a successful Libyan demand for an extra $1.00 in price because of the low sulfur content of its oil and freight advantages—a concession extended to the other "Mediterranean" producers (Algeria, Iraq, and Saudi Arabian oil from Tapline) and Nigeria. Moreover, the Tripoli-Tehran agreements provided for an annual rise of 2.5 percent to allow for inflation, and the devaluations of the dollar caused corresponding increases in price. The OPEC take per barrel rose from 95 cents in 1970 to $2.12 in 1973, and revenues increased from $7.3 billion to $22.8 billion.[10]

As a British observer put it, "After cash must come control," and in the course of the next few years all the Middle Eastern and North African governments took over 50 to 100 percent of the equity of the companies—a process that will not be followed further here.

In the meantime, important developments were taking place in the world oil market. The high rate of increase in world energy consumption that had prevailed in the 1960s accelerated in the early 1970s because of a simultaneous, and unusually synchronized, boom in North America, Western Europe, and Japan. Since the output of other sources of energy increased slowly (see the next section), world consumption of oil grew at the exceptionally fast rate of 10.6 percent per annum in 1969-73—a rate far higher than the projections made by both official bodies and private persons.[11]

But production showed little or no increase outside the Middle East and Africa. Most of the growth in output of the Soviet Union and China was absorbed by these countries themselves. Both the United States and Venezuela peaked in 1970 and thereafter started to decline, and their spare capacity—which in previous crises had cushioned the Middle Eastern shock—disappeared to leave the world very vulnerable. Indeed, United States imports of oil, which in the past had represented only a small fraction of consumption, began to rise rapidly, reaching 25 percent in 1971 and 35 percent in 1973. Moreover, United States oil companies found it more profitable to invest abroad—in the North Sea and elsewhere, but mainly in OPEC; the one major domestic venture, in Alaska, ran into difficulties and delays.

Neglect of Other Sources of Energy

Other sources of energy were neglected because of the belief that cheap oil was available, because of legitimate environmental considerations, and because the Western world—and the United States, in particular—were behaving like spoilt children in thinking that they could have unlimited amounts of energy at no cost. During 1950-70, coal production declined sharply in Europe and stagnated in the United States; nuclear power faced unexpected technical difficulties, escalating costs, and environmental constraints; and the development of natural gas was held up by the very low price fixed by government regulations in the United States.

Change in inter-Arab relations

Another important change was taking place in inter-Arab relations: the growing rapprochement between King Faisal of Saudi Arabia and President Sadat of Egypt. No love had been lost between Faisal and Sadat's predecessor, Nasser, each man fearing and distrusting the other. But gradually

Faisal and Sadat got together. Faisal, believing that unless the Arab-Israeli problem were solved, there would be more wars and revolutions, became increasingly convinced that he had to use the "oil weapon" to induce the United States to put pressure on Israel and thus end the political stalemate. He therefore agreed to supply Egypt with weapons and money and sent several messages to President Nixon; these seem to have received very little attention—Nixon had other things on his mind. Faisal was also motivated by inter-Arab considerations: the desire to draw Sadat away from Qaddafi, who was also offering help and whom Faisal considered a wild and dangerous man. Some agreement seems to have been reached that, if there were no positive action by the United States, the Arabs would launch a two-pronged attack: a military offensive against Israel and an oil embargo on the United States.

The Structure of OPEC

All these factors, by themselves, would have been insufficient had OPEC not fulfilled the conditions normally stipulated for the successful functioning of a cartel:

a. Its members must control a large share of world reserves, production, and exports—for OPEC, the figures in 1973 were about 70, 54, and 84 percent, respectively.

b. The price elasticity of demand must be low—a figure of -0.3 has been suggested for crude oil by M. A. Adelman and of -0.35 by a Ford Foundation team.[12]

c. The price elasticity of supply of alternative producers must be low—Houthakker suggests for North America an "optimistic" figure of 0.5 and a "pessimistic" one of 0.15, and for Latin America and Europe, 0.1 and 0.05.[13]

d. The price elasticity of supply of substitutes must be low—this certainly seems true of coal, gas, shale oil, and nuclear and hydroelectric power, and is discussed further below.

e. The cohesion of the members of the cartel must be strong enough to prevent their undercutting each other; this too is discussed below.

In addition to meeting these conditions, whose absence has wrecked so many cartels, OPEC had three advantages:

a. Oil is an essential commodity in the strictest sense of the word. The difference this makes was soon realized by the Central American countries that tried to emulate OPEC by forming a banana cartel!

b. The framework of the cartel had been established by the oil companies—going back to the days of Rockefeller and Deterding—and could be taken over readymade by OPEC.

c. The price of crude bears only a tenuous and indirect relation to the price paid by consumers of the various products. This is due partly to the high costs of transport—say, $1.00 a barrel (depending on the size of the tanker) from the Persian Gulf to Western Europe in 1973—and refining—say, another 70 cents. But even more it is due to the very high taxes levied on products by the governments of consuming countries, which amounted to $5.00 to $6.00 a barrel in 1973. It will be seen that, in addition to company profits, there were many layers between the producer and consumer that could absorb a large part of the rise in prices—and to a certain extent did.

Even so, the cartel might not have held had it not been for its peculiar structure and the pivotal role of Saudi Arabia. Several groups can be distinguished within the cartel: the Arab core and the non-Arab periphery—that is, Iran, Venezuela, Indonesia, Nigeria, and the smaller countries—and, within the core, the radical group (Algeria, Iraq, Libya) and the conservative countries (Saudi Arabia, Kuwait, Qatar, and the United Arab Emirates). Each of these made its own contribution. The radical Arabs, in conformity with their ideology and the role they had cast for themselves in the Third World, urged strong action; this also fitted with their ambitions in inter-Arab politics; in addition, Algeria and Iraq needed large funds for their vast development plans. The non-Arabs were not interested in the political aims of the Arabs and had no particular quarrel with the United States or Israel, but they had large populations and ambitious development plans and were eager to raise the price of oil; moreover, since their reserves were relatively small, they were willing to limit output if necessary, and stretch out production. As for the conservative Arabs, they provided the cushion and the balancing force—particularly Saudi Arabia, which, with the Emirates, accounts for 40 percent of OPEC and 25 percent of world reserves. It also had huge revenues and monetary reserves and could therefore afford to cut down production drastically without suffering hardship or even serious discomfort; moreover, conserving oil was in its long-term interest since it did not have the capacity to absorb more than a small fraction of its current income. On the other hand, if the activist members of OPEC pushed too far, Saudi Arabia, with its ample spare capacity, could threaten to increase its output and force down the price.

One more point needs mentioning: the negotiating skill of the Arabs and Iranians and their grasp of the economic and political forces at work. This came as a surprise to Western observers; it should not have—the bazaar is the best training ground in the world for bilateral bargaining, and the Middle Easterners are not dumb.

Western Leadership

The Western leaders, however, were both dumb and disunited. Western Europe was in disarray and the Common Market under great strain. Japan was playing a lone hand. The Bretton Woods financial system was breaking down. The Europeans and Japanese distrusted both the United States government and the oil companies, were convinced that the United States Middle Eastern policy was mistaken, and hoped to do better with direct negotiations and deals with the oil producers; this was especially true of France, but by no means of it alone.

There was as much disarray in the United States. A consistent policy was made impossible by the multitude of interests at work: oil independents and majors; coal operators and miners; nuclear power interests; transport; consumers; environmentalists; military and political lobbies; and so on. A very important paralyzing force was the profound distrust of the oil companies that was prevalent in both American political circles and the public at large. Another was the multiplicity of government agencies concerned: in 1975, thirty-three congressional committees, with sixty-five subcommittees, claimed jurisdiction over the United States Energy Research and Development Administration, and the executive branch was no better.[14] In addition, President Nixon had other fish to fry, and Congress was preoccupied mainly with frying him.

There was a complete misreading of the situation; both the power of the United States and the vulnerability of OPEC were overestimated. In May 1973, Nadim Pachachi, a prominent Arab oil expert, had recommended that the Arabs freeze their output at existing levels until the Israelis had withdrawn from Arab lands, and Kuwait introduced a system of rationing. The companies responded by increasing output in Saudi Arabia and Iran, which of course increased dependence on those two countries. On September 5, 1973, Nixon on television was threatening Libya and the radical elements in the Middle East: "oil without a market, as Dr. Mossadegh learnt many, many years ago, doesn't do much good. . . . We and Europe are the market . . . if they continue to up the price they will lose the markets."[15] But by then it was markets that were seeking oil. Again, in mid-September, Kissinger spoke to the Senate about our "excellent relations with our principal Middle Eastern suppliers of oil, Iran and Saudi Arabia," and noted that "we do not foresee any circumstances in which they would cut off our supply."[16] But at the end of September Faisal warned of cutbacks if there were no American response, and early in October both Zaki Yamani, the Saudi oil minister, and James Akins, United States ambassador to Saudi Arabia, formally warned that there could be a Saudi cutback.

Meanwhile negotiations were about to begin in Vienna between OPEC and the companies—with a view toward doubling prices—when the fourth Arab-Israeli war broke out on October 6. On the sixteenth, the ministers of Iran, Iraq, Kuwait, Qatar, Saudi Arabia, and the United Arab Emirates decided to raise the price of Saudi light crude from $3.01 to $5.12 a barrel, thus increasing the government's take from $1.77 to $3.05. The next day the Arab oil ministers recommended cuts in output and embargoes against "unfriendly states." Between October 19 and 28, the Arab states alone put an embargo on exports to the United States and the Netherlands. To make the point more clearly, on November 5 the Arabs imposed a production cut of 25 percent for November with the promise of further monthly cuts of 5 percent; on December 9, one such additional cut was made. This created panic and a scramble for available oil, and the spot price reached $17 a barrel. On December 22, the six Persian Gulf states raised their posted prices to $11.65 for Saudi light crude; this time the initiative seems to have been taken by Iran, and the effect was to raise the government's share to over $10 by the end of 1974. At this point it was clear that the battle had been won; in March-July 1974 the embargoes on the United States and the Netherlands were lifted; the OPEC price revolution was over.

The Aftermath

Years have passed* since the 1973 oil crisis and the world is still caught up in its aftermath. This has taken many forms—shifts in trade flows, changes in terms of trade, balance-of-payments difficulties, acceleration of

---

*This chapter was written in the 1970s. See new conclusion on page 224.

inflation, accumulation of petrodollars and consequent financial difficulties, emergence of new patterns of investment, and so on. These problems are outside the scope of this study, which focuses on only two issues: the cohesion of the OPEC cartel and probable trends in the world oil market.

Cohesion of OPEC

The cohesion of OPEC has so far been tested three times. First in 1973-74; during and immediately after the embargo and production cutdown, the temptation to cheat by failing to reduce output, undercutting price, or shipping to embargoed countries must have been strong. But the need to do so was greatly diminished by the fact that a small number of states, headed by Saudi Arabia, were willing to bear the brunt of the reduction in output. OPEC output in November 1973 fell by 4.13 million barrels a day, or 12.5 percent, compared to September; this was more than accounted for by the Arab countries, however, which cut down by 4.57 million barrels a day, or 25.7 percent, allowing the non-Arab members to raise their output by 2.9 percent. The December figures were almost identical, rising by 300,000 barrels a day, mainly because of the increase in Arab production. A breakdown by country shows that in November Saudi output was lower by 2.3 million barrels a day than in September (a decrease of 26.8 percent), Kuwait's output by 1.06 million barrels a day (30.0 percent), Libya's by 520,000 barrels a day (22.7 percent), Abu Dhabi's by 230,000 (16.4 percent), Algeria's by 200,000 (18.2 percent), and Qatar's by 130,000 (21.7 percent).[17] Iraq alone showed an increase, and there is reason to believe that it offered some oil at a discount during the height of the crisis.

Since then, OPEC production has been subjected to a double squeeze. First, because of higher prices, the recession, and conservation measures taken in various countries, consumption declined in 1974 and 1975 and surpassed the 1973 level only in 1976; the 1977 figure was about 5 percent higher than that of 1973. Second, the share of non-OPEC output rose steadily. This has restrained OPEC from pushing prices up too sharply, in spite of repeated warnings that it would have to do so to offset the appreciable rise in the price of goods imported by the OPEC countries as well as the steady decline in the dollar—in which they receive payments—compared to other currencies such as the yen, mark, etc., which account for a substantial fraction of their imports. On October 1, 1975, the reference price was raised by 10 percent. In December 1976, at the Qatar meeting, there was a split in the ranks: eleven governments decreed a rise of 10 percent (some of the "oil hawks" clamored for 15 or even 25 percent), to be followed by another 5 percent on July 1, 1977; but Saudi Arabia and the Emirates refused to go beyond 5 percent in all. This meant that during the first half of 1977, Saudi crude was selling at $12.09, or 72 cents below Iranian oil of the same quality. In July 1977, unity was restored; Saudi Arabia and the Emirates brought their price in line with that of the other OPEC countries ($12.70), which in turn agreed to forgo the scheduled 5 percent rise in their price. The power of Saudi Arabia was underlined by the fact that in 1977 its output rose by 5.7 percent and that of the Emirates by 3.8 percent, whereas that of every other OPEC country except Nigeria and Libya declined; during the first half of the year, when Saudi crude was cheaper, output rose by 14 percent.[19] Saudi Arabia's influence was reinforced at the Caracas meeting of December 20-22, 1977, by the shift in the position of Iran. Hitherto Iran, with relatively small oil reserves, a large population, and very ambitious development and military programs, had been counted among the "hawks," together with Algeria, Iraq, Nigeria, and Venezuela—whose situation, needs, and policies were roughly similar—and Libya. These countries had pushed for higher prices, accompanied if necessary by a limitation on output, which would stretch out their reserves. At Caracas, Iraq is reported to have proposed a 23 percent rise in prices and Indonesia and Venezuela a 5 to 8 percent rise. But Saudi Arabia, Iran, Kuwait, Qatar, and the Emirates insisted on a price freeze, at least until June 15, 1978, and on June 18 the freeze was extended to December 31.

Saudi Arabia's position has been determined by such economic factors as its huge oil reserves, enormous revenues, vast accumulated foreign exchange holdings, and very limited absorptive capacity due to small population and lack of complementary natural resources. The glut in the oil market no doubt was also a consideration. But political factors, too, have been important: a commitment to world stability and a desire to use its economic power to bring about a change in the United States' position on the Arab-Israeli dispute.

In addition to political considerations, Iran's shift may have been motivated by the realization that the huge influx of funds had been a very mixed blessing; it had converted what had been the remarkably rapid, balanced, and many-sided growth of 1962-73 into an unsustainable spurt, resulting in economic dislocation, high inflation, and social discontent. But it is clear that Iran does not have the same basic inducements to keep prices down as has Saudi Arabia.

As regards the forces affecting OPEC's cohesion, clearly there are political forces pushing its members apart, notably the rivalries between Iran, Iraq, and Saudi Arabia, the antipathy between radical and conservative Arab governments, and the activities of the Palestinians. But the balance of economic forces seems to be definitely centripetal: its members have found that hanging together is far more profitable than hanging separately. Nothing but collective action could have raised the governments' take per barrel some twelvefold in seven years. And, as every intelligent oligopolist knows, and as the oil companies have known all along, once undercutting begins there is no end to the downward trend of prices—especially for a commodity whose marginal cost in all the major OPEC countries was well under $1.00 and in several close to 30 cents. Moreover, even ignoring such important producers as Saudi Arabia, Kuwait, Libya, Qatar, and the Emirates, for whom money is almost no consideration, the chief inducement to reduce price in order to increase one's share of output is absent. For the oil producers can be virtually certain that, barring a worldwide cataclysm, every drop of oil recoverable from their reserves will find a market. This statement is based on two facts. First, the history of the last two hundred years shows that when a new fuel replaces an old one (for example, coal, wood or oil, coal), gaining a rapidly increasing share of the market, the absolute level of output of the older fuel is maintained for several decades. Second, oil has a better use than burning as a fuel—it is the feedstock for the mighty and rapidly expanding petrochemical industry, where it is likely to command a much higher price. Again, given the fact that no OPEC country is in a position to invest rationally at home all its oil income, the choice is either to waste—and this is of course being done on a royal scale—or to invest abroad. But the risk of inflation and of expropriation or freezing of funds by the depository countries greatly reduce the attractiveness of this alternative. This fact largely offsets the very important consideration that the discounted present value of future income can be very low—for example, at an inflation rate of 7 percent per annum, one dollar in twenty-five years is worth only 18.4 cents today. On the whole, it is safer to base one's actions on the assumption that, over the next few years, oil will continue to prove thicker than water and the OPEC cartel will hold.[20]

One final point is worth noting: by now numerous powerful interests outside OPEC support higher oil prices, since they would be seriously hurt by a sharp fall in the price of oil. These include not only high-cost oil producers in Europe—for example, in the North Sea—and the United States, but coal operators and miners, who have greatly profited from the rise in

the price of oil, and other producers of energy, not to mention the bureaucracy and other vested interests that have come into being because of the
energy crisis.[21]

Conclusion

The above article, written in 1977, ended with an analysis of the factors
affecting the probable future price of oil and a study of various forecasts.

The outbreak of the Revolution in Iran, in 1978, shut down production
in that country, sent the price of oil rocketing to $35 a barrel and put a great
strain on both the oil and the financial markets. But it also greatly stimulated conservation in the industrialized countries. That factor, together with
an increase in output in Saudi Arabia and the forces discussed above,
pushed back the price of oil to $10. In the 1980s and early 90s, the price fluc-
tuated around $20 and was only temporarily affected by such events as the
Iran-Iraq war of 1980-89, the Iraqi invasion of Kuwait in 1990, and the U.S.
invasion of Iraq in 1991.

Notes

1. Charles Issawi, *Oil, the Middle East and the World* (New York, 1972), p. 74.

2. This was not the first interruption; during the Arab uprising against the British
    in Palestine in 1936, the pipeline had been sabotaged, and in 1940 the flow to
    Syria and Lebanon, occupied by pro-Vichy French troops, was stopped.

3. See United Nations (1955, ch. 3).

4. Of the abundant literature generated by the crisis, mention should be made of
    the Organization for European Economic Cooperation, *Europe's Need for Oil*
    (Paris, 1958) and Harold Lubell, *Middle East Oil Crises and Western Europe's
    Energy Supplies* (Baltimore, Md.: Johns Hopkins Press, 1963), which examine
    the implications of various possible shutdowns of Middle Eastern oil fields.

5. For a breakdown of investment in Middle East petroleum from the beginnings
    until 1960, see Issawi and Mohammed Yeganeh, *The Economics of Middle
    Eastern Oil* (New York, 1962), ch. 2; in other branches of the economy, British
    and French interests were predominant.

6. See breakdowns in *ibid.,* p. 61; U.S. Federal Trade Commission (1952, pp. 23-
    28); for more recent breakdowns, see Dankwart A. Rustow and John F. Mugno,
    OPEC: Success and Prospects (New York, 1976), pp. 142-43; more generally, John
    M. Blair, *The Control of Oil* (New York, 1976, pt. I), Anthony Sampson, *The Seven
    Sisters* (London, 1975), passim.

7. Neil H. Jacoby, *Multinational Oil* (New York, 1973), p. 177.

8. For details see Fuad Rouhani, *A History of OPEC* (New York, 1971), Ashraf Lutfi,

OPEC Oil (Beirut, 1968), Zuhayr Mikdashi, *The Community of Oil Exporting Countries* (Ithaca, N.Y., 1972), Rustow and Mugno, *op. cit.,* and Mikdashi (1975).

9. For full text, see Rustow and Mugno, *op. cit.,* pp. 166-72.

10. See details in Rustow and Mugno, *op. cit.,* pp. 130-31, and Wilkins (1975).

11. British Petroleum Company, *BP Statistical Review of the World Oil Industry—1976* (London, 1977), and Joel Darmstadter and Hans H. Landsberg, "The Economic Background," *Daedalus,* Fall 1975, 104(4), 15-37.

12. *Petroleum Economist,* September 1977; *New York Times,* April 4, 1977.

13. Hendrik S. Houthakker, *The World Price of Oil* (Washington, D.C., 1976), p. 19; he also gives income elasticities of demand for most products well above unity, which is favorable for producers at a time of rising real income in the world.

14. Wirth (1976).

15. Quoted in *Arab Report and Record,* September 1-15, 1973.

16. Quoted in *Oil and Gas Journal,* September 17, 1973; I owe this and the preceding reference to my former student, Syed Shaban Alam.

17. See tables in Rustow and Mugno, *op. cit.,* pp. 136-37.

18. *Petroleum Economist,* January 1978; Irving Trust Co., *The Economic View from One Wall Street* (New York, December 1977).

19. *Petroleum Economist,* January 1978.

20. A gimmick repeatedly proposed by M. A. Adelman (most recently in *The Economist* of April 8, 1978) deserves attention: namely, that the United States should import its oil by sealed bids, thus giving OPEC members the incentive to chisel. The manager of one of Egypt's largest importing firms in the 1930s informed me that each year they called for sealed bids for chemical fertilizers and picked the lowest, which came from a different European country each year. It was only after the war that he learned that the fertilizer cartel, at its annual meeting, reshuffled markets among producers, assigning Egypt one year to France, another year to Germany, and so on. It should not be beyond the powers of OPEC to do the same.

21. This point is made, humorously but convincingly, by Lewis H. Latham, "The Arabian Oil Bubble," *Harper's,* May 1978, 256(1536).

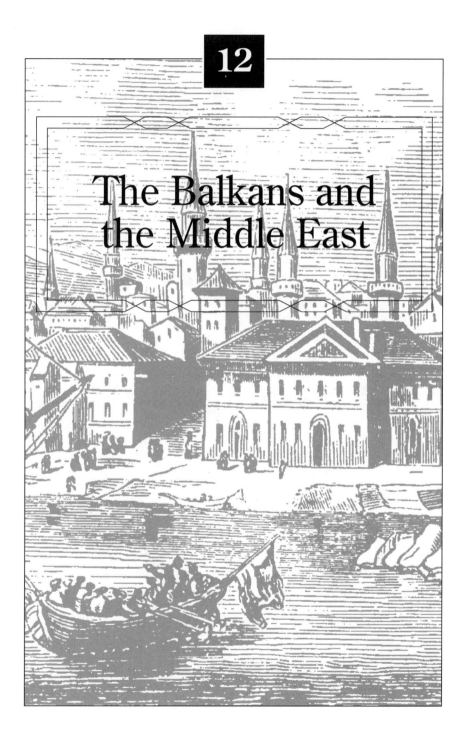

12

The Balkans and the Middle East

he Balkans—Bulgaria, Romania, Yugoslavia, and Greece—are the main European successor states of the Ottoman Empire. Economically and socially, the Balkans are distinctly more developed than the Middle East. Table 121.1 shows selected economic and social indicators for the main successor states of the Ottoman Empire, four in each area; incidentally, most of what is said about the Middle East, particularly Iraq, also applies to Iran. The date chosen for comparison is 1990, before the disintegration of Yugoslavia, the destruction of Iraq and the collapse of the economy in Bulgaria and Romania. Both the economic and social criteria show the Balkans far ahead: among the economic, real per-capita GDP, adjusted for purchasing power; the percentage of the population employed in industry, which gives the most meaningful comparison for industrialization; and wheat yields, which indicate agricultural productivity; and, among the social, life expectancy; adult literacy; and birth rates. The extremely high rates for employment in industry in Bulgaria and Romania reflect the forced industrialization of the communist period. The only areas of overlap are the very high wheat yield in Egypt, due to the great fertility of its soil and its developed irrigation, but also to its excellent farming techniques, and the relatively high literacy rate in Turkey, which reflects the progress made in recent years.

A similar comparison for the beginning of this century (see Table 12.2) shows a mixed picture. In the economic field there is little to choose between the two groups. Per capita foreign trade, a good index of monetization, was distinctly higher in the Middle East. Wheat yields were very slightly lower and railway mileage about the same. As regards National Income, for Egypt, Syria and Turkey the figures for 1913 were about $45-$50 per capita, and for Iraq probably less.[1] Comparable estimates for the Balkan countries were over $40 for Bulgaria and about $50 for Romania and Serbia.[2] The social indicators, however, tell another story. Literacy rates were much higher in the Balkans and birth rates distinctly lower.

I suspect that the more rapid social development of the Balkans in the 19th century, compared to the Middle East, probably explains much of its superior economic performance in the 20th century, and shall therefore

devote the rest of this article to examining the historical roots of this phenomenon. But before doing so, a few general considerations, regarding the
factors that favored or handicapped the Balkans, are in order.

First, there is the geographical. In the Balkans rainfall is far more abundant, better distributed seasonally, and shows less annual fluctuations than
in the Middle East.[3] This not only means better crops but makes it easier
for small farmers to survive since they are less threatened by drought—a
fact of great social importance, as will be mentioned. It also means that
wood and waterpower are more abundant, favoring small scale industries,
and that there are many more navigable rivers, though some tend to dry up
in summer. It may be added that the Balkans are better provided with minerals, except for oil whose importance is only recent.

Secondly, there is religion: The Balkans are predominantly Orthodox
Christian and the Middle East Muslim. Now while the Orthodox church
has not been a dynamic or progressive body for many centuries, and was
estranged from Western Christianity by a millennial hostility, it was somewhat more open to progressive European influences than was Islam.

For instance, the Patriarch Cyril Lucaris (elected 1620) tried to introduce Protestant doctrines and in the 17th century Orthodox theological
students were sent to Gloucester College, Oxford. And it is possible that the
monogamy enjoined by Christianity was more conducive to economic and
social development than the polygamy practiced by the upper classes, and
further down, in the Middle East.

Thirdly, there is the political. Most Balkan countries emancipated
themselves from Ottoman rule, and achieved autonomy or independence,
early in the 19th century. In the Middle East, where the process was complicated by British and French imperialism, this emancipation did not take
place until after the First or even Second World War. It is true that the
Balkan governments were far from being models of stability, efficiency and
enlightenment and they had more than their share of assassinations, coups,
and bankruptcies, but they were more responsive to the needs of their people than the Ottomans had been and carried out many useful measures in
education, industry and land reform.

In this century, however, the fate of the Balkans has been much more
tragic. In the First World War their losses were greater, and in the Second
far greater, than those of the Middle East, which was almost totally spared.
Bulgaria and Romania also had fifty years of Communist rule, which promoted their educational and industrial development, but at the cost of
straining and distorting their economies, leading to a collapse from which

they are just beginning to emerge.

Another factor favoring the Balkans was linguistic. Their languages were much closer to the Western European ones in structure and vocabulary, which made it far easier to absorb Western learning. Moreover, except in Greece with *Katharevousa,* the spoken vernacular was used for writing. Among the Turks, however, until the 1920s—and among the Arabs to this day—the written language continued to be the archaic, classical one, imposing a great burden on students and impeding literacy.

As against these favorable factors, the Balkans entered the 19th century under some severe handicaps to modernization. First, they were much less urbanized: as late as 1860, only Bucharest had passed the 100,000 mark; by contrast, in 1800 Istanbul had some 400,000 inhabitants, Cairo 250,000 and Aleppo, Baghdad, Damascus and Izmir some 100,000.

Secondly, the Balkans lacked the high crafts, producing both quality and mass goods, of these and other Middle Eastern cities. At most, a few villages like Ambelakia, in Thessaly and in the Plovdiv region in Bulgaria produced simple goods for sale in Ottoman markets and they, like their Middle Eastern counterparts, suffered greatly from the flood of machine-made European goods in the 1840s and 1850s.[4]

Lastly, land transport was, if anything, more primitive in the Balkans. The terrain was rougher and muddier and camel transport, which played such an important part in the Middle East, was lacking.

The social factors that favored the development of the Balkans may be studied under two headings: social structure, and earlier contacts with Europe and the development of education.

Social Structure

For our purposes, this has two aspects: agrarian structure and the emergence of a bourgeoisie. Because of the enormous variation in land productivity in the Middle East, due mainly to availability of water and type of irrigation, it is impossible to provide comparable figures on the countries studied here. However, until the series of land reforms of the 1950s, they all had certain features in common. First, the percentage of land in large ownerships (defined differently but appropriately) was about 25 in Turkey, 40 in Egypt, 50 in Syria and 80 in Iraq. Secondly, the vast majority of farmers had less land than was needed to maintain their families, and had to lease supplementary areas, at high rents. Thirdly, there was a large and growing landless population. This situation was the result of a series of developments that began in the 19th century: rapid population growth, unaccompanied by substantial industrialization; integration in the world market; and application of western-inspired Land Codes.[5]

In the Balkans the situation was radically different, except in Romania. As Table 12.3 shows, the bulk of the land was held by small farmers and only a low fraction by large owners.

In Greece, where *Chiftliks* (estates) had been held by Turks, after independence very little land remained in the hands of landlords—until the acquisition of Thessaly in 1881 and Macedonia in 1913. After the First World War, 38 per cent of arable land was redistributed under the land reform.[6]

Serbia also enjoyed peasant ownership with independence. Between 1815 and 1830 *Chiftliks* were abolished and a little later measures were taken to protect small properties.[7] The Habsburg territories benefitted from the abolition of serfdom and other reforms and although large estates survived, by 1900 farms of under 50 hectares accounted for 68.4 per cent of cultivated land, including pastures and forests, in Croatia-Slavonia, 75 in Slovenia, 65 in the Vojvodina and 86 in Dalmatia. In 1918 a land reform distributed about one-tenth of the land in the newly acquired territories to small farmers.[8]

The course of events in Bulgaria was similar. The exodus of the Turkish landowners in 1877 and the law of 1880 transferred the bulk of the land to small farmers.[9] After the First World War, Bulgaria too had a large-scale land reform. Because of this structure, the level of living of Serbian and Bulgarian peasants was relatively high, and attracted favorable comment from foreign observers.[10] It also facilitated the growth of rural credit and marketing cooperatives in most parts of the Balkans.[11]

In Romania, by contrast, independence did not lead to the elimination of landlords, who were native *boyars* and who continued to hold large estates. Numerous dues and exactions continued to depress the peasantry whose situation was only partly relieved by the reforms of 1848 in the Habsburg provinces and of 1864, 1881, 1889 and 1907 in the Kingdom. The cooperative movement made little headway before the First World War.[12] The land reform of 1918 distributed 21 per cent of the arable land.[13]

As regards the emergence of a bourgeoisie, the main difference is that in the Middle East economic development was mainly carried out by an implanted middle class, consisting of West Europeans backed by members of minority groups such as the Greeks, Armenians, Jews and Syrian Christians: these provided both the entrepreneurial and the technical and administrative skill required.[14] In the Balkans, on the other hand, the middle class has been predominantly native, and has been greatly helped by various measures taken by the governments after independence.

Greece began to develop its bourgeoisie in the 18th century, thanks to its extensive shipping and its far-flung trade linking the Ottoman Empire to Europe and Russia. And even after Hellenic independence, Ottoman Greeks continued to form a large part of the bourgeoisie of the Empire.[15] In the other countries, at independence the middle class was much smaller. But in all, its growth was helped by government action. Starting with Greece in 1842, by 1885 all four Balkan countries had successfully established national banks with exclusive powers of note issue. None were primarily in the hands of European investors. By the last prewar decade, all the notes issued were convertible.[16] All these banks, except the Bulgarian, established their independence from both governments and foreign capital. Similarly, the savings and mortgage banks were independent of foreign capital. Indeed the smallness of the role played by the latter is remarkable. By contrast, in the Middle East, until the 1920s all banks, except for a few very small ones, were foreign owned and managed; this includes the note-issuing Ottoman Bank and The National Bank of Egypt.

Another breeding ground for the bourgeoisie was industry. The usual factors impeding industrialization in underdeveloped countries limited its size and scope in the Balkans—but by 1913 it employed more workers, and had more capital investment and machinery installed, than in the Middle East.[17] Except in the Romanian oil industry, foreign capital played a minor part, but in some branches immigrants, many of whom fused with the native population, were prominent. Native banks financed certain firms and the government helped with protective tariffs, industrial legislation, technical education and facilitating linkages between the national railways and industry. By 1913, output was growing at a respectable rate and in the interwar period it rose rapidly.[18] In the Middle East, on the other hand, growth was very slow until the 1930's.

Emigration also swelled the ranks of the bourgeoisie. Remittances from emigrants raised incomes and returning immigrants provided capital, entrepreneurship and skills. This was particularly true of Greece, with its large and wealthy "colonies" in Constantinople, Smyrna, Odessa and Alexandria—as well as the Americas—but was also significant in the other countries.[19] In the Middle East only Lebanon exemplified this phenomenon.

Contacts with Europe, Education

Greece was the first country to establish cultural contacts with Europe, a process that started in the late Byzantine period. From the 16th century on, graduates of the Greek College in Rome and the schools set up by Greeks in Venice returned home, bringing with them elements of European culture. They also brought back Greek books published in Venice and elsewhere, an estimated 2,500 titles between about 1750 and 1821.[20] This was followed by the founding of Greek schools and the setting up of printing presses in Constantinople and elsewhere.[21] The Venetian occupation of Crete until 1669 and of the Ionian Islands until 1797 also had some influence—certainly in painting and perhaps in other fields. Greek merchant communities in the Mediterranean and central European cities were culturally active, and the first Greek newspaper was founded in Vienna in 1790.[22]

By the end of the 18th century a small number of educated Greeks had a sound knowledge of the ideas of the Enlightenment. This comes out clearly in Adamantios Korais' "Report on the Present State of Civilization in Greece," delivered in Paris in 1803; among recent publications, it mentions books on physics, logic and mathematics.[23]

The French Revolution had a great impact on the Balkan peoples, especially the Greeks. Propagandists spread heady ideas and so did the French occupation, and reorganization, of the Ionian Islands and Dalmatia.[24] Since Greek was both the commercial *lingua franca* of the Balkans and the liturgical and cultural language of the clergy and much of the elite, new ideas picked up by the various peoples tended to be transmitted to the Greeks. Almost immediately after independence "steps were taken to establish elementary schools in all the communes, and education was made obligatory." By 1898, 150,000 children attended primary schools (6.6 per cent of the total population) and nearly 30,000 secondary schools.[25] Athens University was founded in 1842 and a Polytechnic Institute at about the same time.

Romania, especially Transylvania, was also subjected, fairly early, to Western influences, emanating from Poland and Hungary. A few landmarks may be noted: the printing of the first book in Romanian in Venice in 1536, the foundation of a Jesuit University at Cluj in 1581 (followed by a Calvinist one in Alba Iulia in 1622) and the setting up of printing presses in several towns.[26] The extension of Habsburg rule over Transylvania coincided with the period of reforms and new ideas were transmitted by both Uniates (Orthodox churches that acknowledged Papal supremacy) and Protestants. Starting around 1750 a more powerful influence began to make itself felt: that of the French Enlightenment. In that year the first translation from French took place.[27] French merchants, secretaries and tutors brought with them, and stimulated the taste for, French books.[28]

Romania was a favorable soil for the reception of such ideas. Ottoman rule was indirect, and from 1711 to 1821 was exercised (with one short interval) by the Phanariots, rich, cultivated and francophone members of the Greek upper class of Constantinople, who welcomed and encouraged Frenchmen and French ideas, many of which were brought in by Greek immigrants. The native *boyar* aristocracy—who, in the absence of Turkish landowners, held large amounts of land—had an aggregate purchasing power unmatched in the Balkans and many of its members came to live in Bucharest, by far the largest city of the region. Lastly, the Latinity of Romania made it more accessible to French (and Italian) works.

The *Histories* of Constantine Cantacuzino (1700) and Dimitri Cantemir (1714) reflect the spirit of the Enlightenment. Education also made progress and students were sent to Europe. A "Compendium of Cartesian Philosophy" was published (in Latin) in Transylvania in 1682 and the "first mathematics book in Romanian" in Vienna in 1777.[29] This influence was greatly reinforced by the French Revolution which, in addition to propaganda, sent many émigrés. Soon national and peasant uprisings broke out.[30] The Revolution of 1821, and Russian help, resulted in autonomy for Moldavia and Wallachia, and eventually led to full independence. After independence, efforts were make to promote education. Schools were opened and the Universities of Jassy and Bucharest were founded in 1860 and 1864 respectively. The development of the petroleum industry after 1857 also led to the establishment of technical education.[31] But, because of the social structure, mass education in Romania lagged behind Bulgaria and Greece until the First World War and beyond.[32]

Culturally, if not politically, the Southern Slavs were fortunate in that, by 1700, most of them had come under Habsburg rule. This meant that, more than any other Balkan people, they were exposed to Austrian and Italian influence. Another window to the West was Ragusa, under its successive Venetian, Ottoman and Habsburg rulers. Since close contact was maintained with Serbs and others under Ottoman rule, some of this culture was diffused. Books in Cyrillic were published by Budapest University Press and the first Serbian newspaper was brought out in Vienna in 1791.[33] These found their way to the Slav provinces successively annexed by the Habsburgs, and presumably to the Serbian Kingdom.

As already mentioned, Ragusa, with its developed and westernized society, also exerted a powerful cultural influence. These, and other seeds, bore fruit. By the 1850s, 352 elementary schools were in operation in Serbia, an Academy of Science was established in 1841 and the University of Belgrade in 1844. After that, progress at all levels was steady.

Of all the Balkan peoples studied here, the Bulgarians were the slowest starters. Unlike the Greeks they had no diaspora in the West and unlike the Romanians and Serbians no large numbers of kinsmen living in an adjacent Western land. There were, however, certain compensations. In the 18th century many Bulgarian boys attended the more modern Greek schools—as indeed did Serbs—and in the 19th century Greco-Slav schools.[34] Bulgaria also benefitted from the government schools opened by its governors, who included the reformer Midhat pasha.

By contrast, the Middle East remained almost wholly cut off from the west. Indeed it is not too much to say that, until the 19th century, its only borrowings were in weaponry, metallurgy and mining. Printing was introduced to Constantinople as early as 1493, but was confined by imperial decree to scripts other than Arabic, and it was not until 1727 that it took off in Constantinople and 1822 in Cairo. Military schools were opened in Turkey in the 1770s and in Egypt in the 1820s to be followed by engineering and medical schools. Student missions to Europe were sent from Egypt in the 1820s and from Turkey in the 1830s. Both governments then set up secondary and primary schools, to supplement European missionary or local (mostly Christian or Jewish) private ones. But it was not until the middle of the 19th century that European culture had a significant impact on a small, but important, elite and not until the eve of World War I that the nucleus of national universities came into being.[35]

I believe this cultural lag, together with the Middle East's unfavorable social structure, explains much of its retardation, economic and social.

Notes:

1. Charles Issawi, *The Fertile Crescent,* 1800-1914 (New York, 1988), p. 35, and sources cited.

2. John R. Lampe and Marvin R. Jackson, *Balkan Economic History, 1550-1950* (Bloomington, Indiana, 1982), p. 160.

3. P. V. de la Blache and L. Gallois, *Géographie universelle, vols. IV and VII* (Paris, 1931 and 1934); P. Beaumont et al., *The Middle East: a Geographical Study* (London, 1976).

4. See Institut d'études balkaniques, *La révolution industrielle dans le sud-est*

européen (Sofia, 1976); Charles Issawi, *The Economic History of the Middle East* (Chicago, 1966), pp. 41-52; *idem, An Economic History of the Middle East and North Africa* (New York, 1982), pp. 150-154.

5. For details, see *ibid.,* pp. 134-49, and sources cited.

6. L. Stavrianos, *The Balkans Since 1453* (New York, 1958), p. 677.

7. Stavrianos, *op. cit.,* pp. 260-62; D. Warriner, *Contrasts in Emerging Societies* (Bloomington, Indiana, 1965), p. 287.

8. Lampe and Jackson, *op. cit.,* table on pp. 289, 352-3.

9. Stavrianos, *op. cit.,* p. 442; Warriner, *op. cit.,* pp. 15, 212.

10. Warriner, *op. cit.,* pp. 302-8, 255-56, 273-75.

11. See table for 1930, Lampe and Jackson, *op. cit.,* pp. 372-73.

12. Ifor Evans, *The Agrarian Revolution in Romania* (Cambridge, 1924), pp. 96-98 and *passim;* see also Lampe and Jackson, Stavrianos and Warriner, *op. cit.*

13. Stavrianos, *op. cit.,* p. 594.

14. See chapters 11, 13, 18 and 19 in Charles Issawi, *The Arab Legacy* (Princeton, 1981).

15. See Dimitri Gondicas and Charles Issawi, *The Greeks in the Ottoman Empire* (Princeton, 1995), *passim.*

16. Lampe and Jackson, *op. cit.,* pp. 203-4.

17. Around 1910 employment in Romanian factories was about 45,000, in Serbia 16,000 and in Bulgaria 16,000. In Egypt it was 30-35,000, in Turkey about 20,000 and in Syria and Iraq it was negligible. See *ibid.,* p. 241, and Issawi, *An Economic History of the Middle East and North Africa, op. cit.,* pp. 155-56.

18. Lampe and Jackson, *op. cit.,* pp. 244-77, 402-33, 482-503.

19. *Ibid.,* p. 196; Stavrianos, p. 606.

20. C.M. Woodhouse, *Modern Greece, A Short History* (London, 1986), p. 126.

21. Nicholas Svoronos, *Histoire de la Grèce moderne* (Paris, 1980), p. 24.

22. Stavrianos, *op. cit.,* p. 146.

23. See text in Elie Kedourie, *Nationalism in Asia and Africa* (New York, 1970), pp. 153-88.

24. Stavrianos, *op. cit.,* pp. 199-207.

25. *Encyclopaedia Britannica,* Eleventh Edition, Vol. XII, p. 433. "Greece". For subsequent figures on Greece and other Balkan countries see Lampe and Jackson, *op. cit.,* pp. 502-4.

26. Horia C. Matei, et al., *Chronological History of Romania* (Bucharest, 1972), pp. 101-6; Miron Constantinescu, *Histoire de la Roumanie* (Paris, 1970), pp. 195-206.

27. Matei, *op. cit.,* p. 139.

28. John C. Campbell, *French Influence and the Rise of Roumanian Nationalism* (New York, 1971), pp. 12-13; N. Iorga, "La pénétration des idées de l'occident dans le Sud-Est de l'Europe," *Revue historique du Sud-Est Européen,* I, 1924.

29. Andrei Otetea, *The History of the Romanian People* (New York, 1970), pp. 292-95; *Encyclopaedia Britannica,* Eleventh Edition, vol. xxiii, s.v. "Romania".

30. Otetea, *op. cit.,* pp. 280-1, 316-23.

31. Constantinescu, *op. cit.,* pp. 246-51, 313-331.

32. See table in Lampe and Jackson, *op. cit.,* pp. 503-4.

33. *Ibid.,* p. 254.

34. *Ibid.,* p. 147.

35. See Andreas Kazamias, *Education and the Quest for Modernity in Turkey* (London, 1966); Niyazi Berkes, *The Development of Secularism in Turkey* (Montreal, 1964); Albert Hourani, *Arabic Thought in the Liberal Age* (London, 1962); Raif Khouri, *Modern Arab Thought* (ed. Charles Issawi) (Princeton, 1983); G. Heyworth-Dunne, *An Introduction to the History of Education in Modern Egypt* (London, 1938).

TABLE 12.1
Indices of Economic and Social Development, 1990

	Bulgaria	Egypt	Greece	Iraq	Romania	Syria	Yugoslavia	Turkey
Real GDP [a]	5,064	1,934	6,764	3,510	3,000	4,348	5,095	4,002
Employment in Industry [b]	37.9	12.0	19.3	7.8	43.5	15.1	23.6	14.6
Wheat Yield [c]	4.3	5.0	2.5	0.9	3.0	1.4	4.1	2.1
Life Expectancy [d]	72.6	60.3	76.1	65.0	70.8	66.1	72.6	65.1
Birth Rate [e]	13.1	38.8	10.1	42.6	16.5	44.6	15.1	29.2
Adult Literacy [f]	93.0	48.4	93.2	59.7	96.0	64.5	72.6	80.7

[a] Per capita, in dollars, 1989, adjusted for purchasing power
[b] Percentage of total employment, 1986-89
[c] Tons per hectare, 1989-91; Iraq 1989-90
[d] Years at birth, 1990
[e] Crude live birth rate, per thousand, 1988
[f] Percentage, 1990

Source: United Nations Development Program, *Human Development Report* (New York, 1992)

TABLE 12.2
Indices of Economic and Social Development, Pre-World War I

	Bulgaria	Egypt	Greece	Iraq	Romania	Syria[a]	Yugoslavia	Turkey
Foreign Trade[b]	11.3	24.0	11.9	—	31.7	—	8.0	15.4
Wheat Yield[c]	1.1	2.0	1.0	0.7	1.2	1.0	1.1	1.0
Railway Mileage[d]	439	357	332	41	355	412	460	498
Birth Rate[e]	33.0	43.7	29.9	—	34.5	—	34.2	—
Literacy[f]	34.5	7	40.3	—	39.3	—	40.3	8

[a] Includes Lebanon, Palestine and Transjordan
[b] Exports plus imports per capita, in dollars, 1913; Turkey includes Iraq and Syria
[c] Tons per hectare; Bulgaria, Greece, Romania and Serbia, 1911-15; Egypt, Iraq, Syria and Turkey 1934-38
[d] Kilometers per million inhabitants, 1913
[e] Per thousand inhabitants, 1926-30; Egypt 1934-38; the figure for Turkey was probably about the same as that for Egypt, and for Iraq and Syria somewhat higher
[f] Percentage, age 10 or over around 1907; Romania 1912; Turkey 1927; the figure for Syria was distinctly higher, and that for Iraq lower than those for Egypt and Turkey; the figure is for Yugoslavia in 1900; for Serbia the rate was 21.

Sources: League of Nations, *International Statistical Yearbook, 1928;* John R. Lampe and Marvin R. Jackson, *Balkan Economic History, 1550-1950* (Bloomington, Indiana, 1982), pp. 188, 333; UNESCO, *Progress of Literacy in Various Countries* (Paris, 1953); L. Colescu, *Stiuorii de Carte din Romania in 1912* (Bucharest, 1947).

Table III
Percentage of Land Held, 1905-08

	Bulgaria	Romania	Serbia
20 hectares or below	80	43	72
20-50 hectares	16	7	16
100 hectares and above	4	49	

Source: Lampe and Jackson, *op. cit.,* p. 185